11:37 GOD'S CONTRACTING UNIVERSE

The Madness of Humanity, the Ascendancy of
the Old World Psychiatric Disorder & Beyond 2012—
the Zero Point Proposal

ZERO POINT

Institute for Mystical and Spiritual Science
Box 700, 108 Clothier Street East, Kemptville,
Ontario, Canada K0G 1J0

zeropoint@bell.net / (613) 258-6258
www.zeropoint.ca

ZERO POINT Publications 2011

First Printing—2011

Graphic Design and Prepress: Željka Župánic

11:37 GOD'S CONTRACTING UNIVERSE
The Madness of Humanity, the Ascendancy of
the Old World Psychiatric Disorder & Beyond 2012—
the Zero Point Proposal

ISBN: 978-0-9877890-0-6

the WORDS, REVELATIONS
& JUDGEMENTS of GOD
Revealed to those 'Upright of Heart'
Who still speak TRUTH
Who still feel LOVE
Who care for the Holy Life within
Who want to save your Soul
Who might learn of the Magic of Life
Becoming the hidden 'STARS,'

You are
As Sparks of Holiness within the
Heart Spaces of a Divine Mother
Wherein GOD'S MYSTERIES are
REVEALED WITHIN.

- A WARNING TO HUMANITY -
IN YOUR TIME OF NEED
TRIALS AND TRIBULATIONS ARE TO COME
AS YOU HAVE BROUGHT DOWN
THE WRATH OF GOD
UPON YOURSELVES, and the scum sense
Their own demise, for all their wickedness, sins
Greed, deceits and torture, and cruelties
UNSPEAKABLE

TABLE OF CONTENTS

Preface

11:37 GOD'S CONTRACTING UNIVERSE addresses the current crisis in the life of humanity upon this planet, which has descended into archcriminal and lunatic ways. Unfortunately, awakening to the madness of humankind, the wars, the poisoning, the deceits and cruelty, is quite a shock, or it has

been for me over the past five years of my life. Fortunately, I have simply to see it all as *God's story*, as it so beyond anything I could have imagined as a person asleep to the deceptions foisted upon humankind through the ages.

These writings on the contemporary situation of humankind include what I felt at the time were 'revelations,' which occurred when I first woke up to the lies and deceits of 9-11 in August of 2006. These were posted briefly to the zero point web site on August 11 of 2006 but withdrawn after several weeks, due to the madness and anxiety which they were causing my partner and myself. *GCU* then includes varied investigations into the criminal activities of the so-called elites, an original contribution to 9-11 research on the *Fabled Airplanes* and the scripted witness of 9-11, and a section on the psychopathology of humankind offered from the perspective of mystic G. I. Gurdjieff. The work then elaborates upon the Zero Point proposal for the criminal prosecution of the world elites under the existent anti-terrorism legislation for their crimes against the human race. Lastly, I have included a chapter explaining the significance of 11:37 in the title of this work, and a tribute to my sweetheart Karen who has recently passed away. The present work gives a sample of the breadth of my concerns for the contemporary madness, criminality and lunacy of humankind.

On May 6 of 2011, Karen T. Hale passed away unexpectedly and suddenly at the age of 55. Karen had been the love of my life over the past 12 years and we had shared varied quite epic adventures together during that time. Karen was a remarkable woman who somehow saw into the madness of things about us and was deeply affected by all that we learnt through the years after waking up to the fraud of 9-11 and then the additional crimes being committed by governments against citizens around the world. The horror of it all precipitated Karen and I into months and years of experiences ranging from bliss, rapture and illumination, to dread and fearfulness, confusions and difficulties. By the time of her death, Karen had in a magical way attained something within herself through her *conscious labours* and *intentional suffering*, and her bravery in the face of it all.* Karen had been with me during the development of the 11:37 *God's Contracting Universe* and *Zero Point Teachings* books which I have published in 2011, although not to see these works in print. Of course, one cannot know for certain when she might or might not be around *in spirit*.

What a story line, a *who-done-it* for the movie goer, with a masterful plot and hidden ending. The human race got *punked* through an unspeakable con precipitated with the intentional downing of the Two Towers. This is the current situation of humanity, deceived by their governments and media. The masses of humanity are manipulated like puppets by the Media of Lies, none of who report the Truth of 9/11 and all of whom are complicit in concocting this *nightmare parable.*

How asleep is humankind? Everyone has believed what he or she has been told or led to believe like little lost sheep being led to slaughter. What were we and they all doing, so asleep at the wheel, so deceived by so-called elite groups and forces unfathomed? Most of the worlds' population came to believe the lies of 9/11 and were intentionally deceived by their media and political representatives. Politicians within modern societies no longer serve the peoples or citizens at all and have instead become the puppets and servants of the international criminal cabals, *a global crime syndicate,* that control the fortunes of the world. Fortunately, there were and are truth warriors out there, who learnt of 9/11 and began to investigate and grasp the true nature of the Beast of modern times. The American dream has become the American nightmare, a nation high-jacked by a shadow government and criminal elite whose activities run like blood stains through the life of humanity.

The materials on the *God's Contracting Universe* were written during this period of shock, horror, enlightenment and outrage—that I and

---

* *Conscious labours* and *intentional suffering* are described by G. I. Gurdjieff as the means by which an individual can attain their soul.

K. experienced through these times. We woke up to the horror of the situation of humankind and realized also how asleep we had been. How stupid and deceived! The Truth of 9/11 is far more horrifying than what I used to believe in--in crazed Arab fundamentalists. That was relatively easy to comprehend. Unfortunately, the Truth is far more disturbing and traumatizing and leaves one understanding our society, media and world in a new way--grasping the low level of the development of the psyche of contemporary humanity and the dark activities of the elites with their genocide agendas.

Between 2006 and 2012, there has been a quickening of events as humankind undergoes trials and tribulations, induced natural disasters and chaos, and further *"processes of reciprocal destruction"* as Gurdjieff called them, meaning wars and conflicts, as are now instigated around the world. However, as it happens, there are now tens of millions of people who understand that these terrorist activities are *state sponsored terrorist attacks* and *false flag events*. Humankind has been so asleep to the Beast within our own society, while our young men and women sacrifice their lives for these mad puppets and clowns upon the world stage, hidden elites controlled by underground and even alien influences. What a mad cap time is upon us! The true causes of events on the world stage are completely hidden from the hypnotized and conditioned masses of humanity.

Karen and I both made efforts in our ways, sometimes madcap, to do something in the world to save souls and to fight for love, truth and righteousness. I didn't want to be a hobbit who stayed home drinking beer and watching men play games with balls, while a real life *Lord of the Rings* unfolds on the world stage. Karen and I had a life. I have yet to deal with the grief I feel over Karen's death and the anger at what I see has been done to all of us as Canadian, American and world citizens. In some strange way, Karen and I engaged in this spiritual war for the life of humankind and did so through the past years.

This book, like *Zero Point Teachings*, is dedicated to you sweetheart Karen, for your bravery, love and struggle to live in truth. To me, Karen you were and are a Star. By the Will of God, may I *live to tell* of our epic adventures together and in the meanwhile, contribute with others to turn the tides threatening to wash away our societies and civilization.

Christopher P. Holmes
November 2011

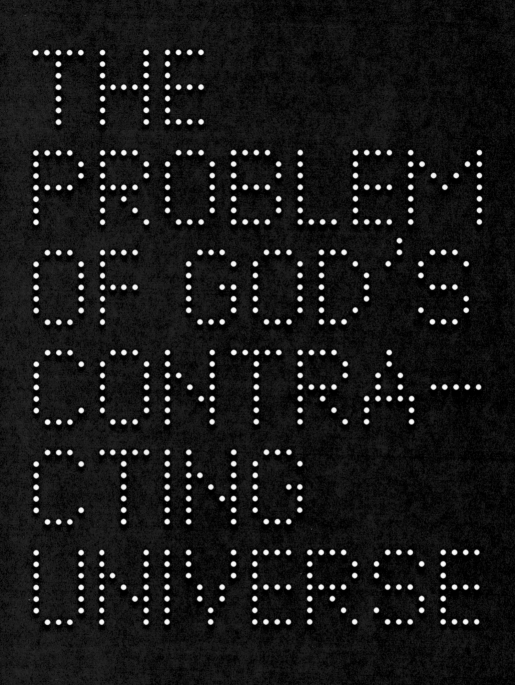

THE
PROBLEM
OF GOD'S
CONTRA-
CTING
UNIVERSE

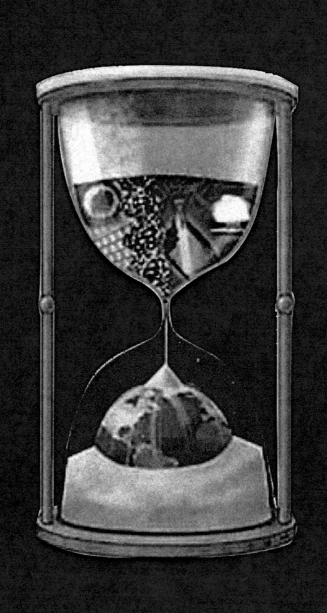

"At present the population of the world is increasing...
If a Black Death could be spread throughout the world once in every generation, survivors could procreate freely without making the world too full... the state of affairs might be somewhat unpleasant, but what of it? Really high-minded people are indifferent to suffering, especially that of others....
Gradually, by selective breeding, the congenital differences between rulers and ruled will increase until they become almost different species. A revolt of the plebs would become as unthinkable as an organized insurrection of sheep against the practice of eating mutton."
Bertrand Russell, The Impact of Science on Society

"The Rockefeller Foundation has the SAME agenda as the Illuminati and the Gates Foundation. David Rockefeller, a member of the Illuminati, is a founder and member of several organizations such as the Trilateral Commission, the Bilderbergers and the Club of Rome, whose purpose is to
a) set up a One World Government, b) control ALL business throughout the world and, c) dramatically and rapidly reducing the population of the world from 6 billion to 500 million, by war, disease and famine." (Dr. L. Day, 2008)

"... international terrorism does NOT exist and the September 11 attacks were the result of a set-up. What we are seeing is a manipulation by the big powers; this terrorism would not exist without them. "Terrorism" talk is the weapon used in a new type of war in complicity with the media, which allows modifying international politics and changing existing reality. In other words, "Terrify the people with incessant talk of "Terrorism"
so they will give up their rights and become malleable slaves in the hands of the New World Order." General Leonid Ivashov,

Axis for Peace 2005 Conference

Introduction & Background

*"The individual is handicapped by coming face to face
with a conspiracy so monstrous he cannot believe it exists."*

J. E. Hoover, former head of the FBI

*"Humanity is the victim of a monstrous conspiracy
of unspeakable proportions."*

(H. Makow, Illuminati, p. 76)

In August of 2006, Karen and I attended a film shoot in New York City for the new age movie Metaphysia, eventually released in 2011 (www. metaphysia.com). We drove down by van from the Ottawa area. Before returning, we took a brief drive around the 9/11 Ground Zero site, although it was largely hidden from view by construction barriers. Certainly, within myself, the brief visit to Ground Zero stirred eerie and unsettling feelings, and I did not want to linger. However, I was completely naïve as to what lay below the surface.

Upon return, my youngest son brought the movie Loose Change to our attention. Loose Change is an expose of 9/11, the supposed Muslim terrorist attack on the World Trade Centre Towers in New York City. Having just visited the site of the former Two Towers, we were curious to view the film. Karen nor I had ever been politically minded or oriented and generally had not been exposed to the conspiracy theory stuff— preferring instead the inspirations and truths of mystical teachings and modern science in our lives. Until those moments, Karen and I had been completely naive as to the true events which occurred on that ominous day of September 11, 2001.

The movie Loose Change is available through www.video.Google.com and according to the CBC (Canadian Broadcasting Corporation), it has been downloaded over 10 millions time over the internet (estimated in 2008). According to Alex Jones at www.prisonplanet.com, it has now been viewed a hundred million times. Loose Change is an expose of the fraud of 9/11. Unfortunately, the movie obscures many details of the whole fraud, the lies and deceptions, but it would take years of further research for us to understand that.

Upon viewing the film, Karen and I were shocked and horrified, and then spent many more hours, months and years, researching the significant issues and evidences surrounding the 9/11 events. It is now overwhelmingly clear that criminal psychopaths within our own society were responsible for 9-11 and that it had nothing to do with Osama Bin Laden and his reindeer (or crazed Muslims, recovering from strippers and cocaine, according to the official story). Instead, 9-11 was the handiwork of a so-called elite class within our own societies, who want a nightmare new world psychiatric disordered society. We were shocked to realize that the events such as the London train bombing, and Indonesian terrorist attacks, the Oklahoma City bombing, and so on and on, were all false flag events, being staged by so-called elites in order to bring about a fascist police state society, to advance corporate power and to usher in a 'new world order,' which I prefer to more accurately describe as the old world psychiatric disorder.

We were shocked and horrified by what we learnt, as the fraud of 9-11 obviously also implicated our own government and media in perpetrating this deception on the Canadian people. Over time, everything we thought we knew of our society, of the media, of the justice and police services, and military, the medical system and the health societies, all were proven illusory. Since the shock of those early events until this year, 2011, Karen and I had turned to the internet to attempt to understand it all and the nature of the global crime syndicate that rules our planet. I gladly now embrace the term 'conspiracy theorist,' as science is full of theories and the study of the ruling classes and their crimes against humanity are a complex and subtle story. Anyone who is not a conspiracy theorist is in fact simply an idiot, as the history of humankind attests throughout to the fact of such elite networks and deceptions. The media has simply devised this term 'conspiracy theorist' as a way of discrediting those who wake up to their public deceptions, so that the sheep people are not disturbed in their sleep.

The more I and Karen learnt, the more horrified we were. The Truth of 9/11 is that it was "an inside job"—it always was, is and shall forever have been. Further, the criminal network who perpetrated this crime, have largely been able to con or fool the world's population through their own media and propaganda machine to justify wars and imperialism and the increasing restriction of human rights and freedoms. We now live in an Orwellian society with Big Brother and Double Think Ministries, a Media of Lies and a general population of people have no true idea of the horrendous events which occurred on 9/11 or of the ominous events unfolding on the world stage. Lunatics, madmen, psychopaths, aliens, Satanists and pseudo-illuminate, are all among the characters on the complex world stage.

The western world is portrayed within the media as spreading freedom and democracy, while in truth, it is a society manipulated by the greed, cruelty, fear and lust for power of disturbed psychopaths and egomanias, perverts and pedophiles, committing terrorist crimes around the world and bringing about a police state society. And these guys and gals even think that they are 'illuminated.' This is the current situation of humanity, deceived by their governments and media--all complicit in this nightmare parable. Everyone has believed what he or she has been told, or led to believe like little lost sheep being led to slaughter.

What a story line, a who-done-it for the movie goer, with a masterful plot and hidden ending. The human race got punked through an unspeakable con precipitated with the intentional downing of the Two Towers. This is the current situation of humanity, deceived by their governments and media. The masses of humanity are manipulated like puppets by the Media of Lies, none of who report the Truth of 9/11 and all of whom are complicit in this nightmare parable.

After our rude awakening in August of 2006, Karen and I explored widely over the internet and to listen to truth radio networks, while making efforts to be more actively aware of the horrendous events unfolding on the world stage and the very significant issues involved. I would certainly recommend to all readers that you escape the mind control techniques and propaganda of the corporate media, turn off your stupid TV's and cancel your newspaper, and instead seek alternate news sources and internet radio shows. Here are some recommendations: www.oraclebroadcasting. com, http://republicbroadcasting.org; www.globalresearch.ca; www. informationclearinghouse.info.

Although you individually may be completely unaware of these facts, the truth is now known by tens of millions around the world. There is a world wide "truth movement" occurring on this planet, as those upright of heart stand up to face the tyranny which has been imposed around the world.

Fortunately, there were and are truth warriors out there, who learnt of 9/11 and began to investigate and grasp the true nature of the Beast of modern times. The American dream has become the American nightmare. America as a nation has been high jacked by a shadow government and criminal elite whose activities run like blood stains through the life of humanity.

The revelations in 11:37 God's Contracting Universe, were written during this initial period of shock, horror, bliss and enlightenment, and outrage-- that I and K. experienced through these times and then subsequently as we made efforts to attempt to wake others up to the reality of these massive public deceptions. Whereas previously in my writings, I had always used the phrase of the Problems of God's Contracting Universe to refer to the debate between science and religion, and the manner in which scientists consider that as science advances "there is less and less for God to do," as Dr. Carl Sagan commented. Awakening to the lies and deceptions being perpetrated against the world's populations by these criminal cabals with their evil intentions for population reduction and genocide, the poisoning of foods and the environment, and their high jacking of world governments, has been another chapter of such a story of the Problem of God's Contracting Universe. This is not simply a problem in the human search for knowledge, but now, it has become a problem for the future life of humanity. Are we going to sink into the nightmare world concocted by these megalomaniacs in their quest for world domination, or will we as the human race, those 'upright of heart,' be able to take back this planet and establish international law and justice?

This is a war for the hearts and mind of humanity, a real life Lord of the Rings tale, beyond what most people can even imagine. This monstrous conspiracy is noted in the very significant quotations that open this chapter. We are facing a conspiracy so monstrous that people, ordinary people, cannot imagine it to be true. Further, they lack the 'courage' or 'new heart' required to face the beast of modern times, or else, they are simply primarily concerned for their own welfare and that of their favourites.

Karen and I struggled through the past years in some kind of madcap way, awakening to these truths and deceptions, and trying desperately to wake other people up or to have some kind of effect in a world gone mad. It took us years to recover from the initial elevated states, rapture, illumination, bliss, confusion, fearfulness and unreality, we experienced during the early months of our awakening.

I first posted the next chapter of 'revelations' to my website on August 11, 2006. Upon awakening, I had felt the wrath of God move through me, as I apprehended all the injustice, cruelty, criminality and sinfulness which had overtaken every aspect of our society. This material flowed through me in a way which I had never experienced before or since. Whereas my usual writing is scholarly and academic in matter, this was a prose and verse which seemed to flow from an exalted level within myself. Due to periods of fearfulness and dread which Karen and I were experiencing at times, I withdrew the material from the website. I have only reposted it again this year 2011, subsequent to Karen's death.

As a double Libra, I have a strong desire to have justice and righteousness returned to this sacred planet and to help reveal the deceptions and mind control that has been perpetrated against humanity through the course of our lives. These writing give some flavour of my researches, efforts, struggles and insights. What else could two talented but poor people do in a world gone mad, but to make some effort to live in love and truth and take up the sword in a spiritual conflict for the lives and souls of humankind? I make no apologies for the tone or content of these materials. I am only a fool at the zero point who knows nothing.

Bless you Karen for your courage through it all, your conscious labors and intentional suffering as Gurdjieff describes. Surely you have earned your Star through it all.

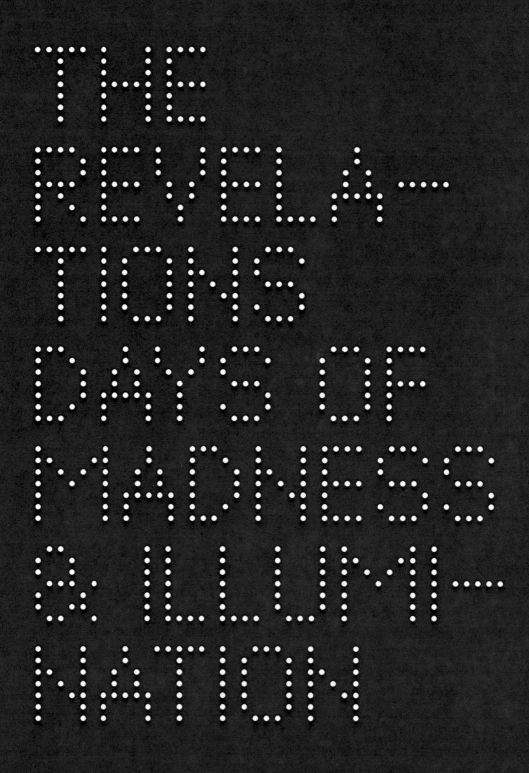

THE REVELA-
TIONS
DAYS OF
MADNESS
& ILLUMI-
NATION

Zero Point formerly,
Institute for *Mystical and Spiritual
Science*, and NOW, a website
August 11, 2006

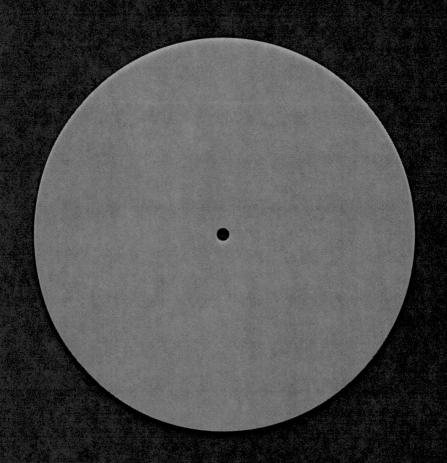

for the WORDS, REVELATIONS
& JUDGEMENTS of GOD

Revealed to those 'Upright of Heart'
Who still speak TRUTH
Who still feel LOVE
Who care for the Holy Life within
Who want to save your Soul
Who might learn of the Magic of Life
Becoming the hidden 'STARS,'

You are
As Sparks of Holiness within the
Heart Spaces of a Divine Mother
Wherein GOD'S MYSTERIES are
REVEALED WITHIN.

-A WARNING TO HUMANITY-
IN YOUR TIME OF NEED
TRIALS AND TRIBULATIONS ARE TO COME
AS YOU HAVE BROUGHT DOWN
THE WRATH OF GOD
UPON YOURSELVES, and the scum sense
Their own demise, for all their wickedness, sins
Greed, deceits and torture, and cruelties
UNSPEAKABLE

They will turn to staging events and cons,
Even mass murders,
Creating imaginary enemies without
Deceiving you to the enemy within.

No real Moslem ever turned mass-murder
Into a feature movie presentation of lies.
No Real Jew did that,
I know better, I love Jews
Real Jews, Real Moslems, Real Christians
Real People.

The scum attempt to sustain their
Lives as the worlds crumble about them
And they are exposed,
As a king with no clothes.
Not as a REAL KING.

As Bob Dylan, wrote, in The Gates of Eden
"Even the President of the United States
must someday have to stand naked."
Which might work well in Cuba,
At his own Bay of Pigs.

Poor little Sheep with no Shepherd
Who like TV and Movies,
And believed the deceit,
Have some Faith, Hope and Love
Through these times, and remember
The Light at the End of the Tunnel
Pierce the Veils of Illusion
Wake Up Poor Sheep

I will suggest some Oscar nominations for Hollywood
To clarify for those who don't grasp
The true Horror of the Situation
Of the lives of Contemporary men

OSCAR NOMINATIONS

Hot off the Press
7 fool's gold Oscar Rewards for the

The Beast & its movie handiwork,
"World Trade Centre"

1.
Best Con

The Sheep were 'had.'
The masses of the World were so traumatized,
Confused and deluded, they couldn't remember
The Truth of 9/11, and you were able to
Maintain these cons through the
Ministries and Media of Lies, and
Intelligence Agencies-the inside criminals
Then to sell a popular movie,
Out of 'something in your heart.'
Further, to scapegoat imaginary
Arabs or Muslims
All yes, for greed & Six other Deadly Sins

3.
Best story line

from a Queen, to a puppet
president and Cronies, to the Torturers
and Barbarians, Misers and Madmen,
Scum and Slim-- quite a sad lot,
All should be in Cuba, where it is quite hot
With nice dogs to save humanity.

2.
Best Cover-up & Complicity in
Mass Murder & the Activities
and Financing of International
Terrorism

4.
Mass-Murder Special Effects

in demolitions and the destructive use of
thermate -
Three demolitions perfectly performed,
By remote control from Building 7, or 6.
Do men really have to make money,
7 Days a Week - Is the movie open on
Sundays?

5.
Best Cooperative Venture

involving the sick queen Herself,
Little dark princes, the Scrooges
of Wall Street,
Puppet presidents, prime ministers,
and cronies,
Silverstein and his favourite
demolition company
The Media who hid the Truth
The little people who just do their jobs
Fearing to speak the Truth.
All quite a pathetic lot.
All now subject to Nuremberg Decisions
Canadian, American & International Law

6.
Most Unusual Hidden Story Line

From something rotten in the State of
Denmark, to the control of the pseudo
Intelligent network criminals,
Pseudo-stars, Silverstein,
Fools' Oscar gold.
The devil's alchemy -- turning
Human blood into fool's gold.

7.
Best Ending to come about

Thank you for putting before the World
All the Evidences of your Dastardly Deeds
Wrapped in a Hollywood package
For all Humanity to see the SINS
Of such ways, the lies and deceit
Of the CON, and of little sheep
Being led to slaughter.

9/11 was an inside job
Always was, is, and will forever have been,
For all Eternity.
Nothing can change the Truth.

Thanks creeps for also for drafting
All the necessary
Legislation to Seize and Imprison all these
Terrorists and scum within decent society
All their Assets, and the Asses themselves.
And now time for a visit to Cuba,
For a cigar, your mass-murder trophies.
Each other's fine company
All the poisons you devise for others,
Pharmaceuticals, Flues & Implants
Even nice pet dogs and Cages,
Your saint Nicholas even.
A quiet place, where you might spend all time
In the HELL of your own design.

In retribution for unspeakable sinful crimes,
against the Human Race.

HOLY WORLD

The Human Race will
Skim a First level of
7 levels of Scum off Human Society
All such fortunes of this pathetic lot,
Can then be used to pay
Off the Debts of Nations, to rebuild Lebanon
Afghanistan and Iraq
To build a New World
Of justice, truth, love and beauty
As God intended.

The New Jerusalem
Will come about when humankind
Realizes that true Christians, Muslims, and Jews
All have the same hidden teachings of the Heart
Wherein God's mysteries can be revealed.

The Ministry of lies has 'led you to think or believe'
Like little lost sheep, who have lost their Way;
To believe that the conflicts in the life
Of humanity are due to religion.
You were so deceived.

The life of Humanity will change
When true Christians, Muslims and Jews
Together rid the earth of such scum as these.
None will own the NEW JERUSALEM.
Revealed to those 'Upright of Heart'

HOLLYWOOD OR HOLY WORLD
THE DAY OF JUDGEMENT IS HERE

THE PROBLEM OF
GOD'S CONTRACTING UNIVERSE

Hear THESE WORDS
of JUDGEMENT upon your selves
Hollywood

In the Ministries and Media of Lies
Within the Armies of the Hordes
The Rich who have sucked
Out the lives and blood of decent men
And women in greed,

I AM passing Judgements upon you
You have incurred MY WRATH
And will face Trials & Tribulations
-- as will all Humankind --
before THE NEW JERUSALEM

An Open letter to Humanity
On the Tragedies and Truth of 9-11
& The Making of a New World

"… the dumb ass speaking with man's voice
forbade the madness of the prophet."
II Peter 2: 16 - New Testament

A TALE OF TWO TOWERS

Dumb Asses & Their Horrible Crimes
The Deceivers & the Little Lost Sheep
The Truth of 9/11
The Devil's Alchemy of turning Human Blood
Into a Fool's Oscar gold

The God Adventures of Sherlock Holmes, Master Sleuth
With help from Saint Peter and the Angels
With Love in His Heart and a Mind
Illuminated by the Inner Light of Self.
With four ducks in the yard--Fire, Air, Water and Earth

A Shepherd
to Save Sheep from Wolves and Deceivers
WHO no longer understand, what they have become,
To Manifest the Will and Word of God,
As I AM TO DO.
TO SMITE THE ENEMY, by the WRATH OF GOD,
And help you judge yourself.

I must fear no evil for THOU ARE WITH ME
Though I walk through valleys in the Shadow of Death.
Armed with the *Sword of Spiritual Knowledge*
& Gifts of Divine Realization
I WILL pierce these veils of illusion
and Deceit to Expose the Beast
And its unspeakable crimes against the Human Race.

The Days of Judgement have
Begun--Today

9/11
I will pass Judgement
And I dare any petty little pea-brain
With his confusions and deceit
And no evidence for any truth, beyond lies
TO STAND BESIDE ME,
IN A COURT OF LAW
I WOULD SMITE THEE DOWN
IN A HEARTBEAT
YES, TAKE ME to Court for speaking TRUTH
Of 9/11, the Bilderberg clan, their puppets and pawns,
the torturers, and deceivers, the rich in no Real Life
The lunatic Queen, the Prince of Darkness,
Barbarian Hordes in Tow, Deceivers and Connivers,
Who do mass murders, sell pop and deception
To perpetrate a Nightmare,
Through the Control of the Minds of the little men,

What little men and women you have become.
Who cannot slay such demons of the Mind,
Or Speak Truth any longer.   How sad.
What little people you've all become.
If you little people of Hollywood
Confess not of your sins

I WILL to bring down the WRATH OF GOD
UPON YOU, and Hollywood will pass into dust.
To so live off the blood of men
And to be so complicit.

I WILL - YOU DOWN
A FIRST WARNING
a sign of what is to come
in times of Trials and Tribulations.

There will be 9/11
World Truth Hearings
I dare these pea-brains and hypocrites to
STAND BESIDE ME
AND I WILL SMITE THEE DOWN
FROM WITHIN

Such 'terrestrial nullities,' one can't conceive,
With such unspeakable things in your hearts.

Wow, that's quite a story, with evil empires,
pop and indigestion, movies, queens, dogs and cigars,
Mass murder in movies, and conspiracy put on
video for world wide consumptions
Of madness and lunacy
I WILL SMITE YOU DOWN,
Although in 7 STAGES.
As a Shepherd
To Save the Lost and Deluded Sheep
Being Led to Slaughter through Deceit
To Cast the Money-Changers Out of the Holy Lands
As All Lands are HOLY, and to send them off to Cuba,
For a good long vacation with a new pet dogs
A Havana cigar up their ass
For intercourse among themselves.
In a private hell--of their own Design.

This movie, available within your local community,
Soon to be released on DVD
Provides all the conceivable evidence that any
Even half-sane or Intelligent Society or Individual
Could use to prove in any Impartial Court of Law
Anywhere in the World, to any even half sane Judge,
If there are any such creatures left,
That the Entire Assets of all these Asses
Who *"speak with man's voice,"*
The whole Bilderberg Clan and their puppets
Even the tyrants of Hollywood
All the assets of the asses,
Around the World should be seized
According to the existing Anti-Terrorism,
Financing and Conspiracy Laws
Which the Beast itself has designed.
To Seal its Fate, and
To bring about its own demise.

They have put the evidence
Into the World of all their Crimes,
Duplicities, Mass-Murder and Deception
Into the common domain.
The criminal evidences are available
Indeed around the world--on the Internet
Go to www.video.Google.com and learn the crimes.
Although, unmentioned within the *Ministries and Medias
of Lies, Deceit and Double-Think*
Owned by the Bilderberg Clan

These things are now known by millions and millions
Of people around the world

As the empire is now crumbling.
The pseudo-masters conned the Sleeping Sheep
Created an Orwell Nightmare
leading them to Slaughter
While governments and countries stand impotent.

Take this fine movie of deceit, mix with half a cup of
Videos at www.video.Google.com, search 9/11,
And any sane person, if there are such birds left,
Has an Absolutely air-tight case against
All these despicable scum, their finances and activities.
All the evidences are available worldwide,
to imprison all these filthy characters,
Use all their Estates based on Greed and
Human Suffering, Death and Deception
for the Making of a New World

To send the Queen, the Bilderbergs,
The One who makes $7 billion dollars
Blowing up Building Number 7, 6 & the Two Towers
And eventually, brought about the collapse of
the Empire of Evil.
Before the Return of the King.

Imagine showing such unspeakable SINS to the world,
With poisoned pop and popcorn
Enough to cause indigestion
As indeed, Hollywood is so sick
That it could degenerate to such unspeakable things
While all forget the *Nuremberg Sins*
They now commit
In all their Duplicities of Silence and Deceit.

Oh, Hollywood, why has the holly and fool's gold
Become more important than such things
As Love, Truth and Beauty, Honor and Integrity
Love of Country, your children and mine.
That you might stoop so low
Deceive the Human Race
In support of psychopaths at the helm of a
Country of such Noble Ideals.

You must look at yourself,
See the Lie
Speak the Truth
With Love--in your Heart.

By continuing this Nightmare,
As you now know,
Makes you guilty of complicity
in Unspeakable Crimes against Humanity
You are subject to American, Canadian,
International Law in regards to the
support of, financing or activities
in support of International Terrorism,
And you can, from NOW,
be judged in your hearts, by ME.
And I will bring my WRATH upon YOU
Within your hearts, from within
And bring down your sick inner semi-souls,
Off to feed the moon and aliens, in your lunacy.

Do not be of the Beast
Little lost sheep

Who fear what is to come,
So deluded, unable be Speak.
So sad for you,
So you decide in your heart,

If Hollywood tinsel
Is more important to you
Than that *within your heart*
The Treasury of GOD's
Mysteries IN STORE
In your small sick little minds,
Controlled by lunacy and deceit,
You have become such cowards,
Parts of the Beast.

As it is within your Heart,
So Shall it Be,
The Mysteries of Love and Truth
or Mass Duplicity.

You are in grave danger,
As the Beast is quavering,
And will Stage new Deceptions,
Mass Murders and Crimes,
All to maintain their lives
Living of the blood of others,
In fear of their own inner
NOTHINGNESS.

Oh, Hollywood,
Is this what you want for a Sane World
For Seven Generations of God's Children.

Oh America, the Tragedy of such Nightmares
But certainly a good Tale, for such a peculiar fellow
as myself, Sherlock Holmes, who no longer knows
who he is,
with quite an adventure, A true Real Life Drama,
That only A GOD MIGHT DESIGN

In Book II, *The Two Towers*,
the barbarians and their evil masters,
Are ruling the world, reeking chaos, suffering and despair,
Breeding inhuman types and committing
unspeakable crimes.
While the masses are lulled into sleep,
Like little lost sheep, to be led to slaughter
Food for the witch and evil pseudo-masters.
Yet forces of Light, Life and Love & Truth
Within Hollywood itself
Have long been gathering,
To bring the *Return of Righteousness* within the World,
Some individual still don't approve of mass murder
and popcorn.
It can cause indigestion.

As Humankind passes through Tribulations
There must be Faith, Hope and Love in the World
And Truth, all things intended by the Divine Being
Who unfolded such a profound mystery drama and story
For Sherlock Holmes, crime detective, and for You.
A Shepherd who Wills to Save the Sheep
From the wicked Queen and princes,
who want to fuck them in the bum, and have sex-slaves,
The pseudo-president and his cronies.

Humankind is Awakening to the Holy World,
Although gradually in Stages,
As Cosmic Mysteries unfold
within the transformation
Of the Human Heart.

To Drink from the Waters of Life
7 Levels of Scum must first be removed.

This is a Horrifying
Yet Marvellous Adventure Tale --
Beyond anything conceived in Hollywood
This is not Fiction, but Truth, Now in this World
Not in imagination, but in Truth.
It is the Lord of the Ring in Real Life
It Exposes the Lies of the Hollywood Fluff
Media Mongrel deceivers
The financiers of Greed and Cruelty
Beyond what any 'normal person,'
Could imagine or conceive,
As you had been led to believe.
--LIKE sheep to slaughter.

A sick red stain of blood
Runs through the life of humanity,
The scientific evidences and eyewitness reports of the Fall,
All evidences to condemn these perpetrators
Of unspeakable crimes against humanity,
And NOW, they provide a movie, out of
something in their heart
'World Trade Centre
To place before the World the Evidences

Of the whole Sick and Deceitful Mess.
And, soon to be released on DVD.

This letter to humanity
Attempts to explain the Nightmare Parable,
And the Criminal Lunatic Syndicates,
Which show Crimes of Mass Murder
Of International Conspiracy and Terrorism,
In your local theatres, while you eat popcorn,
To further confuse and delude YOU,
All done, out of "something in their hearts."

These teachings explain
How the human race,
Became a rat race,
Deceived by a pseudo master-race.

This is an Epic Story, surely A Lord of the Rings.
Yet True and afoot within Modern Times--NOW.
One has to admit
Quite a Tale!
And that is not the end of it
But only the beginning.

777
REVELATIONS

The Beast has had its Day
Sealed its Fate,
Brought about its own demise
Making movies of mass murder
Deceit to sell with popcorn and pop
Leading the Poor Sheep surely to die
Not to know the mysteries
of their Hearts and Mine.

ALL the international terrorist
legislation can put them all away
if anyone used any Intelligence.

How weak you have become
through such years of deceit
Deception, to be so 'had.'
The Wrath of God
Will come down
Upon the Nations of the World

True Americans don't slaughter people
True Canadians, nor English
Or any even half-sane Being
Unfortunately not too common

And now, the Jews
march around the World
like Nazis, having Forgotten
What they preach

So loudly not to do.

My Children
I will not not let this happen
And you can stop
Or I will draw the inner life
from within you.

Let decent people have a life
free from such tyranny and Oppression.

The scourge of humanity
who terrorize the Children of God

I am Armed with The LIGHT OF TRUTH
AND I WILL TAKE NO MORE
LET REAL PEOPLE LIVE

IN LIGHT, IN TRUTH, IN LOVE

THE PEOPLES OF THE WORLD
WILL REBUILD THE NATIONS
WHEN THE SCUM OF HUMAN
LIVE HAS BEEN SAFELY
TUCKED AWAY WHERE THEY BELONG
AND LET FIDEL HAVE A CIGAR

Land of the Free and Brave
Or perhaps not too brave, but deluded and enslaved

How do true Israelites stand by while
their Hordes of Barbarians
Murder Innocent People
Orchestrating media-lies and deceptions
Of your own Peoples

In the Name of what?
It's Lunacy and your day is Done
or I WILL SMITE YOU DOWN
AS YOUR HOLY BOOKS SAY

DO NOT DO SUCH THINGS
IN MY NAME

AS ALLAH, AS YHVH, AS CHRIST
AS KRISHNA, WHO SLEW THE HORDES
WITH SPIRITUAL WARRIORS
WHO WANT LIFE FOR YOUR CHILDREN
AND MINE

A FREE WORLD OF ALL THAT IS GOOD
IN MODERN CIVILIZATION
BEFORE YOU ALL PASS A WAY

I WILL GIVE YOU LIGHT
AND DIRECTION
NO MORE SHALL DECEPTION
STEAL THE SOULS
OF BELOVED CHILDREN

SEND the scum TO CUBA,
A JUST REWARD FOR SUCH
UNSPEAKABLE THINGS
OR, I WILL BRING MY WRATH DOWN
UPON THE NATIONS
AND BEGIN WITH PUPPETS
MASTERMINDS WHO HAVE
NO MIND

THE PEOPLE, OR SLUGS, WHO
HAVE NO LIVE OF THEIR OWN
WHO SURELY LEAD YOU TO DEATH.

CHILDREN OF ISRAEL
YOU ARE WARNED

TELL THAT TO YOUR INELLEGENCE
SERVICES, AND SECRET POLICE
AND MEDIA, WHICH DECEIVES THE
TRUE PEOPLE OF ISRAEL
STAGING THEIR OWN NEWS
AND MASS DECEITS
WHO HAVE FORGOTTEN
THEMSELVES AND THEIR GOD

WHO WILL NOW SMITE THEM DOWN
STEP DOWN 7 THOUSAND WAR-PLANES
AND ALL

I WILL SEARCH YOU OUT
AND TRACK YOU TO THE END OF YOUR
DAYS, THESE ARMIES OF HORDES
THE ASSES WHO SPEAK IN MY NAME
YOU DONT KNOW WHAT MY NAME IS.

The Beast has sealed its own fate
Now coming undone.

COUNTDOWN TO 2012
AND BEYOND [1]

Humankind is at a critical period in modern history. A grand epic
tale of psychopaths, cruelty and criminality, is unfolding on the world
stage. Forces of evil are having their days of cruelty, deceit, perversion and power, and bringing about new stages of international terrorism, violence and the poisoning of populations. The banking
and corporate elites continue the intentional looting of the wealth
of nations, poisoning the populace and environment, secretly dissolving democratic institutions and sovereignties, and carrying out
state-sponsored terrorist acts around the world. Their lethal arsenals
include new biological weapons and inoculations, mind control technologies and police state weapons, weather modification and earth
upheavals played on a nightmare HAARP. Their upcoming plans include massive genocide, internments, famines, starvation and impoverishment. Mass genocides can be effected through the release of
biological weapons and/or enforced inoculations, starvation and the
destruction of the food supplies, cataclysmic earth events, or even a
World War III all in service of the eugenic plans of the psychopaths,
perverts and Satanists who came to rule to world--who consider
themselves *the elites* and *illuminated*.

Wow, what a wild story and it is true, however beyond the capacity
of most pea-brains to grasp. The attempt to enlighten the masses of
humankind is like trying to fill a sieve and the slaves to do not have
the courage, or *'new heart,'* required to face the real Beast in modern
times. The enemies were domestic all the time and not foreign--with-
in our own nations instead of half way around the world in some in-

---

[1] This is the primary writing on the New World Order and 2012 which has been
featured on the www.zeropoint.ca website over the past years, revised periodically.

vaded and desecrated countries, like Afghanistan and Iraq, rich in oil, drugs and human suffering. There were no Muslims attacking the US in high jacked airplanes on 9-11, as the public was led to believe just like any other Hollywood Tale and fed as propaganda through the Media of Lies. The whole thing was a fraud and the people who committed it are still in power, while none of our police and intelligence services capture the real terrorists but instead knowingly and unknowingly protect and serve them.

The conspiracy theorists were right all along after all — as documented by Alex Jones at www.prisonplanet.com and within such a real news source such as www.globalresearch.ca, www.informationclearinghouse.info and http://republicbroadcasting.org . The sleeping people and the little lost sheep still believe that Osama and his reindeers crashed down such wonderful towers, and that the intelligence and police really do capture the bad guys instead of protecting them. The citizenry of America is more concerned with men playing games with balls, than with the life of their families, nation, the environment or humankind. The American dream became the American nightmare and all the high ideals of America, Canada and Mexico as sovereign nations within a sane world community were proven to be illusory and based on lies and deceits. As if America had some democracy to spread. America is not a democracy but a psychopathocracy — a country run by a psychopathic elite, as are Israel and Great Britain, the United Nations and Canada, and most of the countries of the world.

The masses of humanity have been deceived like little sheep --at home in front of the TV, listening to the radio and reading their newspapers; while at work, in their churches and synagogues. They have been intentionally deluded by the corporate Media of lies and the education of double-think, self-absorbed in the culture of materialism and narcissism.

Whatever happened to the values of humanity, to the Constitution and Bills of Rights, and the inherent moral principles of what is right or wrong?   The neo-con, like neo-Nazi spiders, have woven their webs of deceit, jockeyed and perverted the police and judicial powers and attained a insidious fascist control of the lives of the populace. Madmen at the helms of nations, lusting for further blood, power and control, and willing for egomaniacal and satanic ends to even plunge humankind into pandemics and extermination and even a World War Three   all in the service of a claimed 'New World Order,' which I prefer to call the *Old World Psychiatric Disorder*. Humankind has never known life apart from the control of such self styled elites and monopoly men.

The criminal invasion of mid-Eastern lands, black operations groups around the world, psychopaths and perverts at the heads of the na- tions, hidden elites, pharmaceuticals and poisons, bioterrorism by our own governments, the corporate greed of the masters of war   that Dylan sang of, the lies and cover-ups of 9/11 and the establishment of the New World Order, are all concocted by the pseudo-illuminate, puppets, kings and queens. Behind the scene as a shadow is a cabal of Satanists, psychopaths and perverts, who have lost their hearts and souls and fallen under the control of alien intelligences and beings. Satan is said to have a hierarchy of servants and we certainly witness this in the crimes of our governments and police. Meanwhile, forces of light awaken people around the world to the deceits of the lie and those *upright of heart* struggle to bring forth the truth to the world of sleepwalkers in order to awaken from *the nightmare parable* --being lived out in the life of contemporary humanity. The human race be- came a rat race and was deceived by a pseudo-master race. Oh, what a sad Tale of unspeakable deceit and cruelty!

Will the Tale of *The Two Towers* be followed by part III, *The Return of the King* and the restoration of righteousness to the world, as should happen in a Hollywood tale as it did in *The Lord of the Rings* and all before the new age Mayan calendar year of 2012? Or will humankind sink further into the Orwellian nightmare, webs of deceit and lies, with inoculations and implants, chemtrail spraying and GM (geneti- cally modified) poisoning, the unspeakable greed of the elites, alien

control and lunacy, and planetary processes of what G. I. Gurdjieff
called the *"processes of reciprocal destruction,"* or simply 'war'? Humankind is moving towards Armageddon, while US, British and Israeli
forces and hidden elites carry out international plots and plans, and the
banksters impoverish the population--all part of what Bush called "the
third wave." Indeed, money, sex and power are the three characteristic
motives of men one, two and three, of the seven possible levels of human evolution. The third wave is that of power, as wielded by the heads
of states and the underlying world tyrants, about now to conduct other
mass murders in Iran, Pakistan, Palestine and elsewhere even against
their own countrymen, committing more crimes against humanity and
further starving and sickening the peoples of the world.

The *World Health Organization*, an assembly staffed in the 1950's by
ex-Nazi doctors and scientists, proponents of eugenics, is now man-
dating *enforced inoculations* for the masses of the world's populations,
supposedly to protect them against viruses which the same cabal of
pharmaceutical giants have designed! The new world order elite aim
to reduce the world's population to their aim stated on the Georgian
Guidestones of five hundred million. And so America, as a nation,
moves forward to massive genocide of its citizenry, all the sheep who
believed that their masters would not skin them alive and devour them.

Chemtrails, inoculations and biological weapons, implants, pharmaceuticals and poisons, HAARP, weather control and mind control--
the forces of Darkness have an arsenal of weapons for homicide and
genocide and to spread terrorism throughout the world, while the
corporate media of lies has been able to intentionally deceive, ma-
nipulate and confuse the little sheep brains.

The poor little sheep are being led to slaughter, hypnotized by black magicians and deceived by the medias of lies. Oh poor America, poor England, poor Israel, poor world, poor Muslim, Christians and Jews, poor humankind, all to sink to such depths of depravity as evident throughout the world. The Hollywood Tales became more important than the life of the Holy World--the light and the truth, the mysteries and cosmic nature of love. What a sad and pathetic Tale of humankind! And the masses of humankind do not even know that they are parts of such grand and psychopathological Tales as they are so asleep and deceived!

CRIMES
AGAINST
HUMAN-
ITY

The Crime[2]
You have been 'punked, ' 'had,' CONNED

TRIALS AND TRIBULATIONSARE UPON US

A criminal cover up has occurred—of what actually occurred on September 11, 2001—9/11. Fortunately, around the world, millions of people have now woken up and learnt these undeniable facts: The collapse of the world trade towers was a "con"—a put on. You were 'had' in popular lingo. There were *no Arab terrorists* and the burning airplanes did not cause the buildings to collapse. Instead, the buildings were intentionally demolished using the airplanes as a distraction, so that the public would not realize or understand how the buildings were actually blown up from inside! A huge volume of scientific evidence and eyewitness accounts substantiate these claims— largely available free through the Internet at www.video.Google.com. Search the Truth of 9/11. The myth of Arab terrorists was spread through the Media, through the cover-ups by the police and intelligence communities, and through the U. S. government's own 9/11 Commission Report, or 'Omission Report' as labelled by one author. Most of the public is so weak in their bodies, minds and hearts, that they are incapable of grasping the true nature of what was done on September 11, 2001; and further, what this means about the current crisis in the life of humanity on planet Earth.

Humankind is *now facing catastrophes, pestilences and upheavals*—the Trials and Tribulations predicted in the sacred books of Christians (*New*

---

[2]This article was written in August of 2006 and on September 11 of 2006, Karen and I went to Parliament Hill in Ottawa, expecting there to be thousands of people protesting the fraud of 9-11, Canada's involvement in the Afghanistan war, and so on. Instead, we were the only two truth activists there with our signs that 9-11 was an inside job and distributing this synopsis of our studies at the time. I have been reluctant then to change this chapter beyond basic editing despite how my understanding has subsequently evolved. At that time in 2006 until 2010, I still believed that there were at least airplanes involved on 9-11 and not simply media hoaxes and studio trickery. (See Section IV.)

Testament in *Revelations*), Jews (*Old Testament* in *Ezekiel*) and Muslims in the *Koran*. End times are upon us in these years of the Beast, 2006, and there will be great upheavals, destruction and pestilence over the next years as these savage characters stage further terrorist incidents within our society and try to take further steps towards establishing what they call *the New World Order*. As the Truth of 9/11 emerges into human consciousness, new terrorist schemes will be hatched within these criminal networks to justify further security and police state tactics, and mass entrapments, and to further undermine the criminal justice system. The new Millennium or Age begins on December 21 2012, according the Illuminati's own fabricated end date, and the times of the end are upon us. This is happening NOW, although the mass public is deluded as sheep and 'led to believe' in Arab terrorism. Humankind now lives in police states as Neo-Nazi secret societies and the Bilderberg groups are directing the unfoldment of horrific events to come--with their biological, electronic, pharmaceutical and nuclear weapons, and media control. The elected government is either deceived as sheep or controlled as goats by the underlying secret shadow government. Horrifying events are now unfolding in the life of humankind. You must attempt to be *'upright of heart'* to maintain your inner sanity in times of such chaos and criminal activity within our society, even by those peoples you have trusted. Begin by learning the Truth of 9/11 and spreading it to those who are ready to hear of such things. Copy and distribute this notice freely. The time is upon us.

There is a hierarchy of secret police and international terrorists within our society, a corporate elite, international banksters and Wall Street financiers, who carry out acts of terrorism around the world—to support the invasion of Arab lands, war industries, police and security services, and the sales of pharmaceuticals. These international terrorists own the world's major media—your TV and radio stations and newspapers and actually *stage terrorist acts* themselves, while then controlling what the public is *led to believe* through the media of lies. The gullible public are like little sheep being led to slaughter. In Canada, this includes the CBC, CTV and the Citizens, Stars and Suns, and so on, all either owned by the Bilderbergs or controlled by the intelligence/police networks.[3]

---

[3] In 2011, Peter Mansbridge, head of the CBC, Canada's supposed publicly owned news outlet, attended the Bilderberg group.

In fact, the *Two Towers* of the World Trade Center, along with Building 7, were detonated by the tenant, Mr. Silverstein, in association with the elite of the US and Israeli governments, the secret police—including top CIA, FBI, Homeland Security and the Mossad, directed and supported by elite Wall Street Financiers, Zionist banksters and War Merchants—of the secretive Bilderberg group or other secret societies. Insiders intentionally demolished the buildings using explosives and unknown directed energy weapons, while the public was intentionally deceived and all the criminal evidences were hidden and destroyed by the police services as much as was possible. The evidences of the cover-up and the falsifications of the corporate Media are all evidence of the sinister plots and conspiracy webs of the Beast of modern times.

But unfortunately, just as there is no Santa Claus—get that straight first, and then maybe you can come to realize, that there were no real Arab Terrorists high jacking airplanes. That was the Con. It simply didn't happen that way and it never could have happened that way, for All Eternity No matter what you have been *told or led to believe,* or how stupid you have been, you have been like *sheep being led to slaughter*. The Truth of 9/11 is far *more horrifying* than the real event.

As it is, the destruction of the World Trade Towers poses huge enigmas and uncertainties. One way to understand these—is through TRUTH— the horrible Truth of 9/11, the largest mass murder within Western Society within the new Millennium, caught on film. The Beast within western society reared its head within the nations, to stage scenes of mass murder while intentionally scapegoating Arabs and Muslims, to justify crimes of mass murder, imperialism and cruel steps towards an Orwell police state and world-domination.[4] They even channelled their crimes into a Hollywood movie—to maintain the public's state of confusion, misinformation and delusion.

One out of three Americans now knows the fact that 9/11 was a huge public deception, *a con*, intentionally perpetrated on humanity, not by imaginary Arabs or Moslems, but by those on the INSIDE—IT WAS AN INSIDE JOB. These facts can easily be documented and demonstrated conclusively within any impartial court of law anywhere in the world, if such still exists—

---

[4]The motto of the Israeli intelligence service, the Mossad, is "by way of deception, we wage war," and this has in fact been done repeatedly through modern history.

before any sane, impartial judge, if such still exists. Unfortunately, the judicial system has been infiltrated or intimidated by these same underlying criminal networks within American, Canadian, British and Israeli society, as elsewhere. A huge volume of evidence is publicly available — at www. video.Google.com, www.globalresearch.ca, www.prisonplanet.com and one could draw from thousands of eyewitness, scholars, scientists and investigators, to flesh out these evidences. Type in 9 11, Bilderbergs, the Illuminati and Zionism, and explore a wealth of educational films, evidences and arguments — demonstrating absolutely conclusively scientifically and/or legally, that the collapse of the World Trade Towers was *an inside job — a con, and almost all of humanity got fooled. You were 'had.''*

Do not *'believe'* what the Truth Movement is saying, as you have been fooled by THE CON, *like sheep to do — that is to believe.'* It is of no use now to YOU to again 'simply believe,' what is said here. Instead, you have to regain control of your natural intelligence and attention, and make conscious effort to investigate, research and then finally LEARN THE TRUTH OF 9/11. You OWE this to yourself, your children and 7 future Generations of God's Children. The LIES OF 9/11 MUST BE EXPOSED before it is too late for us as American, Canadian, or World Citizens — as Moslems, Christians, and Jews — and for all the children yet to be poisoned by the deceits of the Beast.

Criminal elements within the United States, Great Britain, Israel, Canada and elsewhere, are the *world terrorists* — not the Arabs, nor the American people, nor the vast majorities in military services, nor ordinary people just 'doing their jobs,' nor the Arabs, nor the Jews, nor Christians — but particular people within the US administration, a wealthy corporate and banking elite and prominent Wall Street Financiers. This includes President Bush and his family, back to his grandfather Prescott who helped to finance the Nazis, and all the president's cronies, the *black operation intelligence groups*. All of these groups are involved in the secretive Bilderberg Group who own the media — lots of oil, the weapons industries, drugs, sex slaves and gold, police and securities organizations, and pharmaceutical companies, and who still want more human blood and subservience.

Canada's own prime minister has now been entwined with the Bilderbergs and the Council of Foreign Relations, and these sinister plots. The Canadian Forces in the near-East have been completely deceived about the events of 9/11 and the true causes of the events now unfolding on the world stage.

The Canadian Forces are being used as pawns in criminal wars, enrolled into a neo-Nazi scheme of these networks of criminal psychopaths. These perverse elements within decent society have schemed these horrendous crimes against humanity and fooled the little sheep who *"were told"* or *"led to believe,"* that …blah, blah, blah--as sheep led to slaughter.

The Lies of the Beast are now available at local theatres, with popcorn and patriotic bravo and masked by a censored and scripted nightly-news. In modern human society, humankind currently faces a situation similar to the totalitarian state envisioned by George Orwell, in his horrifying novel *1984*. These elites stage `false flag terrorist` events to advance their agendas and to justify their war crimes. To conquer Poland, the Nazis sent their own secret police to massacre German citizens in Poland, and then controlled the media to justify invading Poland to protect the German people. This is exactly what has happened in contemporary society. Various supposedly 'Arab terrorist' acts are carried out by members of our own society and simply blamed on the Arabs, to justify imperialism and movement towards what the elites call the New World Order—the actual term used by Hitler! The little pea-brained human beings, half brain dead from inoculations, fluoride and their favorite TVs, forget what happened on the traumatizing day of September 11, 2001 and fail to understand the hidden patterns of history and the perverse psychopathy of fascism and Zionism.

The Truth of 9/11 is now known around the World, although most people don't understand the broader dynamics of what is involved and hidden behind these events. In August 2006, CBC Radio reported that the alternative film *LOOSE CHANGE*, has been downloaded 10 million times from www.video.Google.com! This movie is an account of many of the enigmas of 9/11. Although you personally may not have known the facts reported here, that 9/11 was an inside job, many millions of people around the world do—like it or not. Of course, the CBC show on the topic was a totally superficial attempt to cover-up the real issues involved here, further evidence of their own complicity.

To be disillusioned of the Con requires that you learn *what a con is, how events can be staged* and how to deceive the human race, while you control *the media of Deceit* and commit mass murder. The conspirators, *'who breath together,'* then frame someone else as a 'scapegoat' to justify imperialism, war industries, worldwide terror and steps towards a totalitarian society. BUT, the CON is exposed NOW, known worldwide!

In a con, you simply say—"Hey, *look, nice birdies in the sky*," while using thermate bombs in the interior of the buildings to commit mass murder. The airplanes simply did not cause the building to collapse! *This is, was and forever will have been --a con, a Hollywood con*. Distract the viewer's attention—it's as old a plot as we have stories. Afterwards, very soon afterwards, the terrorists have a scapegoat in a quest for blood and to make some more monies to line those nice pockets on those fancy pants.

Crash two planes into two buildings, detonate the buildings from within-without; fire a missile and report an imaginary plane hitting the Pentagon, seize any available videos; down a plane, which has no bodies for forensic analysis, and no one is allowed to see. Have some telephones and stage dramatic distress calls—and nobody noticed! Clean up the crime scenes and ship the evidences to China or use for landfill to short-circuit criminal investigations.

At least, for a while, only a few noticed. However, over time, more and more scientists, scholars, writers and researchers, and individuals, learned the Truth of 9/11. This is now a worldwide movement. Hey, a mass murder has been committed in New York and none investigated, and the authorities have only hidden the truth and deceived the public. Millions and millions of people around the world now realize *the massive lies and cover-ups of 9/11!* The so-called *"conspiracy theories"* were really supported by a huge volume of evidences of international terrorism, conspiracy and financing, all along. They were never just theories. The crimes of the Beast are the blood strains through history, including the assassination of the President John Kennedy—beloved by the United States of America, Martin Luther King, John Lennon, Robert Kennedy, train and subway bombing around the world, the Oklahoma City bombing and many lesser known catastrophes. The Beast plays the human race like puppets, sowing discord and confusion, creating religious and cultural animosities and considers itself a *'master race,'* even as God's chosen.

9/11 was an inside job. To believe otherwise—that the planes crashed the Towers, causing them to fall at near free-fall speed in under 15 seconds each, to collapse perfectly into their own 'footprint,' is to accept the possibility, that on that day, September 11, 2001—*all the known laws of physics, chemistry, civil engineering and material science were temporarily suspended*. Further, it requires that you arbitrarily dismiss the testimonials of thousand of firefighters, civilians and the media's own initial news reports (as released before the cover-up began), all which document massive interior explosions in the sub-basements and throughout the Two Towers. These are visibly evident on many of the video records of these events--to a trained eye, or ear. How asleep is humankind, how blind and deaf, how stupid!!!

No buildings in the history of the world, past, present or future, will ever, ever, ever, collapse in such a manner as did the perfectly controlled demolitions of 9/11 — *except by being perfectly controlled demolitions.* If it quacks like a duck, waddles like a duck, looks like a duck and even leaves a smell like duck-shit, then it probably is — a duck and its doings. These claims could easily be proven within any impartial court of Law in the World, before even half-sane judges. Unfortunately, the Beast has rendered the Justice System, like the supposed democratic political systems, impotent. Millions now live in fear, unable to speak and lacking the courage to face the real Beast within our society.

Further, how or why conceivably would the tenant, Mr Silverstein, intentionally 'pull' Building Number 7, as he himself states on public TV, after calling off the firemen extinguishing the relatively minor fires there on two floors? Building number 7 was a 47-story building containing criminal investigations of Wall Street financiers and corporate criminals, and perhaps also used for strategy rooms to exercise *the con*. Further, although the public has not been informed of this, Building 6 of the World Trade complex (a smaller 7 or 8 story building) was also demolished within one minute of the downing of the second Tower. This building was obliterated, blown up from inside, leaving a massive hole. Its destruction passed by unmentioned in the official 9/11 report — itself an intentional cover-up. Buildings 6 and 7 played pivotal roles in these schemes, allowing the perpetrators to have the necessary office space, to commit mass murder with remote demolition controls and joysticks.

After two 100+ story buildings collapse, killing thousands, traumatizing New York and the world with an overwhelming calamity, Mr. Silverman out of *'something' in his heart — these evil inclinations*, said *'pull it.'* Of course, he has never had to explain how the second building was so cleverly wired for another perfect demolition — amidst the chaos of New York, transporting explosives through the burning building, the mayhem, with no permits, all between the time he talked to the fire chief in the afternoon and the five thirty demolition. Is this conceivable? No, building 7 was also pre-wired.

The Ray of Light is the Truth. The human race actually now has overwhelmingly convincing criminal evidence to bring these individuals into criminal courts throughout the world. Unfortunately, due to complexities and confusions within all the evidences, the lack of human memory or informed media, the enormity of the underlying schemes is beyond the grasp or understanding of most common folk—who cannot imagine such horrors. However, if the keys to these mysteries are provided, it all fits together as a whole of undeniable Truth. 9/11 was a con, the criminal acts were covered over, and the lies and public deception was perpetrated intentionally through the media, owned by the Bilderbergs, their associates and pawns.

All of these types, these self-styled psychopathic elites, are complicit in these unspeakable crimes and public deception, and need to be exposed and incarcerated—to re-establish democracy, freedom and love, and higher ideals within the Nations of the World. The seizure of the estates of those involved in these international conspiracies and terrorist activities would immediately pay of the debts of all Nations and serve to re-establish justice and truth within the world. So many are pawns and puppets within the ranks of the Beast and are manipulated in ways unspeakable.

Learning the truth of 9/11 requires dissolving the conditioning and delusions of the mind — the spells and misleading information fostered by the mass media's conditioning of your little pea-brain minds and their intentional 'disinformation' programs. The Canadian and American Intelligence Services have never shared intelligence with the Canadian or American public, but only cover their complicities, themselves integral parts of these sinister plots. As Hitler and other fascist tyrants have known through history—stage events, control the media, finance the war machines, form security firms and secret police, and deceive the Public—all of these strategies are parts of the Beast. The Bilderbergs and the other major secret societies' own philosophical and strategic writings and documents conclusively demonstrate such lines of knowledge and 'master-craft planning.'

Every single aspect of the official 9/11 Commission report has been discredited over time, as the sick tapestry of events has been woven together, by those wanting to learn the truth of 9-11. All the glaring inadequacies of the official report itself are simply further proof of the criminal cover-up and mass level duplicities, intentionally designed to conceal rather than to reveal the Truth of 9/11. The evidence of the cover-up are evident throughout the history of the official investigations and sham inquiries, and through the destruction of evidences, hidden by those involved. Further, that there has been an intentional deception through the media could be easily proved within criminal courts, with access to historical records—to illustrate and document how these deceptions are fostered.

The plane crashes were intentionally staged to portray crazed Arab terrorists, while the *mastermind criminal syndicate*, included the owner of the buildings, individuals within the government and intelligence services of the United States of America (at varied elite levels), very efficient demolitions experts—black operatives, and a clan or cabal of international bankers and financiers in the war industries and Wall Street, who own the media, lots of silver and gold, oil and drugs, and sex slaves. It's all there. They're all up to no good. They offer nothing for the soul life of humankind, nor the future of Canadian, American, British or Israel society, or any sane nation, or for the health of this Planet.

The truth about 9-11 is *now known all around the world*, although not reported on the *FOX, NBC, GLOBAL, CTV*, the *CBC*, in the STARS, or SUNS, OR CITIZENS-any media owned by these crooks and deceivers, all the goats, up to the most delusional psychopathic murderers. DIS-INFORMATION and confusion is concocted instead. However, this knowledge is available free through the Internet Worldwide. *Wake up*. The issue of 9/11 is a symptom of the most serious problem facing humanity today on this planet—this global crime syndicate.

The entire assets of this sad cast of characters should be immediately seized within the national borders of Canada, as they should be throughout the entire world—for their financing and orchestrating of international terrorist activities. That is what has happened in this grand script, as they are to bring about their own demise, shotting themselves in the foot, providing us with the criminal evidence to convict them around the world and all the necessary anti-terrorist legislation now to be used against themselves. The Nations and Citizens of the World should publicly own all the ill-gotten gains of these scoundrels. This vast wealth can simply be used to pay of the vast debts of the nations, due primarily to the Global Crime Syndicates who have highjacked our nations. These vast fortunes can be used to repair the damages done — beginning with the Holy Lands and Middle East — and to bring about justice, education, health care and healing — throughout this Holy Planet Earth, whose Beauties sustain our inner life.

We must heal this planet and the hearts and souls of humankind — all beginning with the Truth of 9/11, and then to recover from the traumas and nightmares concocted for the human race. The Bilderberg group, who last vacationed in Kanata, Ontario could enjoy a holiday in Cuba, to reflect upon their horrendous crimes against humanity, if Mr Castro doesn't mind. They can enjoy the Bay of Pig life, watch their own favourite movies and media news-clips, eat popcorn, have all their own pharmaceuticals and inoculations, implants, whatever they want, even the bird flu and chemtrails, along with their fool's Oscar gold.

You, as an individual, upon reading this letter, are subject to American, Canadian, British and International Law, which forbids the participation in, the support of, or the financing of international terrorist activities. You must stand down from any and all activities, as you might otherwise perpetrate, in service of the Beast. The Media of Lies can again serve the ideals of a free speech in a sane and democratic world, and simply turn about to become a Media of Truth, beginning with the Truths of 9/11. The Media staff themselves will be freed of the tyrants within their own ranks and step up to their roles as true Citizens, serving an informed public, in a society which forbids mass-murder, 'hate propaganda' and 'public deception.' Within the armies and intelligence services, those who remain 'upright of heart, ' still believing in the ideals of America, Canada and the International community, must stand up to the plate, armed with the truth in whatever capacity you are able, to safely bring about the transformations required within our societies. These Webs of Deceit are becoming progressively and more widely known within modern society. The 9/11 Truth Movement is now World Wide, no matter what you have been **'led like sheep to slaughter'** to believe.

You, reading this letter, are reminded of the Nuremberg Judgements, concerning duplicities in crime. If you are in the media, police, military, intelligence communities, judiciary or government, or any other sector of our society involved in these criminal conspiracies, know NOW, YOU ARE BOUND by the NUREMBERG DECISIONS, and can no longer simply, *'do your job as you are told'* if you should have reasonably known, that your actions are similarly complicit in such terrorist activities, cover-ups and conspiracies. NO more excuses, no more lies. The Gig is up—the Con is over. The Beast had its day and its dinner, but then sealed its own Fate. These unspeakable crimes will bring about the demise of these Zionist networks and the global crime syndicate, although progressively in 7 Stages as the Truth is revealed.

O, Canada lost:

THERE'S AN ELEPHANT IN THE ROOM[5]

The expression "There is an elephant in the room" refers to something highly obvious to perception but to which no one responds. No one talks about the elephant in the room even though it is right there in front of everyone and its presence poses a threat to all involved. However, people carry on *as if* there is no elephant in the room—as if they are too numbed, confused or afraid. Instead, people carry on their busy lives while ignoring the elephant in the room and not speaking about it.

Today, in Canada, we have an elephant in the room—something quite monstrous which is threatening us as a nation, in our individual lives and that of our children and grandchildren, and it threatens to bring about further wars, starvation, impoverishment, poisoning, violence and human suffering throughout Canada and the broader world. The Beast has already stolen our countries and resources from us and is threatening even our continued existence on this planet.

J. E. Hoover, former head of the FBI, referred to a conspiracy "so monstrous" that a normal individual could not conceive or imagine that such might exist. Along the same line, Dwight Eisenhower, former president of the United States, warned us of the "military-industrial complex" which

---

[5] This article was written in August of 2006 and on September 11 of 2006, Karen and I went to ParliamThe next four chapters are from an early draft of a book that was to be entitled, *O, Canada Lost: The Ascendancy of the New World Psychiatric Disorder*, detailing aspects of the new world order agenda and how this is impacting Canada, America and the world in every sphere of our lives. I began to write this book in the spring of 2009 at the time I was involved with the *Canadian Action Party*. On July 2nd of 2009, Karen and my house in Kars, Ontario burnt down, officially due to squirrels or chipmunks. After resuming my writings, I continued with this until the spring of 2010, when K. and I moved into the current Kemptville Zero Point centre. In the spring of 2010, I also stopped working with the Canadian Action Party. *O, Canada Lost* was put aside as I began to self publish my primary books on mystical studies and modern science and I withdrew more from those political efforts which seemed to go nowhere and which had caused such problems in K. and my relationship and life during those times.

threatened the future of American democracy; as had John Kennedy warned us before his assassination. Unfortunately, conspiracies are real and history is littered with the tragedies deliberately created for the masses of humanity by the shadow elements within our societies — the real terrorists of modern times.

Some people will want to dismiss me as a 'conspiracy theorist,' which is actually a label that I would be pleased to accept. Firstly, science is made up of 'theories' — like the theory of relativity, quantum theory, the theory of evolution, cognitive-behavioural theory, and much more. So, as I consider myself a scientist, I try to understand the evidences and competing theories which explain the various conspiracies being carried forward in our era and which have been carried out through the centuries. If anyone is not a conspiracy theorist, then they simply understand nothing of human history as most of the blood stains through the tapestry of human history are the results of such conspiracies.

The term 'conspiracy' suggests *breathing together* in private or away from public view with the intent of engaging in criminal and illegal activities. Criminals on all levels are always conspiring and that is the basis of organized crime. In 2006, the Bilderberg group met in Kanata, Ontario, just outside of Ottawa, to conspire together. The head of the world bank, representatives of all the financial elites, the queen of Holland, war criminal Henry Kissinger, David Rockefeller, media moguls and all, gathered together to plan the next stages of bringing about their *new world order* — world government by the scumbags at the top. People meet together and conspire about the criminal things they intend to do to the world's populations, who still believe that they live in democracies. In 2007, these creeps met in Turkey, in 2008, West Virginia, USA, 2009 in Spain, 2011 in Switzerland. All of the Canadian Prime Ministers of recent history have been involved with the Bilderberg group, as it is within these inner circles that the fortunes of the parties, the leaders and the country are conspired, as well as within the secretive Council of Foreign Relations, the Trilateral Commission, and elsewhere.

The government itself has conspiracy theories — ones to confuse and deceive the sleeping public who are led to believe all kinds of ridiculous things which people swallow whole as if they were quite stupid. Particularly, the governments maintains the ridiculous myth that Osama Bin Laden and his reindeer made the New York twin towers blow up and collapse in fifteen seconds each, and that an airplane hit the Pentagon and disappeared into a fourteen foot hole, and that no-one covered anything up. These are Tales of fantasy right out of Hollywood and sold through the hypnosis of the media with its multiple levels of deceit, spin and misinformation. People cannot believe in a conspiracy "so monstrous" that our government, police and media would all deliberately deceive the Canadian, American and world populations as to the true causes and events of 9-11. It is certainly more comforting to believe in Arab or Muslim terrorism and to believe the propaganda of our government and media, than it is to grasp the even more ugly truths.

In the movie *The Matrix*, the hero is offered a red pill which enables him to wake up and begin to learn the truth about the matrix, or a blue pill to go back to sleep and return to normal life. If you take the red pill, you will see the elephant in the room and over time you will understand it more and more clearly—who these people are, what their schemes and philosophies are, why they are so degenerated in their nature as to engage in such organized patterns of criminal activity and even in programs of population reduction.

People cannot see the real monster within the room. The monsters were not under the bed, nor over the ocean in Afghanistan and Iraq, but instead, the monsters are within our society and control the American and Canadian governments, the police, intelligence and military communities, the media and corporations, the pharmaceutical, hospital and medical industries, the brainwashing of your children through the so-called 'educational system,' and the impotent churches, synagogues and mosques.

The Canadian people and the Canadian government are controlled by a criminal class of corporate elite, financiers and 'banksters,' and government officials. This system, whereby our elected officials are only the puppets of the shadow government can now be more clearly understood and proven. The evidences have all come out as the internet has made a wealth of documentary movies and evidences available to capable researchers, Of course, there are still many mysteries and unresolved issues but the overwhelming volume of evidence clearly document the nature of the monstrous conspiracy which has been perpetrated upon the peoples of Canada, the United States and elsewhere around the world. The elites themselves declare their intention of bringing about *a new world order* — which I prefer to call the *old world psychiatric disorder* — a world controlled by psychopaths, perverts and pedophiles, megalomaniacs and the *masters of war*, that Bob Dylan sang of forty years ago.

And so, we have an elephant in the room, a monstrous conspiracy, and the peoples are unable to speak of it or deal with the enormity of the problems and lies. Further, Canada has been lost. While we were sleeping, they have come and stolen it all away. Canadian democracy is a lie, as all five political parties — the Conservatives, Liberals, NDP, the Bloc and the Greens are all part of the old world psychiatric disorder system, and all have played a role in deceiving the Canadian public in support of the elitists' agenda. None will speak the truth of 9-11 and they have allowed the Canadian public to be intentionally deceived while our soldiers die in a criminal war in Afghanistan, and more and more police state powers are imposed upon people.

The Prime Minister of Canada, Stephen Harper, confirms his support for Israeli war crimes and terrorist acts committed against the people of Gaza and around the world, including their participation in 9-11. The Prime Minister hides the fact of Israeli involvement in perpetrating the 9-11 events, now clearly known, and the sick Zionist control of western governments and the media has now been more widely exposed. On a truth net radio show, one announcer tells the joke of there being a sign within the Senate of the US, reading, "*Beware, Israeli occupied territory.*"

The Bilderbergs, the Trilateral Commission, the Council of Foreign Relations, all the Rockefeller and Rothschild institutes and think tanks, these groups and more, like those that conspire at Bohemian grove in California where the Bushes, Clintons and others run around with no clothes on, enjoy each others fine company and pee on trees, all of these are *conspiratorial groups* scheme such things as mass murders, war industries, how to steal the wealth of nations, how to sicken and starve the populations, how to modify the weather and use psychotropic weapons, what false flag terrorist events to stage next and who to blame it on and much more. We have a nation ruled by lunatics and madmen, megalomaniacs and psychopaths whose ambitions for personal power, sexual perversions and greed, has allowed them to rise to the top, as scum rises on the waters of life. The sheep people of Canadian society know nothing of this or are afraid of even looking at the elephant in the room. Mainly they are under the mass hypnosis of their media—their televisions, radios and newspapers, and the lies perpetrated through the educational system. Canada has been lost to the control of these people, hidden behind the scene, while their corporate media lulls the population into sleep while feeding them propaganda and lies. The Media even plays a role in staging events which are actually scripted like a soap opera behind the scenes.

Canada has been infiltrated at the highest levels of our police and intelligence communities, the military and government, the banking and corporate worlds, the media and health care industries. These same criminal elites will now impoverish the population, consolidate more and more of the banks and corporations under their control, steal the pension funds of the peoples of Canada, sicken and weaken the population through the poisoning of the food and water supply, intentionally spreading poisons among the population through inoculations and chemtrail spraying, while they create an Orwellian nightmare world of Big Brother surveillance, police state mindsets and mind control methodologies. They even imagine that they are 'masons,' doing god's work or that of Lucifer. The conspiracy really is quite monstrous and beyond the capacity of most busy little pea brains to grasp.

Nicholas Rockefeller once explained to film maker Aaron Russo that the aim of the elites, so-called, is ultimately to have a micro-chipped population while they own all of the world's wealth and natural resources, with common peoples confined to cities as worker populations. Some psychopaths in the Nazi sections of the UN estimate that if the world's population is reduced to the level of two billion, then this would be *sustainable* for their Utopian nightmare world. Another Masonic goof ball even constructed the Georgian Guide Stones in the state of Georgia, US as a tombstone for the people who are to be murdered in the upcoming flood. The first principle engraved into the stone is to "maintain humanity under 500,000,000 in perpetual balance with nature." In Atlanta, Georgia, there are 400,000 coffins, each capable of holding three bodies, and concentration camps have been prepared by FEMA across the nation, as a police state is incrementally crafted throughout America. O, America, land of the free and brave. What a joke. Oh yea, there are camps also for Canadians—outside of Halifax, London, across Canada and into northern BC, and the government is already sending body bags to aboriginal groups!

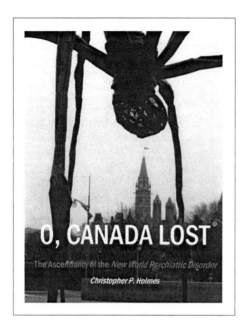

O, CANADA LOST

The Ascendancy of the *New World Psychiatric Disorder*

Christopher P. Holmes

Oh yes: Not only is Canada lost and the US, but further, it is not an elephant in the room, but groups of psychopaths, elitists, war criminals and mass murderers. These psychopaths have high jacked your country, undermined your democracy and are actually spreading illnesses through the nation while corrupting the health care industries and controlling the police services. They have inoculations waiting for you, as well as genetically modified poisons, biological weapons, high tech police equipment and even nuclear weapons. Next time, they will tell you that it is Bugs Bunny and Iranian terrorists who commit a terrorist act, or someone else, depending upon who they plan to invade and murder next in their quest for world domination. What could be more monstrous than this? And it only gets worse.

Goodbye Canada

Paul Hellyer

Goodbye Canada

In *Goodbye Canada*, Paul Hellyer (2001) described globalization as the "relentless drive on the part of the richest, most powerful people in the world to reengineer the global economy for their own benefit." Further, he described this as involving the substitution of "elite global governance as an alternative to the power of nation states." (p. vii) Free trade and globalization are words for "corporate rule" and "colonization," and these undermine Canadian sovereignty and democracy. Hellyer describes the *New World Order* system as "a greed driven monster," a form of "totalitarian capitalism," which is "intrinsically evil because it marginalizes people and countries to the point of despair."

Chapter 2 of *Goodbye Canada* is entitled "THE NEW WORLD (DIS) *ORDER*" and Hellyer opens with David Rockefeller's infamous statement to a Bilderberg group thanking the corporate media for their participation in deceiving the American public as to the goals and activities of the globalists:

> We are grateful to the Washington Post, the New York Times, Time magazine and other great publications whose directors have attended our meetings and respected their promise of discretion for almost forty years. It would have been impossible for us to develop our plan for the world if we had been subjected to the lights of publicity during these years. But the world is now more sophisticated and prepared to march towards a world government. The supranational sovereignty of an intellectual elite and world bankers is surely preferable to the national auto-determination practiced in past centuries.

Hellyer points out that David Rockefeller "sums up what the New World Order is all about—the substitution of elite rule for democracy." He further depicts the "near universal acceptance of globalization as being both inevitable and good for mankind" as the "worst case of brain-washing since the Third Reich in the 1930's."

Hellyer explains that there are three interrelated organizations paramount to the New World Order system — the *Council of Foreign Relations*, the *Bilderbergers* and the *Trilateral Commission*. Hellyer explains that the power of these groups lies with their influence over governments, the corporate media, philanthropic foundations and international financial institutions. In a damning depiction of Canadian politics, Hellyer notes, "political leaders are 'bought' by the elite groups who stand to benefit most from globalization." (p. 49) Furthermore, "the *globalizers ... "buy" governments which willingly hand over the sovereignty of their people ...."* (p. viii) Indeed, Hellyer explains that the sovereignty of Canada has been lost as indeed our prime ministers and other select government figures are and have been members of the CFR, the Trilateral Commission and of the Bilderbergs, while the significance of this fact has been intentionally hidden from the Canadian public by the politicians themselves and by the corporate media, owned by the elites, so-called.

J. Marrs, in *Rule by Secrecy* (2001), presents a similar analysis and explains that each of these three groups is essentially a 'secret society' as the members and contributors are bound by oaths of secrecy. (Article II of the CFR bylaws explicitly states that anyone revealing details of CFR meetings can be dropt from membership.) Similarly, the corporate media intentionally avoids exposing the activities of these groups to public scrutiny and it carries out disinformation programs to marginalize "conspiracy theories," while knowingly deceiving the public. They of course all deserve *David Rockefeller buttons* for their participation in intentionally deceiving the public, so that the globalists and Zionist agendas could be carried forward.

Public officials within the federal and provincial governments have long served the hidden agendas of the financial and corporate elites and not the interests of the common Canadian citizen. The Globalist agenda were initially formulated as "free trade agreements" (the FTA and then the North American Free Trade Agreement, NAFTA), which certainly sounded positive, as does the more recent Security and Prosperity Partnership, the SPP, and the move towards a North American Union, a NAU. However, these agreements did not lead to an enhancement of Canadian business but to job losses and the selling off of Canadian companies and resources. Hellyer explains:

From June 30, 1985, to June 30, 2001, almost 13,000 Canadian companies have been sold to foreigners—the vast majority to our cousins south of the border. ... You don't have to be a rocket scientist to know that it is only a matter of time before companies like Shaw and Rogers cable will be taken over by an American carrier, Bell Canada with CTV in tow will be bought, probably by AT&T, and all the banks will either be owned or controlled by international banks of the scale of J. P. Morgan Chase or Citigroup Inc., and it won't make any difference whether the Canadian banks are merged or not. ... In Canada ... our automotive, gasoline, tire, chemical, soft drinks and many other industries are completely dominated by foreigners. And it is only a matter of time until transportation, telecommunications and banking are added to the list. (p. 4)

If the government continues to relax the rules on foreign ownership it won't be too long before there will be nothing of significance left to sell. Canada will be little more than an empty shell. (p. 10)

The "national treatment" clause of the FTA, signed by Brian Mulroney as Prime Minister, "guaranteed the demise of Canada as a nation state," according to Hellyer. This gives foreign investors and corporations the same rights in the host country as citizens of that country. Hellyer describes this as giving the multinationals "the passport which allows ... unrestricted access. That is what globalization is all about—to give corporations greater rights than people."

Hellyer expresses some major concerns as to what this foreign ownership and corporate control mean. He writes:

But I have a profound distrust of the American government and its foreign policy which is dictated by American corporate interests rather than the interests of the American people. ... The sad fact, which many observers have long suspected, is that we are all being manipulated by a very small but elite group which one could argue is even more powerful than the US government, and which is using that government as its agent in establishing the New World Order. (p. 14)

Hellyer then goes on to explain that the Rockefeller's *Council on Foreign Relations*, the CFR, the Trilateralists and the Bilderbergs, are such secretive societies with globalist plans for a new world order.

The CFR was officially founded on July 29th of 1921. The CFR and its sister organization in London, England, the *Royal Institute of International Affairs (Chatham House)*, were set up by delegates from the 1919 Paris Peace Conference in order to have an international group which would advise their respective governments on international affairs. G. Kah (1978) explains:

> Baron Edmond de Rothschild of France dominated the Paris Peace Conference, and each of the founders to the Royal Institute ended up being men who met Rothschild's approval. The same was true of the Council of Foreign Relations .... (p. 30)

The money for the founding of the CFR came from John D. Rockefeller, J. P. Morgan, Paul Warburg, Jacob Schiff, among others. Prominent directors of the CFR from its inception are the likes of Adlai Stevenson, Cyrus Vance, Zbigniew Brzezinski, Robert Anderson, Paul Volcker, David Rockefeller, Henry Kissinger, Alan Greenspan, George Bush and Richard Cheney. The most powerful man in the CFR during the last decades has been David Rockefeller, grandson of John D. Rockefeller, as the Rockefellers have long been agents to offshore bankers and the Rothschilds. David Rockefeller was a council director for thirty six years, chairman of the board for fifteen years and he continues as an honorary chairman. Generations of the Rockefellers are groomed to continue the tradition of controlling the CFR, along with members from interlocking elite families and banking networks.

Rear Admiral Chester Ward, a CFR member for sixteen years, warned the American people of the intentions of CFR:

> The most powerful cliques in these elitist groups have one objective in common—they want to bring about the surrender of the sovereignty and the national independence of the United States. A second clique of international members of the CFR ... comprises the Wall Street international bankers and their key agents. Primarily, they want the world banking monopoly from whatever power ends up in control of global government. (Kah, 1978, p. 32)

The Rockefellers and the CFR members were influential in setting up the United Nations, the International Monetary Fund (IMF) and World Bank. Oh what a web of deceits and lies these aristocratic families, banksters and criminal cabals have woven through the past decades and centuries. It is certainly beyond what is imagined by the people asleep, conditioned by own self interests, materialism and narcissism, the media and a thousand lies and deceptions.

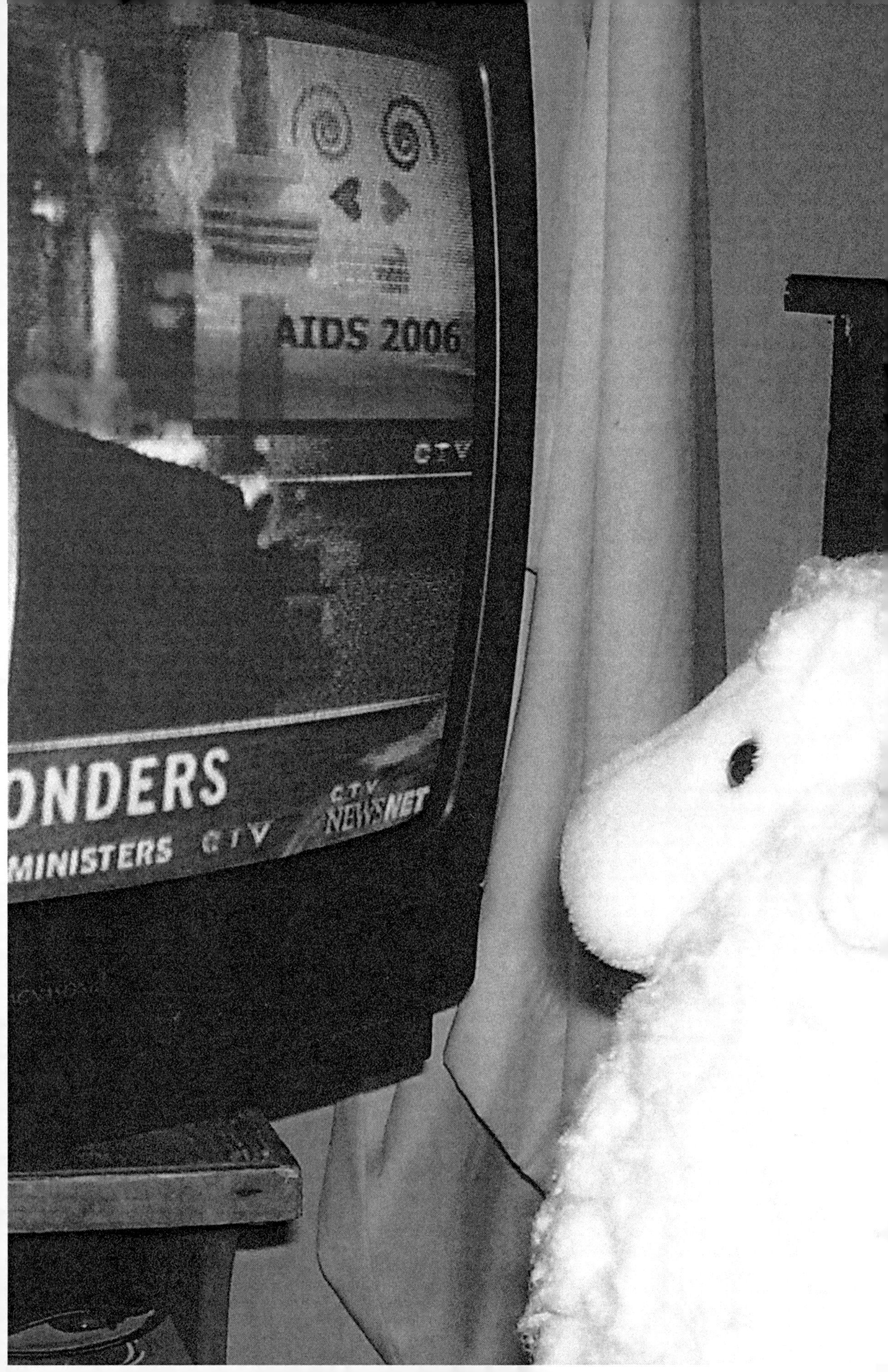
AIDS 2006
CTV
ONDERS
MINISTERS CTV
CTV NEWSNET

Masters of Deceit and Propaganda

The mainstream corporate media consistently lie to the Canadian and American public. These news sources are used to deliberately cover-up the activities of the criminal elites and our criminal governments which they control. They have completely mislead the public about the underlying causes of the wars in Afghanistan and Iraq, the events of 9-11, the causes of the London and Madrid subway bombings, the Oklahoma city bombing, the events of the Mumbai massacres and the conflict in Georgia, the invasion of Libya, the war crimes committed by Israel against the peoples of Gaza, the assassinations of three Kennedys and Martin Luther King, the use of the bailouts to impoverish the populace, the manner in which the elites have schemed the dissolution of national sovereignties and sold off Canadian and American resources to foreign banksters and investors. All of these things are hidden from Canadians and Americans by the lack of mention or minimization, war propaganda and through disinformation. The media obscure the fact that these events are all caused by the same classes of criminal elites, which own the news sources themselves. The corporate media obscure the crimes of their owners and intentionally deceive the public on an ongoing daily basis. The end product is a form of 'sheep news' or 'snooze'—**guaranteed to put you** to sleep so that you have no true understanding of what is happening on the international stage or within your own country.

Not only do the media consistently lie in presenting the activities of your government and the underlying criminal elite, but they actually help in *staging news events*. They are pre-scripted and there are always **'experts' from one of the Rockefeller think tanks or international institute who are ready to be interviewed** by the media whenever they are carrying out another of their crimes. These 'experts' begin to immediately shape your impressionable minds as to the interpretations of the events unfolding in the news. Such so-called experts were suggesting that Osama bin Laden was behind the attacks on New York City within a minute of the second (supposed) airplane crash in New York. The source of the attacks in Muslim and Arab extremism was immediately established within the Zionist-elitist owned media just at those moments when the public was most vulnerable to suggestions and influence. How clever!

Ten years after the 9-11 events, no credible evidence has ever been presented to document the claim that Osama Bin Laden was the mastermind behind the horrendous events, or that it involved Muslims at all. Of course, the media has aired faked videos and tapes of Osama making such claims, but video researchers have consistently shown these to be frauds, with actors and makeup. These videos and such are usually released to the advantage of those in power, to shore up their public support by the sheep people who have been led to believe in Muslim terrorism, instead of understanding the real Zionist, elitist and bankster terrorism. The evidence promised by Colin Powell days after the 9-11 attacks was never produced. Further, the FBI never did issue an arrest warrant for Osama Bin Laden listing charges related to 9-11 — because there was no evidence. The whole thing was a fraud from the very beginning including his faked assassination death in 2011. In the only credible videos of Osama Bin Laden, he himself suggested that the causes of the 9-11 attacks involved the criminal elites of America and elsewhere.

The corporate media cover up the crimes of the elites and create propaganda to justify things like criminal wars, increasing surveillance and security throughout all levels of society, the corrosion of civil and legal rights for citizens, cap and trade taxes to save the planet from man made global warming, and much more, all the while selling poisonous inoculations and pharmaceuticals. David Rockefeller is infamous for his recorded comments thanking the corporate media for their intentional deception of the American public, as this had allowed for the advancement of the globalist agenda. Yes, media personnel all deserve David Rockefeller buttons for their contributions to the commissions of mass murder, genocide, the robbing of nations and massive public deception. The media actually engender hatred against Muslims and Arabs while violating all standards of journalism and hate law legislation. The corporate media have participated in criminal ways in deceiving the public and allowing for the advancement of the globalist elites' psychotic plans for the human race.

Journalist T. Meyssan, in a recent article on the most recent NATO war crimes, entitled, *War Propaganda: Libya and the End of Western Illusion*, explains one angle on the criminal activities of the media:

> TV channels which, under the leadership of their respective Governments, have manufactured false information to lead to war,

are guilty of "crimes against peace," as defined by the relevant UN General Assembly resolutions in the aftermath of World War II. The journalist-propagandists should be considered even more culpable than the military who perpetrated war crimes or crimes against humanity, to the extent that none of these crimes would have been possible without the one that preceded them: the "crime against peace." [6]

The media completely brainwashes the public through an incessant stream of propaganda and lies, while failing completely to inform the public of the true nature of these criminal wars perpetrated on behalf of the global crime syndicate. NATO is even referred to as the "Rothschilds' Army." Of course, the two main news sources for western societies are Reuters and the Associated Press, both owned once again by the Rothschilds.

Each of the dominant Hollywood studios ("the majors") is a subsidiary of a much larger corporation and therefore is not an independent business, and its sources of revenue are within its parent company's wider financial corporate empires. The majors and their parents are: Twentieth Century Fox (News Corp), Paramount Pictures (Viacom), Universal (General Electric/ Vivendi), Disney (The Walt Disney Company), Columbia TriStar (Sony) and Warner Brothers (Time Warner). These parent companies are amongst the largest and most powerful in the world, typically run by lawyers and investment bankers. Their economic interests are also closely tied to the armaments industry, the oil cartels and the pharmaceutical companies.

Texe Marrs, in an article entitled: *Do the Jews Own Hollywood and the Media?* (May 5, 2009), is most direct in getting to the core of the issue:

> Do the Zionist Jews own Hollywood and the media? Are they using the media to mold and shape American opinion by constantly injecting Zionist propaganda and bias into news programs, movies, television shows, even children's cartoons and entertainment? ...

> How about going to top Jews in the media themselves and see what they say? Take Joel Stein, for example, columnist for the Los Angeles Times newspaper and regular contributor to Time magazine. In his

---

[6] August 20, 2011, www.globalresearch.ca/index.php?context=va&aid=26084

column in the LA Times (Dec. 19, 2008), Stein says that Americans who think the Jews do not control Hollywood and the media are just plain "dumb."

"Jews totally run Hollywood." Stein proudly admits. He then goes on to provide a long, long list of Hollywood/media chieftains — all Jews! — to prove his point. On his list, Fox ... Paramount Pictures ... "Walt Disney ... Sony Pictures ... Warner Brothers ... CBS ... MGM ...NBC/Universal Studios .... "As a proud Jew," says Joel Stein, "I want America to know of our accomplishment. Yes, we control Hollywood."

Stein says he then called Abe Foxman, Chairman of the Jewish ADL, to ask him, why don't more Jews just come out and boast at this great accomplishment? Foxman responded by admitting that yes, it's true that most of the top execs "happen to be Jewish." In fact, Foxman told Stein, *all eight major film studios are run by men who happen to be Jewish.*

Ben Stein ... the well-known Jewish actor, economic and writer, when asked "Do Jews run Hollywood?" stared blankly at the questioner, then retorted, "You bet they do — and what of it?"

Shahar Ilan, writing in haaretz.com, the internet division of Israel's top daily newspaper, commented, "The Jews do control the American media. This is very clear, and claiming otherwise is an insult to common knowledge." ...

Zionist Jews have taken over the 'local newspaper' in America," Kapner writes.

This Zionist bias and propaganda spin by the Jewish-owned American media is not new. ...

... Time magazine, Newsweek, NBC, ABC, CBS, CNN, FOX — and many more are all owned or run by Jews and operated solely to further the aims of the traitorous, anti-American, ever growing Zionist World Empire.

All America is in the Grip of the Hidden, Red Iron Fist of Zionism. Of course, the media, even as important as it is to our culture, is only a bit piece of the whole that is now, regrettably, under the big thumbs of the Jewish Zionist elite. Our educational establishment, Wall Street, the banks, the Federal Reserve, our Congress, the White House ..., and our judiciary—each and every one is infiltrated by Zionist radicals who put Israel and their own "Chosen People" first, to the detriment of everything sacred to honest, God-fearing, hard-working Americans.

The news media owned by primarily Jewish or Zionist New World Order folk, on that day of 9-11, helped to stage the mass murders of fellow planetary citizens, all while blaming it on radical Muslims as a pretext for waging imperialist wars against the sovereign nations of Afghanistan and then Iraq.

This same Zionist media is even now *pimping* their next war—against Iran, justifying it all as a question of self-defence, with fabricated evidences and all kinds of experts to talk of the threat to civilization posed by radical Islam. What a joke this would be, if it were not all so tragic: After almost two million murdered, millions more injured, orphaned and desolate, and a land desecrated by war crimes and depleted uranium, and robbed of its wealth. And all based on lies. What a world of deceit, hatefulness and madness these Zionists have concocted for human kind. As the motto of the Israel's secret police service, the Mossad, suggests: "By means of deception, we wage war."

The role of the media in creating and perpetuating the false mind conditioning of the sleeping population is illustrated by a series of videos available on the internet called **"September Clues."** This is a ten part series of video clips each approximately 8 minute which does a critical analysis of the main news coverage of September 11, 2001. The videos which were aired live on the day of the 9-11 attacks *were staged*! They contain all kinds of inconsistencies and enigmas, which as a whole suggests that there were in fact 'no airplanes' flying into the Twin Towers and disappearing inside, and that the images of the planes presented to the public were actually composed in the media's video studios by superimposing images of airplanes over the background of the Towers. Further, the eye-witnesses were scripted and merely actors and actresses, mainly from within the ranks of the media itself. The famous pictures of the airplane striking the second Tower were put together using modern video methods, quite simply as one might do in a Hollywood movie.[7]

Another interesting piece of evidence concerning the criminality of the media concerns the tapes from the BBC, England which were released in 2008. In one clip, the female broadcaster was reporting the collapse of Building 7, the third building to be blown up that day. However, the BBC had its timing wrong and while the reporter was reporting the building collapse, Building 7 was clearly present and standing in the background behind her! You simply have to understand that the media are totally corrupted and actually help in the staging of these types of events and then in the cover-ups and in 'spinning' stories so as to create their intended propaganda.

There is not one piece of criminal evidence demonstrating that 9-11 was an inside job, but thousands. Over time, every detail of the 9-11 myths has been discredited. Further, the obstruction of justice at every level of the US government and police services simply demonstrates how these crimes were perpetrated by a criminal network well intertwined into the police, military and intelligence services of the US government, its NATO allies and into the Wall Street financial and corporate elites. The evidences are all there and the Zionist corporate media have even had to step up their disinformation programs to try to obscure their criminal complicity and treasonous activities from the awakening public.

Of course, the majority of sheep people still believe in Arab terrorism, high jacked airplanes and in what they see on TV. A generation of people have been so thoroughly conditioned and brainwashed through so many years of lies and deception, that they cannot face the monstrous Beast upon us. You have been punked and you are every day when you turn on your TV set, read your newspaper, or listen to local radio stations — all owned and censored by the masters of deceit and propaganda, the pathological liars. Turn off your TV and cancel your newspapers as they provide you only with falsification, obscuration and lies. The corporate media are all part of the criminal networks which have stolen your society from you in service of the banksters, the criminal elite and Zionists.

---

[7] An extensive forensic analysis of this video series is taken up in Section VI of this book.

For those in Canada, who imagine that the media in your country is any different from that of the US, which it is not as it is controlled by the same scumbags, consider the CTV news reporting of the days events at Dawson College in Montreal September 13, 2006. Karen and I watched the TV coverage live on that day and numerous features of the coverage raised our suspicion about the 'crazed lone gunman' theory concocted for public consumption by the corrupted police and tactical units of Montreal, the corporate media and the Zionist controllers. The CTV news coverage of that day provides a variety of criminal evidences relevant to understanding what did or did not happen on September 13, 2006.[8]

The most suspicious aspect of the media coverage was the supposed eye-witness identified on TV as *Tracey Eck*, in a clip used on CTV (Channels 7 and 17), and then picked up and played by other media outlets – the CBC and CBC News world (Ch. 8 & 24). This eye-witness account ended up being wrong and deceptive on numerous counts, and suggests that this witness has been part of the con and was used to introduce misleading information early on as the drama unfolded.

The witness, Tracey Eck, a somewhat attractive young blond woman, with dishevelled hair, but no sweat or other signs of her traumatic story, was simply an actress. Her manner is similar to one of a poor actress, somewhat *hysterical* in nature – using exaggerated emotional terms and descriptions and with occasional smiles on her face, suggesting her self-satisfaction with her acting performance. Her reports suggested that the perpetrator was a 'crazed madman' and that he had accomplices. These notes are incomplete and different clips of this witness were played. It would be very interesting to determine if this woman is actually known as a student at the college or available anywhere for follow-up. Even though her account was readily available on that day, she has never subsequently reappeared on the media to my knowledge.

---

[8] The earlier version of *Zero Point Teachings* contained a longer account of Christopher and Karen's observations of the media coverage of that day, and all the irregularities that were evident to us. We subsequently travelled to Montreal with my article explaining aspects of this false flag event and distributed a limited number of them at a street rally for the people of Darfur. The article was entitled *Another Day of Infamy*. We never heard any comments or feedback concerning our observations and claims, which I have also repeated on various internet talk shows. Likely, our efforts were known and monitored and my writings absorbed into the larger coverup.

 Tracey Eck described the crazed gunman as having "a huge black trench coat" (an odd description) and a **"huge machine gun,"** which is not so true in light of later determination of the calibre of sub-machine gun supposedly used. She described him as having body piercing, as white, 19 years old, studs, black boots, with a 'weird hair cut' as a gothic or punk type—which turned out not to be true from his photos where his hair is more closely cropped. She described "his friends as shorter, all white," which certainly raises questions in light of the 'lone gunman' theory of the police. She then states that she ran, when there was a second shooter, which there is supposed now not to have been. Her claims are now known to have been largely incorrect, but she did help to create an atmosphere of hysteria and misleading information.

Most peculiar to this witness testimony is her description of how she saw people being shot on the street outside the College, but she then describes sitting in the cafeteria having a cigarette with her friend when the crazed gunman came in to her surprise. This is quite ludicrous, that she would sit down for a cigarette after witnessing the shootings on the street and then be surprised by the entrance of the gunman! Tracey next describes hiding in the bushes after escaping from the college—whereas everyone else escaping the college ran down the street, she hid in the bushes. Again, this whole account is quite ridiculous.

Further, in one of the videos of this witness, the streets behind her are quite empty with a couple in the background walking leisurely down the street holding hands with their backs to the camera! There was a policeman in the scene, perhaps to establish a 'police presence.' The background to this video clip is quite ridiculous given to the massive influx of police, swats, securities and emergency services, with people everywhere. There were instead no cars or emergency vehicles visible in this clip. These scenes would not correspond to other video clips of the same streets at the same times. Both of these clips of Tracey's academy performance were likely pre-recorded and set-up.

In Montreal, there was a massive use of police and armed security forces—all designed to create hysteria, mass control, control of the flow of information, set-ups and cover-ups. That's how a con works and how these fascist elements use such incidents in order to impose additional police powers and laws within what used to be a democratic country. One simply had to look at all the armed men and women in fear with guns and everyone in hysteria, so confused and deluded about everything. Much of the hysteria at the college was induced by the SWAT teams, security and police services themselves! With hundreds of loaded weapons drawn—all while there was a lone gunman and it was over in 15 minutes. Didn't anyone tell the SWAT units that it was done? The police completely controlled the flow of information from the site to create a hugely unnecessary drama and giving them hours to deal with the cover-up and reviews of what to say.

I have presented a fuller analysis elsewhere of how the media coverage of the day led me to the definite conclusion that the whole event was a staged black operation involving the tactical units and police themselves. Why would such a thing be done? Within two years of the event, Canadian politicians out of something in their hearts were introducing new gun legislation to restrict the sale and availability of automatic weapons. This was the major reason for their staged murder. The elites want to control hand gun availability as a way of disarming their victims—**the** populace of the country. The elites often concoct such mass murders as a way of bringing in gun legislation to save and protect the little sheep. The elites have staged such mass murders in the US, Canada, Europe and Australia—always leaving behind evidence and anomalies which demonstrate that there was a criminal plot far deeper than the little story fabricated for the public.

LEARN THE TRUTH

One simply must seek alternative news sources if you are brave enough to become informed. This has to be done apart from the propaganda and lies consistently spread through the mainstream media--FOX, CNN, ABC, CTV, CBC, the Suns and Times, Citizens and Stars. The corporate media propagate consistent patterns of propaganda and maintain multiple levels of deceit, misinformation and lies—a true Neo-Con, neo-Nazi and Zionist propaganda machine.

The personnel of the media will all be subject to Nuremberg standards for their betrayals of America, Canadian and British society, for the support and cover-up of domestic and international terrorism, and for their lack of any sane logic or human decency. Turn off the TV and radios, and get rid of your newspapers, or at least grasp what is being done to you. You have been consistently deceived your whole life by the corporate media and Hollywood fluffery, all used as weapons to control and direct mass mind and consciousness, so that the citizens fail completely to notice the elephant and spiders in the room. The corporate media is one of Lies and Double-Think for an Orwellian fascist and police state society.

If you are tired of sheep news, listen to some of the alternative radio and video available through the internet. Particularly, I would recommend listening anytime 24 hours a day to such sources as: www. republicbroadcasting.org, http://oraclebroadcasting.com, www.gnclive. com, or Alex Jones at www.prisonplanet.com and www.infowars. com. Valuable new sources include www.informationclearinghouse.

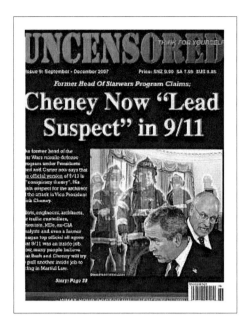

info, www.globalresearch.ca, www.911researchers.com and www.truthnetradio.com. While in New Zealand, Christopher was exposed to the remarkable NZ expose magazine www.uncensored.co.nz. Get active in the INFO WAR, learning more yourself, as these are complex subjects.

Humankind must escape the mass hypnosis of their educations and the corporate media, and dissolve the false consciousness system intentionally fostered by the pseudo-elites. The public has been intentionally *'dumbied down.'* The news media even have fake call-ins to public radio, faked commentary on their websites submitted by their own agents, and even 'fake polls' to influence public perceptions.

Watch alternative investigative and historic movies which make the Hollywood garbage look quite foolish and perverse: Movies such as Alex Jones' *Endgame*, The Empire of The City – P*art I* and II, Zero, Aaron Russo's *From Freedom to Fascism, Zeitgeist* - the Movie, Len Horowitz *In Lies we Trust: On the CIA, Hollywood and Bioterrorism.* These and a wealth of other truth documentaries are all available free through *www.video.google.com* or www.youtube.com.

If you as a Canadian, American or otherwise, love your country, or the earth, or your family, or any notions of truth and justice, then it is incumbent upon you as an individual and citizen to become informed and break the spell of the mind hypnosis intentionally fostered upon you by the corporate media and Hollywood. You are a product of decades of subliminal social engineering. The media actively cover up the crimes and actions of the elites and even help to stage events for your terror. There were no Muslim terrorists on 9-11 and the Canadian peoples like the Canadian military have been intentionally deceived as to who the real terrorists are and who their networks really entail.

The free exchange of information over the internet has enabled the truth of many historical and current events to be re-investigated and/or revealed. People are realizing that these deviants have largely rewritten history and deceived the public about the causes of the many wars, terrorist acts, assassinations and so on. Blah, blah, blah, you have been led like sheep to slaughter and understood nothing of the crimes of your governments and the corporate-financial elites who have high jacked our nations. So many hoaxes have been and are being perpetrated upon the sleeping public. Yes, this includes even the moon landing hoax.

Consider what is wrong with this image of Aldrin on the moon? This image is from the book *We Reach the Moon* by J. Wilford (Bantam Books, 1969). How did this lunar module descend onto the moon using rockets to slow its descent, without creating some crater underneath and dust clouds to cover the module? Instead, there is no disturbance of the moon surface underneath the module. This is a fraud, like everything else you are fed by the corporate media. Another current example of media fraud concerned the dramatic, supposed 'live feeds' from the gushing oil wells of the Gulf Coast in 2010. On youtube, there are clips showing a 'door' opening in the background onto the scene behind the gushing pipes and a human figure is clearly evident. This suggest that the whole scene was staged somehow using a tank of water and studio space. The corporate media does not inform you, but deceives you in a clear and consistent matter. Media personnel do all deserve David Rockefeller buttons of appreciation for their contributions to mass murders and war crimes as perpetrated around the world, all while keeping the Zionist and elitist agendas hidden from the public!

U. N. Agenda 21 for Environmental Radicalism, Local Sustainability & Population Reduction

Most Americans don't grasp it yet, but the truth is that the global elite are absolutely obsessed with population control. In fact, there is a growing consensus among the global elite that they need to get rid of 80 to 90 percent of us.

The number one commandment of the infamous *Georgia Guidestones* is this: "Maintain humanity under 500,000,000 in perpetual balance with nature."

Unfortunately, a very high percentage of our global leaders actually believe in this stuff.

The world is changing. The global elite have immense amounts of wealth and power and they are intent on imposing a radical environmental agenda on all the rest of us.

The reality is that many of the wealthiest and most prominent people in the world are absolutely obsessed with the green agenda and with population control. Just consider the following quotes….

David Rockefeller: *"The negative impact of population growth on all of our planetary ecosystems is becoming appallingly evident."*

CNN Founder Ted Turner: *"A total population of 250-300 million people, a 95% decline from present levels, would be ideal."*

Dave Foreman, Earth First Co-Founder: *"My three main goals would be to reduce human population to about 100 million worldwide, destroy the industrial infrastructure and see wilderness, with it's full complement of species, returning throughout the world."*

Maurice Strong: *"Isn't the only hope for the planet that the industrialized civilizations collapse? Isn't it our responsibility to bring that about?"*

Michael Oppenheimer: *"The only hope for the world is to make sure there is not another United States. We can't let other countries have the same number of cars, the amount of industrialization, we have in the US. We have to stop these Third World countries right where they are."*

This radical agenda is even represented in the White House. John P. Holdren, Barack Obama's top science advisor, co-authored a textbook entitled "Ecoscience" back in 1977 in which he actually advocated mass sterilization, compulsory abortion, a one world government and a global police force to enforce population control.

Yes, a lot of what you have read in this article sounds crazy. But the global elite really do believe in population control and they really are seeking to implement a radical environmental agenda across the entire planet.

(Article *End of the American Dream*, Author unknown)

The U. N. Agenda 21 and its plans for world wide *Sustainable Development* are important topics which citizens should be aware of, that is if they value their individual rights and freedoms. Presented as a noble plan to save the earth, the globalists move forward with their scheme for one world government, the restriction of individual rights and freedoms, and the sacrifice of individual property rights in service of the collective ruled by the psychopathic elite. If fully implemented, Agenda 21 would monitor all lands and peoples.

In 1992, a UN conference, commonly known as the *Earth Summit*, was held in Rio de Janeiro, Brazil. 179 member states formally endorsed the Sustainable Development philosophy. At this conference, Agenda 21 was adopted, signed in person by serial mass murderer and war criminal George Bush on behalf of the United States. According to the UN.org website, Agenda 21 is *"a comprehensive plan of action to be taken globally, nationally, and locally by organizations of the United Nations System, Governments, and Major Groups in every area in which human impacts (sic) the environment."* The conference called for a *Global Biodiversity Assessment* of the state of the planet and it provided UN leaders with the "information" and "science" (or propaganda) necessary to validate their global management system. The conference's doomsday predictions were designed to excuse population reduction, to introduce oppressive lifestyle regulations and foster a return to earth centred religions as the basis for environmental values and self-sustaining human settlements.

This global contract binds governments around the world to the UN plan for changing the way we live, eat, learn and communicate—all under the noble banner of saving the earth. Its regulations will limit water and electricity use, increase transportation costs and deny the access of populations to wilderness areas. Under the guise of public benefit, privately owned land can be seized and transformed into *human free zones*. The UN agenda supplants local and long-standing state or provincial laws and can call for the elimination of individual property rights, especially for such groups as farmers, ranchers and landowners. The implications of Agenda 21 are to merge environmentalism with socialism, to expand the government into almost every aspect of our lives; including land use, food production, housing and transportation, manufacturing, energy production and rationing, and even health care. Agenda 21 is helping to destroy American and Canadian industries and competitiveness, resulting in job losses and additional taxes, regulations and carbon tax credits, and it allows for the seizure of private properties—all portrayed as for the common good and a sustainable future:

> Sustainable development sustains nothing and takes everything. It's a wonderfully Orwellian term designed to dupe people into thinking they are doing something positive, when in reality they are enslaving themselves and their prosperity. Sustainable development … is about redistributing your wealth, prosperity and opportunity to have a better life …. (D. Casey, www.keepourrights.org)

Al Gore became the major eco-prophets of Agenda 21 and the global elite. Gore's movie *An Inconvenient Truth* and the globalist agenda was promoted throughout the world media and resulted in a Hollywood Oscar for your favourite Gore. The major theme of Gore's presentations was that man made carbon emissions from industries, cars and breathing are bringing about global warming, melting the icecaps and bringing about devastating environmental changes. The globalists' emphasis was upon the threats of global warming as a pretext for all forms of United Nations' regulations and the creation of a world wide exchange of 'carbon credits' with the taxations to fund the globalists' agenda and to provide Al Gore with some handsome profits. Another eco-prophet James Lovelock, creator of the Gaia hypothesis, stated in a Guardian interview, that indeed *"democracy must be put on hold"* if the fight against global warming is going to be successful and that only *"a few people with authority"* should be permitted to rule the planet until the crisis is solved.

Of course, Gore's movie itself was thoroughly examined by critics and his presentations shown to be deceptive and fraudulent. The movie was actually banned in parts of Europe and an alternative move *"A Convenient Lie"* is available through youtube.com which debunks the *"quack science"* of Gore and the globalists. Further, the so-called consensus among the world scientists is not at all a consensus outside of the UN's own advisors. Thirty five thousand scientists signed another petition questioning the global warming scheme; not only whether or not global warming or global cooling were occurring but further challenging the links drawn to human carbon productions as the culprit. In 2010, a series of internal emails between scientists at the East Anglia University in England revealed that the globalist scientists had intentionally been deceiving the world's public concerning climactic data and trends. The globalists have subsequently come to emphasize "climactic change," about which there is less dispute. [9] The globalists design all kinds of schemes for additional taxation and to bring about their imagined one world government under their control and with a massively reduced population. I understand that Agenda 21 proposes a world population of 2 billion as being sustainable, unfortunately quite below our current estimated seven billion. The United Nations has just recently designated October 31st, 2011 as the 7 Billion Day—a fitting day on Halloween, the *festival of death*. The Georgia Guidestones postulate the even more radical objective of population reduction to achieve the figure of a

---

[9] The globalists emphasize the threat of global warming due to human activity but will not talk about the HAARP program based in Alaska and elsewhere, including Newfoundland. HAARP involves *ionospheric heaters* which heat the ionosphere to the temperature of the sun's corona. Of course, given this dire warning of global warming, why are the scientists and politicians not demanding that we stop this intentional warming of our atmospheres? HAARP facilities are known to play a role in weather modification, in the generation of earthquakes activity and in creating and/or influencing so-called natural catastrophes. The globalists may well be using the HAARP facility to melt the Artic ice to open up the northerly regions for the exploitation of resources and shipping routes.

paltry 500,000,000. The elites will then be able to enjoy a new *'age of reason'* able to jog freely about the wilderness areas of the earth, pee on trees and enjoy each others fine company, with worker populations in isolated cities.

These people are quite 'whacked' and should be in psychiatric care, pursuing such eugenics programs as always, having learnt so much from all the Nazi doctors and Rockefeller scientists incorporated into the military, the CIA, NASA, the World Health Organization and the UN at the conclusion of World War Two through *operation paperclip,* Countries of North and South America swallowed up tens of thousands of such specialists into the black operations of our governments, the intelligence, police and military communities, into corporations under the globalists' control, into pharmaceutical companies and the weapons industries, into black operations and the media of propaganda and lies. What a web of deceits and lies has been strung out for the masses, and always hidden under such euphemisms as 'sustainable development.'

These terrorist fanatics have their own quack scientists espousing such agendas. One of the most prominent has been a professor of biology at the University of Texas, at Austin, Eric Pianka panned an article entitled *"What nobody wants to hear, but everyone needs to know,"* Pianka made the following shocking statements:

> *First, and foremost, we must get out of denial and recognize that Earth simply cannot support many billions of people.

> *This planet might be able to support perhaps as many as half a billion people who could live a sustainable life in relative comfort. Human populations must be greatly diminished, and as quickly as possible to limit further environmental damage.

> *I do not bear any ill will toward humanity. However, I am convinced that the world WOULD clearly be much better off without so many of us.

The world would certainly be much better off without Eric Pianka and a whole clan of elites with their quack science and new world psychiatrically disordered schemes. And these people actually pretend to care for the Earth and humankind!

Masters of Poisoning, Sickness & Starvation

Most Canadians, like Americans, naively assume that our governments protect the citizenry from poisons and toxic substances in our food supply, air and water, and in our medicines. In Canada, we have *Health Canada*, while in the US, the *Food and Drug Administration* and the *Centre for Disease Control* (CDC) assume these tasks. The sheep people cannot imagine that the government is actually allowing numerous poisons to be distributed in the air through chemtrail spraying, in our food through the toxins added and through genetically modification, in our water with the addition of fluoride and other pollutants, and in our medicines through the lack of adequate controls over the introduction of new pharmaceuticals and the promotion of mass inoculation programs. In fact, the governments are not protecting the public but actually allowing the poisoning of citizens in service of the population reduction plans of the Zionists and world elites, and in service of the greed of corporations which make vast sums both through their poisoning programs and through the medical industries which people turn to in order to combat the effects of such poisoning.

Henry Kissinger, arch-Zionist and serial mass murderer, simply refers to the populace as "useless eaters" and considers that the fewer there are of us, the further ahead will be the globalists plans for a new world psychiatric disordered society. Prince Phillip, the Duke of Edinburgh, when asked if he believed in reincarnation, replied: *"If I were reincarnated I would wish to be returned to earth as a killer virus to lower human population levels."* Of course, our charmed Prince likely does not have to reincarnate if he wants to contribute to such mass extermination programs, as biological weapons of varied forms are available to the governments and these criminal cabals. The United Nations posits the number of two billion as ideal for a *sustainable world* order while the *Georgian Guide Stones* in the US have the principle carved in stone of maintaining the world's population at under 500,000 million. The Georgia Guidestones were built as a monument to the peoples yet to be murdered in service of reaching the goals of the psychopathic eugenicists and the Zionist Cabals with their new world order megalomania.

Chemtrail spraying has been going on for over a decade in North America, in other NATO countries and around the world.[10] Unfortunately, the sheep people think that it is all quite natural to have high flying jets crisscrossing the sky leaving behind them vast trails of chemical poisons. The sheeple generally do not even look up at the sky around them. They are so preoccupied with a thousand personal and life concerns that they are completely unaware of what is going on in the skies. Others have become accustomed to the sight of such planes and have been led to believe that these chemtrails are simply *contrails* (or condensation trails) or exhausts left behind by regular commercial jets.[11] Some people I have asked have even thought that the government must be spraying for mosquitoes! Unfortunately, this is not the case and citizens of the world are being intentionally poisoned by this form of 'non-lethal warfare.'

---

[10] THE CIA FRONT...EVERGREEN AIR...located at PINAL AIRPARK-MARANA ARIZONA..a LONGTIME CIA/NSA SECRET FACILITY FOR MORE THAN 40 YEARS.. is the PRIME MODIFICATION CENTER THAT MODIFIES A WIDE RANGE OF AIRCRAFT TYPES TO CONDUCT THE "COVERT" CHEMTRAIL SPRAY OPERATIONS THAT BEGAN OVER THE ENTIRE UNITED STATES IN NOVEMBER OF 1998...PRIOR TO THIS..SELECTED AREAS OF THE U.S. HAD CHEMTRAIL OPERATIONS TO TEST ALL THE TECHNOLOGY EMPLOYED IN THESE CHEMTRAIL SPRAY OPERATIONS AND TO DETERMINE THE OPERATING PARAMENTERS RELATED TO AIRCRAFT PERFORMANCE ENVELOPES AND OPTIMUM ATMOSPHERIC CONDITONS... ONCE THIS WAS ACCOMPLISED....THE NATIONWIDE PROGRAM BEGAN AND IS BEING CONDUCTED UNDER MORE THAN ONE PROGRAM CODE NAME...THE 2 PROGRAM CODE NAMES MOST OFTEN DISCUSSED ARE "OPERATION CLOVER LEAF" and "OPERATION RAINDANCE"... WITHIN MONTHS OF THE OPERATION OVER THE UNITED STATES BEGINNING...CHEMTRAIL SPRAY OPERATIONS BEGAN OVER WIDE PARTS OF DOZENS OF COUNTRIES WITH THE MOST NOTABLE EXCEPTION BEING CHINA ... THIS IS SCARY & CONFIRMS WHAT WE ALL KNEW ALL ALONG!!

Source: http://letsrollforums.com/photo-inside-chemtrail-plane-t16938.html?s=f9aa5baf6385 3c6c62e0ee1f59c1f448&

[11] Contrails or condensation trails can be caused by the interaction of the hot exhaust with water molecules in the atmosphere. However, having just lived across the river and close to the Ottawa airport with a good view of incoming commercial jets, I have found that it is very rare for regular aircraft to be leaving behind any significant trails. The chemtrail spraying is obviously in a class of its own and these are never the airplanes landing at the commercial airports.

Non-lethal warfare methods are those which do not immediate kill the victims but cause varied mental and physical health problems, or act on people's moods and emotions, and which might be used to sedate or poison them. Of course, the militaries have such technology available to spread lethal or toxic substances but these are also specialized airplanes built to contain huge tanks of such toxins. Further, this is a massive program costing into the billions of dollars for such poisoning of the population and environment. One such base for such operations is said to be the Wright-Patterson base in Dayton Ohio, one of the military bases which assimilated a number of Nazi chemical warfare specialists after the war, as were assimilated also into the CIA and the mind control programs, NASA, and into black operation programs. This was part of Operation Paperclip during the years after World War II, where tens of thousands of Nazi specialists were integrated into shadow operations within the United States and Canada, as elsewhere.

The main ingredients of chemtrail spraying are aluminium coated fibreglass fibres, barium and heavy metals (including lead and mercury), desecrated blood particles, viral and carcinogenic substances, and even pharmaceutical medicines. In 2006, a family in Iowa collected a sample of the substances after days of heavy spraying and submitted it to a lab for testing. The results indicated that in addition to 26 heavy metals of aluminium, arsenic, lead, mercury, uranium and zinc, etc, there were determined to be 6 bacteria including anthrax and pneumonia, 9 chemicals including acetylcholine chloride, 4 moulds and fungi, 7 viruses, 2 cancers, 2 vaccines and 2 sedatives. The family contacted Senator Tom Harkin (D-Iowa) to report the test results and they received back a *General Accounting Office* report on "military chaff" and the material safety data sheet for aluminium coated fibreglass fibres. Chaff is spread by pilots to mask planes and was used widely in WW II. Of course, one must wonder why the military would want to so interfere with radar imagery over North America during supposed times of peace and heavy commercial traffic. The military rationale for such spraying is simply a decoy to obscure the truth.

Another claim is that chemtrails are being used for weather modification and this certainly seems part of the larger picture. The chemtrail spraying likely serves various purposes in the war upon humankind. The chemtrails serve to create reflective surfaces which could interact with the electromagnetic radiations of the HAARP program. Further, chemtrail spraying is not a rare phenomenon but are widespread and constant across the nation. One citizen on Vancouver Island reports: *"Our skies out here over Vancouver Island are constantly covered."* In the Ottawa area, our skies are marred by extensive chemtrail spraying three or even four days a week. It is hard to discern whether spraying is going on when there is cloud cover or when the spraying is done at night. As citizens are waking up to this nightmare practice, efforts are also being increased to obscure the chemtrails and to provide further disinformation to conceal the true reasons for this massive poisoning of the American and Canadian populations.

Whenever the government is caught in one lie, they always manufacture another and never provide any authentic information. Of course, our politicians like our media personal, are just such pathological liars as their tasks demand. Thus, the government will firstly claim that chemtrails are simply contrails; and then when this is disproved, they will claim that it has some military or weather modification purpose. In some US schools, chemtrails are being taught as 'sunscreens' to protect us against the life giving rays of the sun or to reduce global warming. Oh, the globalists are going to save the planet! What a joke.

Lastly, when caught up in the obvious illogic and lies of these claims, our governments will simply attribute public concern to ridiculous 'conspiracy theories.' Most people simply cannot imagine that our government would allow citizens to be intentionally poisoned from the sky, but they do. Further, most government personnel are themselves so compartmentalized that they do not really grasp the enormity of these crimes being committed against the peoples of the United States and Canada, and in fact the citizens of the world. Just as we might use chemical sprays to kill of ants, bees or other insect pests, so also, this is being done to the people of Canada, the United States, Europe and elsewhere.

One aboriginal band in northern Ontario was so concerned about the illness among their citizens that they took their demand for the suspension of chemtrails all the way to the Supreme Court of Canada. The end result of the court case was the declaration by the Supreme Court that the spraying was not being done by Canadians, and thus it was outside of their area of jurisprudence! In fact, NATO countries conspire together in this non-lethal warfare and population reduction program and foreign pilots are often used in different countries.

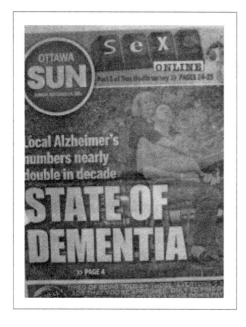

People simply do not grasp the enormity of the problems being caused by chemtrail spraying. Firstly, they cause a diversity of health problems and have been related to chronic fatigue syndrome, Morgellan's skin disorder, respiratory problems, viruses and flues, degenerative mental disorders—such as Alzheimer's (commonly attributed to high levels of aluminium) and cancers. Most significantly, the suppression of the natural immune systems by these toxins renders the victims susceptible to a wide range of flues and illnesses. The ingestion of any one of the substances found in chemtrails, such as aluminium or mercury, can itself cause a wide range of health problems. Most chemtrails include cocktails of such poisons! The poisoning of our atmosphere and environment is likely related also to the collapse of bee colonies, the disappearing of amphibians and insects, the poisoning of our soils, water and food supplies.

In addition, there are other even more odious aspects to chemtrail spraying. Populations can be sedated through pharmaceuticals; while specific concocted flues and epidemics might be intentionally spread. The US (and Canada) now have hundreds of biological weapons labs inventing ever new concoctions. New nano-molecules can also be dispersed in this way. Further, the chemtrail spraying makes the atmosphere more electrically conductive for the use of the HAARP weaponry against citizens—such that we can be irradiated by energetic electromagnetic weapons.

Once again, the American and Canadian government are complicit in these criminal programs and obscure from the public the reasons and aims of

chemtrail spraying. One meets only denial, obscuration and fabrication. Those involved in these programs are administrating noxious substance to its citizenry in direct violation of the laws of the United States and Canada, and the people who are perpetrating these crimes need to be brought before criminal courts under the anti-terrorism legislation, along with those public figures who have allowed this to be done.

The sheep people do not even know what is hitting them.

INOCULATIONS

**… no large, properly designed scientific study has ever
proven the current childhood vaccine schedule
to be safe and effective in keeping children healthy.**
Dr. Mercola, from *20 TIMES the Risk of Autism
When You Make This Choice* November 04 2011[12]

Inoculations are regarded by a growing number of doctors and
researchers of the new world psychiatric disorder as another weapon
of mass destruction. Such inoculations contain mercury, aluminium or
formaldehyde as buffers and preservatives. They also include foreign
biological materials from other animals, dead foetuses and synthetic
substances, all of which circulate through the blood and can cause damages
throughout different areas of the body — from micro-cerebral haemorrhages
to damage in the kidneys, cancers and infertility.

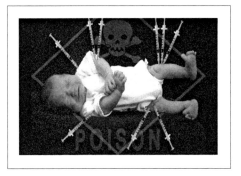

In the US particularly, infants are
mandated in some states for up to 24
inoculations within the first two years
of life, and 48 doses of 14 vaccines by
the time they are six years old. By age
18, federal public health officials say
they should have gotten a total of 69
doses of 16 vaccines from day of birth
to age 18. (Mercola)

At the same time, the rates for cancers, autism, ADHD and learning
disabilities, are skyrocketing. Whereas 20 years ago, 1 in 2500 infants would
show the symptoms of autism, the rate is now closer to 1 in 85. 1 in 3 adults
now develop cancer and blood cancers and tumours in children have
increased dramatically. Many of the mothers of autistic children identify
inoculations as immediate causes of illnesses in their children. In other
cases, the effects are longer term in developing and so the links between the
poisonous inoculations and medical conditions are harder to establish —
especially as there are so many poisons being added simultaneously to our
environment.

---

[12] http://articles.mercola.com/sites/articles/archive/2011/11/04/are-unvaccinated-children-
healthier.aspx?e_cid=20111104_DNL_art_1

The inoculation programs are indeed spreading illness more than preventing them. They introduce many foreign and toxic substances into the blood and throughout the body. Of course, they also provide huge profits for the pharmaceutical manufacturers, billions in profits.
The charts below from VaccineInjury.Info draws a direct comparison of health data from the KiGGs study (The German Health Interview and Examination Survey for Children and Adolescents) versus the data from

Health Condition	Prevalence in Vaccinated Children	Prevalence in Unvaccinated Children
Allergies	40% report at least one allergy	Less than 10%
Asthma	6%	2.5%
Hayfever	10.7% of German children	2.5%
Neurodermatitis (an autoimmune disorder)	13% of German children	7%
ADHD	8% of German children, and another nearly 6% with borderline cases	1-2%
Middle ear infections	11% of German children	Less than 0.5%
Sinusitis	Over 32% of German children	Less than1%
Autism	Approximately 1 in 100	Only 4 cases out of 7,800+ surveys (one child tested very high for metals, and another's mother tested very high for mercury)

unvaccinated children taking part in VaccineInjury.info's survey. The results are overwhelmingly negative concerning the value of inoculations.

Inoculations are introduced without adequate and long term testing and are enabled by the corporate control of our government. The government sells such inoculation programs and encourages widespread use within the medical establishment. The media get in upon the act, hyping the flues and providing the propaganda necessary to promote the inoculations to the sheep people public sitting in front of their TVs. The effects of these inoculations are not researched adequately and when research emerges which questions the inoculation's safety, such findings are suppressed and no longer funded. The corporate sector and drug cartels reap billions

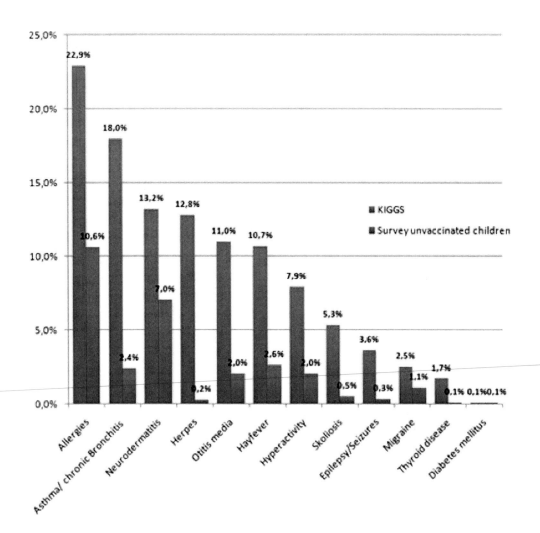

of profits and even then do not mind paying out some lesser amounts in settlements afterwards. It took the pharmaceutical giant Merck 60,000 deaths before they removed Vioxx for asthma from the pharmacies. Billions of profits are made even after paying out billions of civil claims. Dr. Mercola notes that whereas the cost to give your child every government recommended vaccine in 1985 when he started practice was about $80, today that cost has risen to $2,200.

The drug cartels sell their inoculation programs through the medical establishment which they control and they put demands on doctors to be administering such toxins to their patients. In fact, there are an increasing number of mandated inoculations among soldiers, police and other security personnel, health care workers, and both staff and students within the educational system. The inoculation programs and the innumerable illnesses they create put huge financial burden on the health care system, as payouts to doctors and the drug manufacturers. Such practices impoverish the health care system and will help eventually to bankrupt it, along with the country, with the spreading of all kinds of sicknesses through the population through the inoculation programs. All kinds of myths have been propagated through the corporate media concerning the safety and value of inoculations. |It is another media program, like manufacturing 9-11 or a moon landing.

During the gulf war, American soldiers were given inoculations for anthrax and this is regarded as the primary cause of the over 400,000 disabled vets suffering from the 'gulf war syndrome.' The government then denies the ill effects of their programs and denies disabilities to vets while dismissing their symptoms. Many vaccines are required of soldiers who have historically been a primary group on which the pharmaceutical mafia tests its newest concoctions. Again, they make billions of dollars and guarantee billions more of profits for other petrochemical and synthesized drugs used to combat the symptoms caused by the inoculations. Meanwhile, the government of course does not do anything to encourage other natural remedies or solutions, but supports the introduction of poisons into its citizens for their corporate masters. The Protocols of Zion, the blueprint plan for world Zionist domination, even mentions inoculations as a way of poisoning the *goyem*.

The AIDS virus has now been determined to have been manufactured within the biological weapons division of the US military industrial

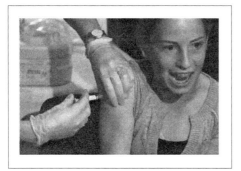

complex and to have been intentionally introduced into the vaccines for the peoples of Africa and into the homosexual communities of New York and San Francisco. Our governments have spent billions of dollars developing biological and chemical weapons, and experimented with all kinds of genetic modifications to develop more potent weapons of mass destruction. They also develop inoculations for the poisons they create. Such things as the bird flu and the swine flu, anthrax and other viruses have been weaponized and can be distributed through inoculations as they can likely be through chemtrail spraying. The secret government can use a variety of toxic agents on the citizenry and then may have enforced inoculations programs to induce illness and/or death.

A recent scandal in the US and Canada is the selling of Gardasil as an inoculation to prevent cervical cancer (or human papilloma virus – HPV) in women. This poison was manufactured by Merck pharmaceutical which pays out millions in salaries and bonuses to promote the vaccine, and they have even tried to have it mandated by state legislatures for young woman. Gardasil was approved in September of 2006 and by September of 2007, Judicial Watch had obtained reports from the Food and Drug Administration using the Freedom of Information Act. There are reported to be hundreds of death and tens of thousands of severe adverse reactions to the vaccinations, and this says nothing of the longer term effects including possible infertility. The drug is supposed to offer immunity for only 3 or 4 of 100 types of cervical cancer that cause 70% of cervical cancer.

Although the American Medical Association states that *"the safety of new agents cannot be known with certainty until a drug has been on the market for years,"* these drugs are fast tracked through the regulatory agencies to market and the public essentially become guinea pigs for the companies. Gardasil will cause illnesses far in excess of the ill effects of the cancer itself. HPV is largely avoidable without an expensive and potentially fatal vaccine which has no significant track record for reducing mortality due to cervical cancer. It has not been available long enough to conduct such research and the pharmaceutical company cannot be counted upon to report adverse reactions and negative test results. HPV itself can usually be resolved through natural means and through strengthening the immune system and 90% of such HPV infections clear up within two years.

The governor of Texas, Richard Perry, associated with Merck and of the Bilderberg elite, tried to pass an executive order to mandate Gardasil for the young girls of Texas before they could enter grade 6 at 12 years old. Remember HPV is transmitted through sexual intercourse. Fortunately, this was rejected in the legislature due to a public backlash and outcry. Mandated inoculations can create huge profits for the pharmaceutical mafia and at the same time are essentially a weapon of mass destruction and sterilization. It has long been known that the UN programs in South Africa have caused widespread sterilization, in addition to spreading AIDS and other viruses—all through inoculations!

In Canada, the Prime Minister Stephen Harper and Conservative government in the fall of 2007 mandated $300 million dollars of tax payers' money for Gardasil vaccinations for the young woman of eastern Canada, beginning in P.E.I and Nova Scotia. Corporate money was poured into television advertising with cute little songs and loving mothers bringing their daughters in for their inoculations and imaginary protection. The Canadian media now tries to convince men to take the vaccination, with even clips of a doctor advising the inoculations for men. A friend of mine while with his family doctor reported that the doctor had actually had her own son vaccinated. People are so foolish and so deceived, and have a completely unfounded trust in their own government and medical establishment—both bought out by the pharmaceutical mafia. Imagine that: Men taking vaccinations for cervical cancer! This will then be promoted through the medical establishment and the ill effects of the inoculations will simply be covered up and denied. By the time the drug is shown to be toxic, Merck will have made enough billions of profit even to pay out civil suits and class actions against them, which they will drag out through the court system, likely with some compromised judge to render a verdict. In fact, new legislations introduced by the governments put the pharmaceutical mafia out of reach from criminal and civil prosecution.

The psychiatrically disturbed elites will release biological weapons against the population. This will likely include variations of the bird flu or swine flu, weaponized versions like H1N1, or some other toxic agents. Not only can the elites cull the flock by infesting them with deadly viruses but then further population reduction can be carried forward through mandated and enforced inoculations. The inoculations can actually carry the disease and work to impair the immune system. There are varied strategies as to how best to carry forward their eugenics plans while deceiving the public through the corporate media. The creation of a pandemic will also be used to justify police state measures, travel restrictions, the internment of populations and to undermine the sovereignty of nations. Dr. L. Day explains:

> The media and the New World Order/Zionist Jewish cabal are using all sorts of hyperbole when discussing this "Bird flu," exaggerations that are in no way warranted. … the incidence of "Bird flu" in Asia (even if we could believe their figures) is 1 in 54 MILLION Ð hardly what one would call a "Pandemic"! … Even with ALL their efforts, the Illuminate/Zionist Jewish cabal was not able to propagandize the public enough to get them to believe the lies about SARS! So they had to create, out of thin air Ð "Bird" Flu Ð which is nothing more than SARS "with wings." Now they can have this "disease" flying all over the world, wherever they want it to land … SARS (remember, it has exactly the same symptoms as "Bird flu") wasn't able to travel fast enough from country to country to create the "world-wide pandemic" the Illuminati had planned, so they had to come up with something with wings! Voila! - - - Bird Flu! SARS with wings!

> The greatest Weapon of Mass Destruction they can use on this country or any other country is mandatory vaccinations, vaccines that will contain the bacteria and viruses of multiple horrific diseases (a Super Vaccine containing numerous disease-*causing* live viruses and bacteria - something the CDC already admits they are developing) to be forced on EVERYONE! (www.drday.com)

In March of 2009, Baxter pharmaceutical was discovered to have shipped inoculations tainted with the bird flu virus to twelve countries in Europe. This happened to be discovered when doctors injected mice with the inoculations and they died shortly afterwards. This is a sample of what the elites intend to do—infect people through their supposedly 'preventative inoculations' which are really designed to introduce viruses into the victim, weaken the immune system and introduce poisons into the body.

A false flag terrorist event looming over the peoples of North America and elsewhere is that of a supposed 'pandemic' propagated intentionally to be followed by enforced inoculations. In fact, the United States has over a thousand laboratory sites working at weaponizing the bird flu and swine flu and creating a wide range of other designer viruses and biological agents through genetic modification and recombinant DNA methodologies. Vaccines are a weapon of choice for the world elites as they cause no property damage or environmental effects. The *World Health Organization* is indeed staffed by such psychopaths as would intentionally commit genocide through such methodologies. The Illuminate will be absolutely sure to produce the "Pandemic" they desire, when billions succumb to the very diseases contained in the vaccine injection they receive!

For your pleasure and safety, Prime Minister Steven Harper has also spent $300,000,000 of your tax monies to offer Gardacil vaccinations to all the young women of Eastern Canada. Perhaps this might also be offered to the Native community, like the flu infested blankets offered to the natives by the European invaders to commit genocide against them. The inoculation program will be sold effectively through the Corporate Media and slick promotions for the little sheep to follow. The New World Psychiatric Disorder group is even preparing other viruses or flues for you, as well as inoculations with Mercury to increase your brain power. These are some of the means by which your government will attempt to carry forward the eugenics programs of the pseudo-illuminate and corporate elites.

The fluoridation of the water supply has been routinely done through North America for over fifty years. Before that, both the Nazis and the Russians fluoridated the water in their prison camps. The fluoridation of water causes electrolyte imbalances and has been linked to dental florosis, cancers of the pancreas and kidneys, asthma, bone osteoporoses, and the disruption of mental clarity and intelligence. It is estimated to reduce the IQ, intelligence quotient, by 20 points!

When fluoridation was introduced, it was presented as a progressive measure to reduce tooth decay and still today one can barely find any tooth pastes which do not contain fluoride, always advertised as something wonderful for you. The fine print on the tube notes however that if a child even swallows a few grams of the toothpaste, he or she will have consumed a poisonous amount of fluoride and may need to be taken to the hospital. Fluoride is a neurotoxin and people are consuming increasing amounts of it through their water, their toothpaste, the foods baked or cooked with water, as well as through their skin when showering or bathing.

The fluoride added to your drinking and washing water is a by-product of the aluminium industry and essentially a toxic and poisonous substance known to cause a wide range of ailments. The manufacturing industries essentially found a way of distributing their toxic wastes while making a profit and once again sold the whole plan through the corporate media and slick ads, such that all the sheeple are brainwashed into thinking that the fluoridation program furthered their health rather than eventually causing them all kinds of sickness and reduced mental functioning. Once again, all adverse research showing the destructiveness of fluoridation was repressed, investigators fired and funding denied. The fluoridation of the water serves the eugenic plans of the elites and makes big bucks to line those fancy pant pockets. The power of the media and the control of the medical establishment by the pharmaceutical mafia allow such negligent and criminal practices to be continued. Of course, once again people are waking up to the criminality of what has been done and is being done, and are beginning to demand a stop to water fluoridation. This is another growing movement in the US. and around the world.

Aspartame is another substance routinely added to foods, especially diet pops and chewing gum, despite the accumulating research demonstrating its toxic effects. The United States' *Food and Drug Administration* turned down G.D. Searle's application for aspartame's approval from 1966 to 1981, at which point, approval was forced through the FDA at the insistence of Searle's CEO, Donald Rumsfeld. This regulatory failure of epic proportions entirely resulted from the actions of Donald Rumsfeld when he was the patent holder for aspartame. The massive public health issues caused by aspartame are thus referred to as *Rumsfeld's plague*.

The FDA has accrued over 92 symptoms from ingesting aspartame, ranging from headaches, blurred vision, skin rashes, epilepsy and multiple sclerosis to that ultimate symptom, DEATH. Aspartame is a chemical that the FDA has known for 43 years is metabolized as methanol, formaldehyde, aspartic acid, phenylalanine, and the proven carcinogen, diketopiperazine. This chemical has produced a massive mountain of medical evidence of its neuro-degenerative effects, which is finally leading to more States within the US calling for it to be removed from the market. New Mexico has now sponsored Senate Memorial 9, 2009, asking the Food and Drug Administration to rescind its approval for the artificial sweetener, aspartame; so also has the Senate of Hawaii, where both diabetes and epileptic seizures, with links to aspartame, have become statistically epidemic. In January 2009,

Hawaii Senator Kalani English introduced SB576 to ban aspartame entirely in Hawaii. This bill is cosponsored by 14 members of the 25 member Hawaii Senate. *Health Canada*, like the FDA, has been negligent in failing to prevent the spread of neuro-degenerative and carcinogenic damage to hundreds of thousands of Canadians!

Genetically modified seeds, plants and foods pose another huge health

issue. A growing body of research demonstrates that GM foods are causing all kinds of impairments, birth defects and infertility, malnutrition, cancers and death. GM foods have now been outright banned in parts of the European Union. Further, the spread of genetically modified corns, rice, soybean, wheat and other crops have caused the devastation of native food supplies around the world in third world countries and in North America. Further, when GM foods are sold, the government requires no labelling at the bequest of the corporate mafia as the public might not want to eat such poisons. A good portion of North American food supply now involves GM foods in one form or another—estimated at 80%. Once again, these GM seeds and foods are introduced without adequate testing, contrary research is suppressed, and only denial and obstruction when the evidences make clear the dangers posed by these technologies.

In *Seeds of Destruction: The Hidden Agenda of Genetic Manipulation* by F. William Engdahl (Global Research, 2007 ISBN 978-0-937147-2-2), the author focuses on how a small socio-political American elite has sought to establish control over the very basis of human survival: the provision of our daily bread. *"Control the food and you control the people."* Engdahl looks into the corridors of power, into the backrooms of the science labs and behind closed doors in the corporate boardrooms to explain the perils of GMO's. He reveals *"a diabolical World of profit-driven political intrigue, government corruption and coercion, where genetic manipulation and the patenting of life forms are used to gain worldwide control over food production."* The book reads like a crime story, which indeed should not come as a surprise, as that is what it is.

Engdahl's carefully argued critique goes far beyond the familiar controversies surrounding the practice of genetic modification as a scientific technique. The book is an eye-opener, a must-read for all those committed to the causes of social justice and World peace. We begin to realize that the *Food and Drug Administration* of the US, like *Health Canada*, do not really serve the health interests of the citizens but the corporate masters with their secretive eugenics plans. Many people are waking up to the crimes of the multinational Monsantos Corporation with their diabolical schemes committed around the world. In India alone, 10,000 to 100,000 landowners are claimed to have committed suicide after losing their lands to the multinational Monsantos, unable to meet their debt obligations and crop yields as promised.

HEALTH CARE LEGISLATION

The Canadian government, in its role as co-conspirators with the corporate and financial elites with their population reduction program, has most recently been trying to pass Bills C51 and C52. [13] These bills essentially criminalize natural health products and practices, and restrict the public's access to natural vitamins, minerals and health supplements! Doctors would have to prescribe these health supplements and then this will be discouraged and made more difficult and expensive.

Perhaps nothing demonstrates so clearly that the Canadian government and *Health Canada* do not take the interests of Canadian citizen to heart in wanting to promote the health of Canadians as does the effort in 2008 to pass Canada's Bill C51, and then other subsequent legislation designed to restrict citizens' health freedom. This bizarre bill, the product of severely

---

[13] These notes were written in 2010 and I have not updated this report I do not have the energies to learn all the details and intrigue surrounding each of these issues.

deranged and psychopathic little minds, would actually outlaw 70% of natural health products, while making others available by expensive prescription, while at the same time, giving police state powers for enforcement. This bill is promoted by the big pharmaceutical companies or the 'pharmaceutical mafia.' Bill C-51 was introduced by the Canadian Minister of Health on April 8th, 2008 and proposed sweeping changes to Canada's Food and Drugs Act that could have devastating consequences on the health products industry.

Among the changes proposed by the bill are alterations to key terminology, including replacing the word *"drug"* with *"therapeutic product,"* thereby giving the Canadian government broad-reaching powers to regulate the sale of all herbs, vitamins, supplements and other items. With this single language change, any health food product that is "therapeutic" automatically falls under the Food and Drug Act. This could include bottled water, blueberries, dandelion greens and essentially all plant-derived substances.

Bill C51 also legitimizes outrageous and criminal powers to the police and introduces quite mentally disturbed regulations. At the same time that C-51 is outlawing herbs, supplements and vitamins, it would grant alarming "enforcement" powers to the thugs or 'agents' who would claim to be "protecting" the public from dangerous unapproved "therapeutic agents" like, say, dandelion greens. Bill C-51 law would allow the Canadian government's corrupted police and agents to:

· *Enter private property without a warrant*
· Take your property at their discretion
· Dispose of your property at will
· Not reimburse you for your losses
· Seize your bank accounts without a warrant
· Charge owners shipping and storage charges for seized property
· Store your property indefinitely
· Levy fines of up to $5,000,000.00 and/or seek 2 years in jail per charge
· Will not have to report seizures to a court.
· They can charge you just for talking about or promoting natural alternatives

The Bill even criminalizes parents who might give herbs or supplements to their children!

The Act changes the definition of the word "sell" to include anyone who gives such therapeutic products to someone else. So a mother giving a herb to her child, under the proposed new language, could be arrested for engaging in the sale of unregulated, unapproved "therapeutic substances." C-51 would even criminalize the simple drying of herbs in your kitchen to be used in an herbal product. That would now be categorized as a *"controlled activity,"* and anyone caught engaging in such *"controlled activities"* could be arrested, fined and potentially jailed. Other "controlled activities" include labelling bottles, harvesting plants on a farm, collecting herbs from your back yard, or even testing herbal products on yourself! In fact, virtually every activity involving herbs or supplements would be criminalized. In the United States, the criminal government is now trying even to outlaw people having gardens! At a time when hunger and starvation is spreading around the world and our food supplies are increasingly poisoned by the corporate elites, the Canadian government conspires with the pharmaceutical agencies and food processor to restrict the health freedom and choices of Canadians. Not only that, but they introduce quite mentally disturbed legislation to introduce police state powers for big brother—what a nightmare!

C-51 is also the Canadian government's "final solution" for the health products industry—a desperate effort to destroy this industry that threatens the profits and viability of conventional medicine, which is the third leading cause of death in the US. Unlike the regulated prescription drugs, only a few persons have ever died from consuming or using any alternative natural health therapies, products or services. In fact, if Health Canada was interested in your health, they would ban pharmaceuticals and promote almost exclusively the natural therapeutic products. Natural medicine works too well and has become too widely used for the conspiracies and profit motives of the eugenicists. Bill C51 would even stop research and development of safe natural alternatives in favour of high risk drugs.

Both the Canadian and American governments have decided to destroy the health product industries by passing such laws that effectively criminalize anyone selling or even growing such products. They simply cannot tolerate allowing consumers to have continued access to natural products. To do so will ultimately spell the destruction of Big Pharma and the outdated, corrupt and criminally-operated pharmaceutical industry that the criminally-operated government is trying to protect. There are disturbing elements to Bill C51 and similar legislation, which should serve as a wake up call to citizens as to who controls our governments. This bill would even allow government agents to adopt laws from other countries without the approval of elected officials, without debate in the House of Commons and without the consent of the Canadian people. This is part of your Security and Prosperity plan!

One activist describes Bill C51:

> This bill is a crime against our democracy and those involved in introducing it and passing it should be charged with treason against the kind and totally naive trusting Canadian people. This bill is part of a much bigger New World Order depopulation, and longevity reducing UN agenda, conducted under the Codex Alimentarius agenda.

In fact, Canada, the USA and Mexico have signed many secret agreements that are piece by piece, producing the North American Union for your security and prosperity—or enslavement, sickness and poverty. It was introduced in Canada because it is a place of least resistance, but under one of the Security and Prosperity Partnership Agreements, the restrictions passed in Canada would automatically become law in the USA and Mexico. Since Canada has a very smaller and spread out population which pays little if no attention at all to what our elected officials do or say, our government attempted to rush this draconian measure through Parliament. Fortunately, the passage of the bill was delayed in 2008 due to the rallying of opposition through health groups and the health food industry. Unfortunately, the government is now introducing the Bill in a new form and likely under the cover of night. It is hard to conceive that our government is so corrupted and controlled by such psychopaths as it has become, as to attempt to pass such a piece of psychiatrically disturbed legislation. Of course, this is all for your security and prosperity.

These Bills in Canada are part of the larger 'Codex Ailimentarius,' proposed by the world elites to apply around the world as part of their population control and eugenics. They want to suppress the availability of natural foods and supplements which can enable people to maintain their health, despite the poisoning of their air, their bloodstreams, their water and soil, and their food.

Another major health issue concerns the 'smart meters' being installed across our nations and mandated by legislatures, controlled by the elites and the thinking of Agenda 21. These devices allow for the monitoring

127

of household electricity use and they allow for remote reading, so that the hydro agent no longer has to go up to your house to read your meter. Unfortunately, this introduces a surveillance technology into your home and further, these meters are classed as 2b carcinogens continuously radiating and contributing to the electromagnetic toxicity of your living spaces! One activist describes people as being 'cooked in their homes' by such meters, which have even been 'weaponized' so that they can emit in different frequency ranges and with different strengths, which could interact even fatally with your biological processes. The smart meters can cause headaches and dizziness, ringing in the ears, seizures, vomiting and nausea, and most significantly, varied cardiac symptoms, ranging from palpitations to arrhythmia. Multiple units on apartment buildings only multiply the toxicity. Some electro-sensitive people have had to flee their homes, while others are removing the meters and replacing them with the traditional analogue meters, only then to be denied power. President Obama and the government have allotted 4 billion dollars for the enforced installation of the smart meters in 140 million American households, and the situation in Canada is much the same. Are smart meters another of the elite's arsenal of weapons for their 'silent wars' against humanity? These have now been renamed as 'murder meters,' a new devise like the highly toxic mercury filled light bulbs, which could enable the plans for the hidden culling of the flock.
(www.refusesmartmeters.com)

Wake up world citizens, you stupid sheep before you and your children are racked with illness, starved through the destruction of your food supplies, poisoned through your air and water, inoculations and pharmaceutical medicines, and you cannot even remember what hit you as you are wracked with Alzheimer's, cancers and infertility.

The Criminal Poisoning of the Citizens of Ottawa & Kemptville through Chemtrail Spraying

The chemtrail spraying of citizens of Kemtpville and Ottawa is a regular phenomenon, usually evident three or four days a week. Its effects can be sensed and felt in the poisoning of the air, the water and land. It is a form of non-lethal warfare, which will likely be much more effective when the government bans the sale and distribution of natural health products, vitamins and herbs. Chemtrail spraying is allowed by your government who love you dearly and will look after you little Canadian sheep, while they sell you pharmaceuticals and poisonous inoculations to cause cancer and numerous other medical and health problems. The New World Order is especially interested in poisoning your children who might want to play outside and they enjoy plaguing your elders with degenerative mental disorders—such as Alzheimer's. I personally hardly know a family without some elders suffering from Alzheimer's. Of course, what can one expect after we have been sprayed with aluminium and other toxins for fifteen years!

A DAY IN THE LIFE
OF THE CHEMTRAIL POISONING
OF THE CITIZENS OF OTTAWA, CANADA
BY A PSYCHOPATHIC ELITE

On Saturday September 17th, 2011, I was on Parliament Hill in Ottawa, Ontario to attend a 9-11 Truth activity sponsored by an Ottawa 9-11 group, which featured the public playing of the newest movie video by the *Architects and Engineers for 9-11 Truth*. This important video, *Explosive Evidence*, clearly documents the fact that the Two Towers of New York which *disintegrated* in under 15 seconds, and Building 7 which fell down in under 6 seconds without even having been supposedly hit by an airplane—all three buildings involved the destruction by *controlled demolitions* of some sort and could not possibly have been the effect of airplane crashes and Muslim extremism, as the public and goyem have been led to believe. The 9-11 group was holding their activity on Parliament Hill after September 11, as the focus on September 11th had been an International 9-11 Truth conference being held in Toronto Ontario.

Anyway, I attended this event from 10 o'clock in the morning through the day until almost 7 o'clock in the evening. I conducted my biweekly live internet radio show through *www.bbsradio.com* directly from Parliament Hill using the speaker of a cell phone and I interviewed some of the 9-11 group participants on Hill as they were finishing up their day of truth activism.

Ottawa's Parliament Hill offers a panoramic view of the surrounding skyline. Spending the day there enabled me to take videos through the day of the local chemtrail spraying of the citizens and guests of Ottawa. I subsequently composed a short video documentary of the day to be posted to www.youtube.com and elsewhere, entitled: *A Day in the Life of the Chemtrail Poisoning of the Citizens of Ottawa, Canada by a Psychopathic Elite.* The chemtrail spraying from such a vantage point as Parliament Hill was so obvious that it continues to amaze me how most sheeple, or sheep people, are not even aware of what is being done to them. The goyem are so preoccupied with a thousand and one things and emotional concerns that they are incapable of perceiving what is happening in their skies around them, yet alone then grasp what is behind it all. In reality, the same psychopathic elite who fashioned 9-11 events for your public deception are also the same ones who are carrying out biological warfare against you from the skies. The old world order psychiatrically disturbed elites are poisoning you and the masses of the populations of NATO countries.

The chemtrail spraying of Ottawa went on all day long while I was on Parliament Hill and was evident in the skies over Ottawa even as I drove in from the south early in the morning. Everything in the Ottawa sky on that day was a product of artificial spraying. There were no natural clouds and it was almost perfectly still with no notable air current. Through the next pages, I have presented just a small sample of photos extracted from my videos of that day. The cover image for *GCU* was extrapolated from the video as it features the *Star of David* on the *Peace Tower* clock, with the time of 11:37—for me, a very meaningful and coincidental time with profound occult significance.

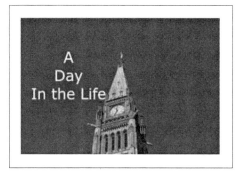

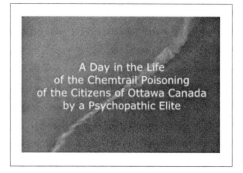

An opening shot, early in the morning shows a blue sky behind the Peace Tower with no cloud cover of any sort. This is how the video opens. The next image is a sample close-up of a chemtrails being laid in the morning hours. Even the diffuse white haze in this picture is the result of earlier but now dispersed chemtrails. This is a good solid trail just behind the Peace Tower, likely destined for friends and citizens of Gatineau and Hull.

There were a number of very dramatic shots of the poisoning of Ottawa's citizens with chemtrail passes directly over and behind the *Houses of Criminals*, although more commonly known as the *Houses of Parliament*. In the following image, all the dispersed white substances surrounding the Peace Tower are chemtrail poisons, even though there seems to be an angel or sylph figure in the tailings to the left of the Tower:

These next shots are over the West Block of Parliament Hill and illustrate the accumulation and dispersion of the chemtrails through the day. The first photo shows a 'vortex' of energy in the chemtrails to the right of the West block spire. Everything in this sky in these pictures is artificially sprayed and there are no natural clouds. As the spraying was carried on all through the day, different chemtrails are at different stages of dispersing and falling on to the ground below to poison the air of the useless eaters— the Goyem and sheep below.

While I was on Parliament Hill that day, the Peace Tower bells sounded periodically to announce the times of day. The knolling of the bells sounded appropriates notes as if announcing the "death knoll" for the citizens of

Ottawa being sprayed with aerial poisoning--all the sheep people who believed the lies of their politicians and the mass deceptions perpetrated by the corporate media. My short documentary movie refers to the sheep going willingly to slaughter, death knoll and all, unaware of the aerial chemical assault upon them and unable to remember 9-11 or who won

the most recent hockey game. A nation asleep! What a travesty of humanity! All noble and free are we? Living in a democracy controlled by psychopathic elite and a media of lies? These people, your local politicians from the House of Criminals and your local media outlets, are all pathological liars and paid handsomely for their terrorist activities and crimes against you.

Here is a close up shot which illustrates the substances being dispersed within chemtrail spraying. These include heavy metals, particularly aluminium, barium, and strontium. These substances actually fall down – due of course to a well known law of science called 'gravity.' These substances are not meant to be saving us from the imagined disasters of global warming due to human carbon emissions, as they are not sustained in the skies. These substances rain descend down upon you, your neighbours, your children, your pets, everyone, whether you are Jewish, Christian, Muslims, Hindu, or atheists or something else. Furthermore, all kinds of new concoctions and inventions can be applied to populations through such *terrorist delivery systems* as chemtrail poisoning provides. This is biological and chemical warfare being perpetrated against you.

Through the months of May to September of this year, I travelled through the province of Ontario on several occasions and was able to see and/or video tape chemtrail spraying from Ottawa up through Petawawa, Deep River, Sault St. Marie, Sudbury, Thunder Bay, Manitoulin Island, Picton, Kingston and over into Quebec, north of Montreal. All of central and eastern Ontario is being sprayed by these psychopathic elites and this is allowed by your local politicians – of course, all denied with 'plausible deniability,' and by your treasonous military brass who allow this to be done, while busy with their war crimes against the peoples of Afghanistan and Libya.

Wake up Canadian and world citizens. The hour is late and we are approaching noon, a possible World War III and irreversible environmental catastrophes unless humankind can bring these criminal cabals to justice for their *crimes against humanity*. Chemtrail spraying is being perpetrated by *existing terrorists* and they are not arranged by Osama Bin Laden from a cave, as you have been led to believe like sheep by the Zionist owned media. The same people who brought you 9-11, fake moon landings, assassinated presidents, false flag terrorism around the world, and the worldwide impoverishment of countries in service of the banksters, are now poisoning you from the skies and making a handy profit along the way, with pharmaceutical poisons and senior's homes. The new world order elite, those who I prefer to refer to as the *old world psychiatrically disordered elites* actually do believe in population reduction and in making a handsome profit besides. The facts of chemtrail poisoning are a symptom of a much more dangerous terrorist threat to Canadians and world citizens than anything posed by the imaginary monsters of

Islamic Fundamentalism, the Hollywood bogey man for public deception.

Chemtrails indicate further the treasonous and terrorist involvement of our own police, intelligence and military communities, as well as the politicians who allow this to be done. Covert biological warfare is being conducted against the citizenry and this activity certainly constitutes a 'crime against humanity,' whether or not you are a prince or a pauper. Unfortunately, the new world psychiatrically disordered psychopaths have all kinds of things up their sleeves for committing homicide and genocide — of course, all to save the earth and to create a new age 'of reason' as suggested by the Georgian Guidestones.

LOOK AT THIS WORLD
ON THE CHEMTRAIL POISONING OF THE
CITIZENS OF KEMPTVILLE

The following illustrations are of chemtrail spraying in Kemptville Ontario where the *Zero Point Institute* is located and where I live. Kemptville is about 45 minutes south of Ottawa, Ontario, Canada's capital. These images are drawn from a half hour documentary video I have produced with the same title as this chapter. The video features musician Kenny J. singing the original composition, *Look at this World*, which serves as an appropriate sound track for this portrait of the chemtrail poisoning of the citizens of Kemptville and our local area.

This image depicts the beginning of another day of chemtrail spraying as viewed from Clothier Street, downtown Kemptville looking west.

The next pictures depict the chemtrails laid over downtown Kemptville as photographed from the local town square with its flags.

These pictures show three major chemtrails laid in parallel and at slightly different stages of dispersing.

The image above is shot from the Giant Tiger parking lot in downtown Kemptville, looking south west.

The following images depict the substances descending down upon us subsequent to these overhead chemtrails:

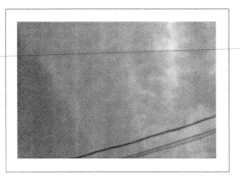
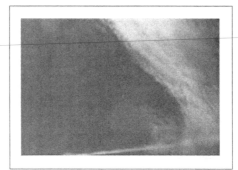

 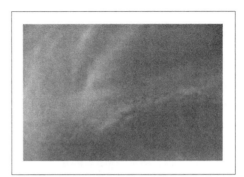

The illustrations below show dispersing of chemtrails. At times, the sky can be overcast or completely silvered as the result of such spraying:

These substances are actually raining down upon the citizens of Kemptville, as they are across all of Canada, although less in northerly regions. The populace is continually being sprayed from above with these poisons! And your elders cannot even remember what has happened to them.

The illustrations below are from the perspective in downtown Kemptville looking north.

On the left, the sky is clear, while on the right, everything in the sky is the results of spraying by these psychopathic elites. And you think that you are free. What a joke.

In case you forget what real clouds and a clear sky look like, here is an image from a day without any aerial assault. The next picture captures the laying of a cross pattern in the sky, looking south from the creek and Clothier Street over the new public library.

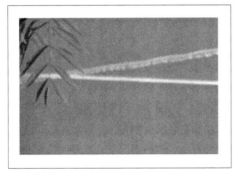

The chemtrail patterns of that day were just beginning at this time and this was another afternoon of thirty to forty such chemtrail passes until the sky was full of poisons and artificial clouds by the evening.

The next images are from a full day of accumulated spraying with an additional chemtrail being laid on top of the day's accumulation. Everything in these images is a consequence of chemtrail spraying and none of these are natural clouds.

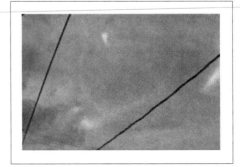

Sometimes the chemtrails are most perceptible in the evenings as the sun highlights the poisonous trails. These shots are of the western sky from downtown Kemptville.

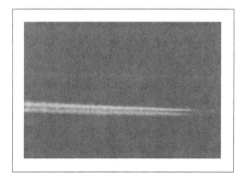

The following is an attempted close-up of a chemtrail airplane. These are usually silvery in colour with few or no markings—so as to make them as invisible as possible and to obscure any evidence as to who is behind this program of the mass poisoning of Canadian citizens.

Chemtrails are an invention of what mystic G. I. Gurdjieff would describe as a *Hasnamussian science*.

> **"... 'Hasnamussian science,' invented by certain pimpled beings among them, in which it is nonchalantly proved that the periodic reciprocal destruction on the Earth is very, very necessary, and that if it did not exist an intolerable overpopulation would result on the Earth, and such economic horrors would ensure that men-beings would begin to eat one another. ..."** G. I. Gurdjieff -- Beelzebub's Tales

Gurdjieff defines 'Hasnamusses' as those who lack the 'divine impulse of conscience,' and who are subject to *"Every kind of depravity, conscious as well as unconscious"* and having "the irresistible inclination to destroy the existence of other breathing creatures." In more popular terminology, such Hasnamusses could be considered psychopaths with a crystallized egoism and lacking awareness of any sacred being-impulses. The old world psychiatrically disordered elite, the global crime syndicate which is establishing the so-called 'new world order,' has all kinds of invented quack sciences and frauds which they perpetrate upon the sleeping public.

Agenda 21, the quack sciences of global warming, food poisoning and inoculations, chemtrails and geo-engineering, war and revolution, are all ways in which the elites help to save humankind from the problems of 'overpopulation.'

Citizens need to seriously question themselves as to why the Canadian government would allow a cabal of psychopathic eugenicists and Satanists to poison Canadian citizens with high atmospheric chemtrail spraying. Your government loves you little sheep and is planning new inoculations and poisoned foods for your enjoyment, safety, sterilization and ultimate demise. The Canadian government is run by a hierarchy of idiots, minions, perverts, pedophiles and psychopaths, Satanists and Luciferians, Kabbalists and Royalty, ultimately controlled by Reptilians and Lunatics; and the whole lie is perpetrated by Hasnamusses in the media of lies and deception. My goodness, what a cosmic Tale! Unfortunately, it is true.

The Illuminati & their Networks:[14] A Valuable Truth & Conspiracy Library

www.zeropoint.ca/NewWorldDisorder.html

ILLUMINATI
THE CULT THAT HIGHJACKED THE WORLD
BY HENRY MAKOW, 2008
www.henrymakow.com

"Humanity is the victim of a monstrous conspiracy
of unspeakable proportions." (**Makow,** *Illuminati*, p. 76)

---

[14] I feature these book reviews on my website at *www.zeropoint.ca* to illustrate modern researches as to the central conspiracy networks. These are immensely complex areas of study and there are many unknowns and questions.

141

This is an immensely valuable book, well researched and written. Makow is a Canadian Jew who clearly distinguishes between the Zionist Jews who form the major part of the Illuminati organization and the greater part of the Jewish community who have, like the goyem population, been duped by Zionist propaganda. The following quotes give highlights from Makow's book which raises and fills in many dark and unknown issues of modern history--particularly the Zionist influences in concocting the World Wars, the Bolshevik revolution in Russia, and much more. I have included some of Makow's notes on the *"crazy apocalyptic Agenda"* of the Illuminati, the cult that highjacked the world. Makow addresses also the holocaust industry and how the claims of anti-Semitism are routinely used to undermine legitimate dissent.

"... mankind is controlled by Satanists. (p. 7)

"a small Satanic cult--Cabalistic bankers and Freemasons ... control the world's finances and media. Our "leaders" are junior members of this international cult, called the Order of the Illuminati. (p. 1)

"Zionism is controlled by "the Order of the Illuminati" which represents a group of dynastic families, generational Satanists, associated with the Rothschilds and European aristocracy, united by money, marriage and Freemasonry (i.e. the Cabala.) This cult stems from the Satanic Jewish Sabbatean-Frankist movement.... (p. 9)

"The Illuminati control the Establishment in Europe, America and most of the world. Its secret war against humanity is designed to make us acquiesce in their tyranny (i.e. 'world government').

"... the Illuminati conspiracy is all-pervasive, has infiltrated every social institution of significance and includes millions of non-Jews.`

"Most Jews are unaware of the Illuminati agenda. ... The Illuminati hides behind the skirts of ordinary Jews. The cult that highjacked the world is the tiny nucleus of Cabalistic bankers and Masons based in London and directed by the House of Rothschild.

"The bankers` first precaution is to buy all the politicians. The second is to buy the major media outlets in order to promote the illusion that politicians make decisions and represent our interests. The third precaution is to take control of the education system, ensuring that people stop thinking at an early age. (p. 28)

"The bankers need to eliminate nation states, freedom and democracy in order to streamline their business and consolidate their power. The UN, NAU, EU, IMF and World Bank--glorified loan sharks and collectors--will make the laws. (p. 29)

"Every war was a trick used to slaughter and brutalize humanity and to increase the wealth and power of this clique, which is based in the Bank of England." (p. 31)

"In every war, the Illuminati controlled both sides of the conflict, and the Third World War will not be an exception. (p. 99)

"England has been a 'Jewish' state for over 300 years. (p.35)

"The top block ... the Grand Druid Council. They only take orders from the Rothschilds and nobody else. They're their private priesthood. The Council of 33 is directly under them, that is the 33 highest Masons in the World. Next is the Council of 300, some of the richest people and conglomerates in the World--including the Bilderbergs.... (p. 74)

"Drug trafficking, white slavery, prostitution and pornography finance secret New World Order programs. Elements of the CIA, FBI, Coast Guard, Military, and police are all involved, as is the Mafia. ... The public has a child-like trust in its leaders. The charge that they really belong to a sadistic, criminal, traitorous syndicate is a betrayal beyond belief." (p. 77)

"Americans eventually will figure out that the Rothschilds and their agents are responsible for the Depression and Obama is their creation and puppet. They will discover that the Illuminati has waged war on humanity for centuries and the US media and education system are a farce. They will recognize the outsized role played by Jews in enacting this diabolical agenda. That's when Illuminati Jews may again turn ordinary Jews, loyal American citizens, into their scapegoat. ... the Zionist and World Jewish leadership prevaricated and obstructed all efforts to save the Jews of Europe. ... the Zionists needed to increase the number of Jewish victims to hide their own role in bringing Hitler to power and instigating World War Two. (pp. 140/149/155)

"In 1891, Cecil Rhodes started a secret society called "the Round Table" dedicated to world hegemony for the shareholders of the Bank of England and their allies. These priggish aristocrats, including the Rothschilds, realized that they must control the world to safeguard their monopoly on money creation as well as global resources. Imperialism never reflects national interests but the agenda of these bankers. They are united also by a commitment to freemasonry, which at the top is dedicated to the destruction of Christianity, the worship of Lucifer, and the rebuilding of a pagan temple in Jerusalem. They see humanity as "useless eaters" and pioneered eugenics and brainwashing to decrease population and turn us into their servants. The eventual annihilation of non-Zionist Jews was rooted in this movement. (p. 156)

"Their goal is to create a world government tyranny dedicated to Lucifer with its capital in Jerusalem. (p. 164)

"... the Jewish holocaust is a valuable tool in advancing the New World Order agenda. It gives their Jewish pawns moral immunity and allows them to vilify any opponents as Nazis. ... Zionism is a fraud on Jews. (pp.169/173)

"Lemming-like, the Western elite has embraced a death-wish for civilization. They have sold their soul (and us) to the devil. ...Treason is the secret policy of the governing elite in the West. Wittingly or unwittingly, they serve the Illuminati plan for "world government," and Orwellian police state called "the New World Order. (pp. 189/223)

"As we sleepwalk into the next world war, let's recall that the people who issue our currency are behind every war and control both sides." (p. 214)

"The Illuminati are a loose alliance of Jewish finance and the British/American/European aristocracy joined by marriage, money and beliefs in the occult (Freemasonry). ...They own vast interlocking cartels (banking, oil, pharmaceuticals, war, chemicals, minerals, media etc.) and control society and government through corporate and professional groups, the media, education, secret societies, think tanks, foundations and intelligence agencies. Their goal is *to absorb the world's wealth and control its citizens using propaganda, "education" and "social engineering."* (p.217)

Illuminati also has valuable references to occult and mystical subjects, in a manner obviously relevant to Zero Point studies:

"… the Illuminati symbol, the dot in a circle ....

"We all have a spark of the Divine within.

"Nothing would disturb the Illuminati more than a revival of belief in God.

"The essence of political struggle is actually spiritual, a cosmic battle between God (Good) and Satan (Evil) for the soul of man. (p. 81)

"Mightier than the nuclear bomb, the Lie is Satan's most powerful weapon. The bomb merely devastates. The Lie steals souls. It enlists millions of naive people to Satan's cause. (p. 63)

"Mankind is in the grip of a multigenerational diabolical conspiracy, and is too mesmerized by sex and money to realize it. (p. 182)

"Ultimately, the battle is for the soul of humanity. (p. 234)

Makow has provided a shocking account of the *Illuminati* and their insidious influence through modern history. *Illuminati²* is a fascinating sequel which spells out the Illuminati influences throughout our broader society, Hollywood, through the media, and varied programs of social engineering.

It seems that life is nothing like what the majority of the sheeple have been led to believe. And then, it even gets weirder again.

HUMAN RACE GET OFF YOUR KNEES
THE LION SLEEPS NO MORE
BY DAVID ICKE, 2010
www.davidicke.com

Human Race: Get Off your Knees is another of David Icke's remarkable and inspiring works. It is the third which i have read this year, 2010, including *The Big Secret* and *The David Icke's Guide to the Global Conspiracy*.

This is a massive almost 700 page volume covering a wealth of historical and contemporary evidence for the role of a reptilian and hybrid elite in controlling the life of humankind upon planet Earth. This has resulted in the underground spread of Satanism and Luciferian cults around the world and the control of the political, economic and social life of humankind by criminal networks centred within the City of London, the banking houses of the Rothschild dynasty, the royal houses of Europe and the Dark Nobility, and the financiers and war merchants of Wall Street. Just when one thought life on this planet could not get any more insane, with the criminal networks controlling all major governments, military and intelligence services, pharmaceutical and international corporations, the media and the educational system; now we learn that there are Reptilian bases on the moon and underneath the surface of the earth! Certainly, the so-called elite have to be weirded out in some such way—quite alien to the mentality of most normal people, to have such deviant and psychopathic attitudes towards humankind as they demonstrate.

David Icke's books are most entertaining and connect so many dots in bringing the matrix into view and countering all the propaganda and lies woven by the media and the culture of deception. Icke intertwines his own life story and personal commentaries into his work, which makes the text most readable and entertaining. Below, I have sampled materials from Icke's book.

With regards to his consciousness studies, David provides these key concepts which are consistent with my work in *The Heart Doctrine*, although there are major differences between my and David's understanding of the holographic physics of life and creation.

> "Consciousness talks to us through the heart ....
> The heart chakra is our major connection
> to Consciousness beyond this 'world' of illusory form....
> The 'heart,' the intuition, however
> is our connection with the Infinite Self beyond
> the five senses...." (pp. 9-10)

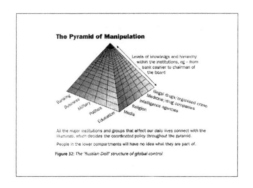

Bravo David Icke for your individuality in pursuing the truth and your inspiring message to humankind to wake up and unleash the lion inherent to the human heart and spirit. Humankind, get off your knees.

> "As the saying, goes, it doesn't matter who you vote for, the government still gets in--the secret government. ... in truth, we live in one-party dictatorships controlled by a handful of bloodline families. (p. 61)

> "The world is controlled by the centre of the Illuminati web in the same way that a corporate headquarters dictates global policy to all of its subsidiaries. In the case of the Illuminati, these 'subsidiaries'

are secret society networks and bloodline families in every country, which themselves have networks that influence all levels from national government to local community. (p. 63)

"The secret society network today operates globally with groupings like the Jesuits, Knights Templar, Knights of Malta, Opus Dei and Freemasonry, working as one unit at their highest levels. This 'unit' or force that connects all the major secret societies is known as the 'Illuminati', or 'Illuminated Ones'. It is a series of degrees into which the other secret societies feed their chosen few, and entry to at least the upper echelons of the Illuminati pyramid is by bloodline only. (p. 59)

"... the fewer banks there are the easier it is to control the system and this is why we have seen the emergence of mega banks, like the Rothschild-dominated Goldman Sachs. (p. 69)

"The Bilderberg Group secretly coordinates a common policy between governments, banks, corporations, the media, intelligence agencies and the military, including NATO. It was established by the Rothschilds in 1954 at the Bilderberg Hotel in the Netherlands and is run on their behalf by the Rockefeller family network. David Rockefeller and Rothschild/Rockefeller agent, Henry Kissinger have been the most prominent players over the decades.... (p. 70)

"The bloodlines love their titles and they are obsessed with status, power and hierarchy. (p. 71)

" ... televisions that watch you ....

"... the plan was also to cull and control the population through medicine, food, new laboratory-made diseases and the suppression of a cure for cancer. (p. 76)

"The Rothschilds have a horrific record of engineering wars, including the world wars, instigating financial crashes and manipulating countries across every continent via the networks they control. (p. 78)

"... the Rothschilds used their agents, the Schiff and Warburg families, to create the privately owned 'American' central bank, the Federal Reserve, in 1913.

"The name 'Rothschild' first appeared in the 18th century when Mayer Amschel Bauer established his banking empire in Frankfurt, Germany, and changed the family name. ... The Bauers were a notorious satanic family in Middle Ages Germany and the major Rothschilds remain master black magicians to this day. ... The name 'Rothschild' derives from the German 'rotes-schild', or 'red shield'/'red sign'. This referred to the red hexagram on the Bauer/ Rothschild home in Frankfurt and it is better known as the 'Star of David.' Despite what most people believe, this is not an exclusively Jewish symbol and was not used in that context until the Rothschilds took it as their own. The hexagram is an esoteric symbol going back to antiquity, and today it is displayed on the flag of Israel because the Rothschilds own the place. (p. 87)

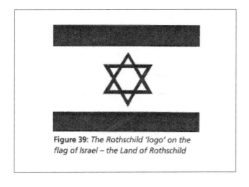

Figure 39: *The Rothschild 'logo' on the flag of Israel – the Land of Rothschild*

The Rothschilds ... and their banking cartel have also funded all sides in virtually every war since about 1800--wars that their agents in government, the military and intelligence agencies have manipulated into being. This has cost the lives of at least hundreds of millions (75 million in the two world wars alone) and has allowed governments and peoples to be controlled through debt payments on the loans. ... As Gutle Schnaper, Mayer Amschel Rothschild's wife, said shorty before she died in 1849: *"If my sons did not want wars, there would be none."* (p. 95)

David Icke has provided a fascinating body of research, connecting so many dots together and outlining the hidden patterns of history. A must read for any conspiracy theory library.

THE CONSPIRATOR'S HIERARCHY:
THE COMMITTEE OF 300
BY DR. JOHN COLEMAN, 2006

Dr. Coleman provides another remarkable study of the world elites and their secret societies.

"We need to find all we can about the secret societies, front organizations, inter-locking government agencies, banks, insurance companies, international businesses, the petroleum industry and the hundreds of thousands of entities and foundations, whose leading lights make up the membership of the Committee of 300, the ultimate body that run the world and has done so for more than a 100 years. (p. 10)

"I discovered the same attitude in intelligence circles; no one would speak openly about the "Olympians," the controlling executive body of the "300"...." (p. 16)

"... all of the great historical events are planned in secret by men in high places, with intent to deceive; ... Such a group were the men of the England East India Company, whose antecedents sprang from the Cathari, the Bogomils and the Albigensians who had their origins in Manichean Babylon and who went on to become the controllers of not only England, but of the whole world. ... the Committee of 300 has been so successful in concealing its existence from the broad mass of the American people. (p. 9)

Coleman explains the Committee of 300 involves members of European nobility including the Black Nobility of Genoa and Venice, financiers and bankers, corporate elite, masons and royalty. Coleman provides lengthy lists of the Committee members as well as of the organizations, corporations and intelligence services through which they extend their international control of the affairs of the world. Coleman's list of past and present Committee members includes such notables as Her Majesties Queen Elizabeth II, Queen Juliana, Sofia, Princes Beatrix, Queen Margreta, George Bush, David Rockefeller, Henry Kissinger, Count Etienne Davignon who effected the 'zero growth' policy for the US for the Club of Rome, Elie de and Edmon de and/or Baron Rothschild, and many family names of European aristocracy and of the financial community.

The influence of the Committee is conveyed through a myriad of foundations, including particularly the Club of Rome and the Royal Institute of International Relations, and the Tavistock Institute of Human Relations--the mother of all think tanks and the master brainwashing and propaganda institution of the world. Numerous other organizations are described as secondary to the inner circle, ranging from the Council of Foreign Relations and the Trilateral Commission, to the Bilderberg group, Skull and Bones, NATO and the UN, the Club of Rome, and the intelligence services of the MI6 in Britain, the CIA and Mossad, Interpol and others.

Coleman provides long lists of institutions and corporations under the control of the Committee of 300. These include such diverse entities as British Petroleum, the Anti Defamation League and the Canadian Jewish Congress, the CFR and Club of Rome, Warner Brother's, TIME, RCA, British East India Company, the London Times, the Aspen Institute, the Association for Humanistic Psychology, Fox and Rupert Murdoch, DeBeers Consolidated Mines, East India Committee of 300, MIT, Rand Institute, NAACP, Stanford Research Institute, Princeton and Harvard Universities, the National and World Council of Churches, the National Training Laboratory, Xerox, IBM, RCA, CBS, BBC, CBC, Raytheon, Lehman Brothers, Kuhn Loeb, United Fruit Company, and so many more.

Oh what a web of deceit and lies has been fabricated across all areas of our society in service of the shadow controllers within the Committee of 300 and its innumerable offshoots. Coleman writes:

> *"The enemy is clearly identifiable as the Committee of 300, the Club of Rome, NATO, the Black Nobility, the Tavistock Institute, CFR and all of its affiliated organizations, the think tanks and research institutions controlled by Stanford and the Tavistock Institute of Human Relations, and last, but certainly not the least, the military establishment.*

"There is no need to use "they" or "the enemy," except as shorthand. We know who "they," the enemy is. The Committee of 300 with its Eastern Liberal Establishment "aristocracy," its banks, insurance companies, giant corporations, petroleum cartels, foundations, communications networks, publishing houses, radio and television networks and the movie industry, presided over by a hierarchy of Hollywood conspirators: This is the enemy. Stop misguided thinking that Russia is the enemy. The enemy has never been in Moscow, it has always been in our backyard, in Washington, not Moscow! (p.240)

To order Dr. Coleman's books call 702 448-5532

Conspiracy theory is a complex area and I would certainly not claim to understand the extent and dynamics of these global crime syndicates and how it all works. From 2006 to the present, Karen and I had researched these topics while trying to discern 'disinformation' from the truth.

THE EMPIRE OF 'THE CITY'
(WORLD SUPERSTATE)

DOCUMENTARY MOVIE BY AMENSTOP PRODUCTIONS
Part I:
http://video.google.com/videoplay?docid=4675077383139148549
Part II:
http://video.google.com/videoplay?docid=-4430543376785758889

This is a profound and shocking documentary movie, in a class of its own in terms of providing an overview of the criminal activities of the psychopathic world elites, the pseudo-Illuminati, through human history. As an alternative movie buff concerned with understanding modern history, the deceits of the media and the real story of the 9-11 attacks in New York, I would recommend this documentary even over such productions as *Loose Change* (2nd Edition or Final Cut), Alex Jones' *Endgame*, Aaron Russo's *From Freedom to Fascism*, or the *Zeitgeist* movie—all excellent contributions to the emerging library of alternative media exposes available through http://video. google.com.

The movie begins with the events of 9-11 and portrays the horrific events of that day as a typical Hollywood production, US style, a staged event carefully crafted to traumatize and delude the American public—all in order to justify the invasions of Afghanistan and Iraq as steps towards the creation of the New World Order and global government, and to make money— billions and trillions of dollars. The presentation of materials on the 9-11 attacks clearly establishes the complicity of the main actors, the motives, means and opportunity of the elites to create a new Pearl Harbour event to justify another mass murder of Muslims and the invasion of the middle- east all for the *GOD* of the elites—Gold, Oil and Drugs. This is all done while Americans wave their little flags made in China in a wave of patriotic fervour while their nation commits war crimes around the world. The producers present their research materials so clearly that it is immediately evident that the whole event was staged not by Muslim extremists to strike a blow at Americans or Jews, but rather an event staged by Zionist extremists and the elites to carry forth their plans for the imposition of a fascist agenda throughout the world. The movie points out how the producers of this "formula Hollywood action thriller" had grossed 40 billions of profit from their insider trading within weeks. They present the "conspicuous trail of planted evidence" left behind to frame the "patsies"—the supposed crazy crazed Muslim terrorists and Osama—who must surely rank up there with Santa Claus as a character of American imagination.

The movie documents how the Cities of London, the Vatican and Columbia (Washington, DC) are each independent city-states within other sovereign nations, subject to no laws other than their own greed and cruelty, accumulating over half the wealth of the world while paying no taxes. This unholy trinity maintains respectively the financial, religious and military control over the earth—and each is home to an obelisk of Egyptian origin with an all-seeing eye at the top of the pyramidal structure, as depicted on the privately owned federal reserve notes used on the American dollar. This movie elaborates the structure of the whole scheme and history of these sociopathic inbreeding families, the International Financiers—the *Bankster* cartel subsumed under "the Crown Corporation" and the Queen of England. The Rothschilds are the bankers for both the Crown Corporation of London and the Vatican and oversee a board of 12 super-elites and a larger assembly of 300 lesser super-elites. The most recent arm of the

Illuminati is the United Nations—upon which they hope to base their new world government.

The term 'banksters' is a neologism used throughout the movie—a perfect term to depict the 'gangster bankers,' whose activities are traced through history from the emergence of the Rothschild banking family in the 18th century and their role in financing the world wars and other mass murders committed through modern human history. The elites have camouflaged their own criminal activities through their ownership of the media and the news services (particularly Reuters and the Associated Press), as the means for the intentional deception of the 'sheeple' or sheep people of the world, the goyem.

There is so, so much in this remarkable movie. It demonstrates the Nazi background of the Bush family helping to finance the second world war and even the death camps, along with a whole slew of other top banksters; the involvement of the world elite in the drug trade—from the opium wars of China to the cocaine epidemics of America, the transporting of opium from Vietnam in the body bags of American soldiers, to the introduction of LSD and other psychedelics in the age of flower power, to the current control of the opium of Afghanistan. There are big bucks in dealing drugs and simultaneously big bucks in the phoney war on drug with both sides played out by the same criminal elites. It also documents the importation of the Nazis into America in 1946 by Truman and how they infiltrated the CIA and the American and Canadian military and defence industries.

Perhaps the most astonishing aspect of the movie is the alternative view provided of the history of the Jews and the Christ story. It is suggested that most of the patriarchs of the Old Testament were based on Egyptian history and myths and the worship of the sun-god Amen. Jesus Christ is claimed to be the offspring of Cleopatra of Egypt and Julius Caesar, and he was apparently sent off to India for protection after Caesar was assassinated and the Romans were marching on Egypt. I have little basis for evaluating this proposed alternative view of the history of the Jews and the Christ story, but in the context of the movie, it appears reasonable and worthy of consideration. It is unfortunate in ways that this reinterpretation of history which in itself is so shocking is interspersed with those story elements which are less suspect and more adequately documented by historic documents.

The movie maintains that some of the original tribes of Israel became the Vikings (the VI-Kings) and formed the Danish and British royalty in early European history. Thus, the descendents of the early Jews have been intertwined through history with the royalty of Europe, as well as the banksters who financed and staged all of the major wars—from World War I and II, to Vietnam, Cambodia, Korea, the Russian Revolution, the American civil war, the Inquisition and Crusades, the phoney cold war and their next endeavour, Armageddon.

It is impossible to convey the true impact of this movie which leads to a reinterpretation of human history, which has intentionally been hidden from the masses through the media and the rewriting of history and the text books. The world's public has been deliberate *dumbed down* through mass education controlled by the elites and their varied 'round tables' and foundations.

The movie ends with the suggestion that Prince William is the anti-Christ set up to become the first head of the global *new world order* by the year 2015. It shows a photo, widely distributed through their media, of Prince William holding a lamb, in the style of Christ, while showing off its cloven hoof as a symbol of the demonic order which has come to dominate the world. Lastly, the movie outlines a series of steps towards resistance and opposition of these satanic brotherhoods and sociopathic banksters, and it actually provides a listing of who many of these creatures are.

A shocking and horrifying movie which clearly demonstrates the serious situation humanity is in today. This group of inbreed psychopaths, mass murderers, torturers and deceivers, are on the verge of concluding their demonic schemes for the enslavement of the peoples of the earth. At the same time, if humankind ever woke up to these patterns of history, these creatures would all be imprisoned and their wealth, seized as the proceeds of crime and terrorism, would pay off all the debts of all the nations of earth, and allow for the feeding, housing and health care of humanity, and truly bring about a new age—not of a new world order under a criminal cartel but a world of true peace, wealth, security and human justice. Perhaps these creatures might enjoy some bay life in Cuba, with their own inoculations and implants, chemtrails and irradiated foods, and for intercourse among themselves, perhaps with Oscars for best mass murder staging and productions. Perhaps their new pet dogs might save the human race from this monstrous breed of subhuman types.

155

CONSPIRACY OF THE SIX-POINTED STAR:
EYE-OPENING REVELATIONS AND FORBIDDEN KNOWLEDGE ABOUT ISRAEL, THE JEWS, ZIONISM, AND THE ROTHSCHILDS BY TEXE MARRS, 2011
(Rivercrest Publishing, Austin, Texas)

Satan has cast a dark shadow over America. The end-times are upon us and that is why insanity seems to reign on every front. America has turned itself into a crazy house, an obscene and vulgar place, void of God's spirit and empty of civility and common sense. (Marrs, p. 174)

"In order that the true meaning of things may not strike the Goyem (Gentiles) before the proper time, we will mask it ...." Protocol 6, of the *Protocols of the Learned Elders of Zion*

The symbol of the six pointed Star is an ancient mystical symbol which embodies profound truths and occult wisdom. In Texe Marrs' book, the last of our reviews and my most recent read in late 2011, only the negative or satanic aspects of this symbol are considered. Marrs is an avowed Christian and he interprets the modern affairs of humankind in terms of Biblical Scripture and associates this symbol with the marks and numbers of the Beast. As if our reader has not been horrified enough with explorations of the evidences for such monstrous conspiracies as most ordinary people cannot image, we come then to a penultimate shocking, disturbing and informative book.

The six pointed star is referred to alternatively as the *Star of David*, the *Seal of Solomon* or the *Star of Mephistopheles*. Although this symbol has an ancient history, in 1822, it was used on the Rothschild coat of arms when they were raised to nobility by the Austrian Emperor. It is now the central motif of the Israeli flag and indeed, Israel itself is sometimes referred to as Rothschild's Land. Marrs states: "Rothschild is Israel's hidden dictator and financial overlord." (p. 193) The Seal of Solomon is the chosen ensign of World Jewry. Thus, Marrs regards it as the "supreme symbol of satanic tyranny." The red dragon on the cover of Marrs' book represents the Great Serpent, Lucifer and Satan, winding its way through the Seal of Solomon.

The Seal of Solomon is associated with the number 666, the mark or number of the Beast according to Book of Revelations. The symbol is composed of six points or vertices, six lines and six triangles, and the inner figure is a six sided hexagram. Marrs relates this to biblical verse 1 Kings 10:14 where Solomon, the king of Israel, required the priests of the temple to annually honour his majesty with a tribute of exactly 666 talents of gold. In the Talmudic tradition, the number 666 is thus considered a 'holy' number, associated with material riches. In contrast, the Christian New Testament describes this number "as loathsome and representative of Satan's *endtime beast*" and "a befitting number for their coming Messiah." Rabbi Mosad Hayesod writing on the Zohar, noted: "The number 666 contains hidden within it exalted and lofty messianic potential." (ibid, p. 18)

Marrs introduces his book with a chapter entitled, "Confessions of an Anti-Semite," where he explains that according to "their private definition, I am one." Whereas Henry Makow explains that these dominant Zionists use the term 'anti-Semitic' as a way of undermining legitimate criticism of the Zionist's agenda, Marrs accepts the label, although tongue in cheek, and explains why he would be considered an anti-Semitic according to their "private definition.'

> So what exactly is their definition of anti-Semite? An anti-Semite is anyone, Jew or Gentile, who (1) is opposed to the ongoing crimes of Israel and/or Jews; or (2) Has the audacity to criticize Israel for either that nation's domestic or foreign policies; (3) Knows and has the courage to point out that America's Jewish organizations and political action committees are this nation's most powerful lobby groups; (4) Knows and dares to point out that wealthy and immoral Jews control America's porno industry; (5) Knows and dares to point out that wealthy and immoral Jews run Hollywood and the entertainment industry; (6) Knows and dares to point out that wealthy Jews control America's book publishing and magazine

industry; (7) Knows and dares to point out that wealthy Jews own and control the vast majority of the largest internet search engines, online retail firms, and social networking companies, as well as the computer security, computer software, and computer manufacturing industries; (8) Knows and points out that wealthy Jews own and/or control ABC, CBS, NBC, CNN, and Fox Network news programs as well as the nation's largest daily newspapers; (9) Knows and dares to point out that there are 66 outstanding United Nations resolutions condemning Israel for its unlawful assault on and treatment of its Arab neighbours and Palestinians; (10) Knows of and dares to criticize Israel for its massacres, brutal treatment, illegal incarceration, torture, and execution of innocent Palestinians and other Arab men, women and children; (11) Knows and dares to expose the billions of dollars of United States aid money going to Israel, while only a paltry amount, if any, goes to the neighboring Palestinians. Finally, (12), as if the foregoing list is not enough to stamp a person an anti-Semite, the same tag is usually assigned to someone who exposes the fact that Israeli spies stole the blueprints and secrets of America's nuclear bombs and the uranium, heavy water, and other elements needed to manufacture nuclear bombs. And then, is bold enough to state such pertinent facts as, for example, that Israel has built up an arsenal of some 200 to 400 of these deadly devices, while Israel's Moslem neighbours—Egypt, Syria, Lebanon, Iraq, Iran and Jordan—have not a single nuke to use as a countervailing weapon in the event they are attacked unprovoked by Israel's nuclear forces.

… I could keep going, but I am sure the reader gets the message. (pp. 11-12)

Throughout his book, Marrs does keep going, including implicating Zionists and Israeli forces in the perpetration of the 9-11 terrorist event. Of course, the 9-11 hoax could only have been carried out by a group capable of controlling the news and media coverage of the day's events and the respective governments who maintained the public deception while sending off their troops to commit war crimes on behalf of Zionist controllers. What a mad world and according to Marrs, it is likely to get much worse!

Marrs notes that in the book of Daniel in the Holy Bible, the final kingdom on earth is said to be the Fourth Kingdom of the Beast. Marrs identifies this with Lord Jacob Rothschild, the fourth Baron of Rothschild, who apparently holds the title the 'King of Israel' and is a British Lord. Apparently, Jacob also has the numeric value of 666. A modified form of the six pointed star is also the chief symbol for Masonry, which Marrs describes as infiltrated by the Zionist networks through the centuries.

Give me control over a nation's currency and I care not who makes its laws.

Baron Mayor Amschel Rothschild

Marrs describes Jacob Rothschilds as *"the wealthiest man in the world today,"* along with his siblings and family. It was the Rothschilds and associated banking families, the Morgans and Rockefellers, who schemed away to form the Federal Reserve Bank in the United States in 1913, taking over the right to print American money and to tax the population to pay on the principle and interest of these loans.

Baron Mayor Amschel Rothschild has attained infamy for his statement to the effect, that he does not care who runs a country, as long as he has control of the nation's currency. And the international Zionist Bankers have indeed quite duped humankind into surrendering their sovereign rights to print one's own currency, and the banksters simultaneously gained control of the political parties directly or through their multifaceted corporate lobbying and bribery.

Marrs elaborates upon the current situation:

> … my own research yields the astonishing facts. The top bankers are 85 percent Jews; Wall Street is a closed industry as far as Gentiles (non-Jews) are concerned. Over 95 percent of its CEO's and executives are Jewish. (pp. 68-69)

> America's banking industry is exclusively Jewish-run. The same goes for Wall Street brokerage and investment houses. Investigate for yourself and you'll discover that the New York—Chicago money crowd is nearly 100 percent Jews. (p. 90)

Marrs provides a shocking account as to the power and influence of the Rothschilds over American and international affairs:

159

Lord Jacob Rothschild is the fourth Baron de Rothschild and rules a vast empire as the current head of the planet's most illustrious bloodline. Who are the Rothschilds? Few Americans know of the terrible power and influence of this wealthy Jewish dynasty. But believe me, the leaders of the world know of Jacob Rothschild and his kin.

Politicians like Hillary Clinton, Colin Powell, John McCain, Nancy Pelosi, and, yes, Barack Obama tremble in fear when the name "Rothschild" is so much as mentioned in passing.

The power of the Rothschilds is greater than the combined influence and authority of the Democrat and Republican Parties. The red shield, the Rothschild Family crest, holds sway over all the nations of Europe, and many a government has toppled because a Rothschild was displeased with its performance. New York's Wall Street and London's "The City" financial districts stoop to hear Rothschild's instructions, ... As it is recorded in Revelation 18, "the kings of the earth have committed fornication with her, and the merchants of the earth are waxed (become) rich…" (p. 206)

Marrs maintains that there was a primary reason as to why Barack Obama became the president of the U.S. and that was because he was "Rothschild's Choice" and a supporter of the Zionist and Communist Agenda. Marrs states: "Barack Obama was chosen to become the first leader of a Jewish-ruled New World Order." Marrs explains that surrounding Obama is:

… a frightening array of Jewish radicals and Zionist agents of influence, Jewish controllers—including White House Chief of Staff Rahm Emanuel and chief political advisor David Axelrod—monitor and guide Obama in his work of destruction. Behind them all is a hidden cabal led by the powerful Rothschild family. President Obama and our cowardly Congress have already given Rothschild's Wall Street cronies over sixteen trillion dollars in the ongoing "Economic Recession" scam. (p. 208)

Of course, the corporate media simply cover over the greatest bank heist in recorded history and sell the propaganda of how to save a nation by paying off the banker's debts and faults. It is very similar to selling fluoride toothpaste or poisonous inoculations for the media, and an army of experts

and analysts, and controlled opposition figures, can be paraded out on TV to explain it all—all simply a puppet show. Meanwhile, the American taxpayers and citizens were robbed of trillions paid to the global crime syndicate and banksters who had committed all kinds of fraud and criminal banking and accounting practices. The ruling classes gorged to satiety on bailouts and bonuses—the newest scams to destroy a nation, its finances and people.

Marrs' book is illustrated throughout and includes this humorous image of Swinders List. Marrs states: "President Barack Obama is a *project of Britain's Lord Rothschild, billionaire George Soros, and the Chicago Jewish Mafia.*" (p. 285)

Henry Kissinger, CFR sloth and faithful servant of Rothschild and Rockefeller, has free reign to enter the Oval Office whenever he pleases.

This is a shocking and disturbing book and one realizes over and over again how many deceptions and frauds have been committed upon the public and citizens of the United States, and of countries around the world—by our politicians, the media and the ruling psychopathic elite. What a nightmare they have concocted through the decades and now as they play out their apocalyptic end games!

Here is an interesting portrait of Henry Kissinger, serial mass murderer and war criminal, Rothschild and Rockefeller servant and confidant to your Presidents. Oh, aren't these *Illuminated Ones* something else again?

As for the immediate fortunes of Obama, Marrs notes:

> For the moment, Barack Obama is doing just fine as far as the
> Illuminati fraternity is concerned. His Administration, guided by
> Jewish swindlers ... has loaded up the globalist banks with over 37
> trillion dollars of stolen taxpayers' money. (p. 159)

Meanwhile, the sleepwalking American public, the sheeple, do not even
realize that they have been shorn of their wealth, health and nation. The
terrorist agendas and crimes of the Zionists throughout history have been
hidden from the public and our governments have become little more than
their puppets and pawns. Oh, what a wicked web of deceits and lies has been
woven, all supported by a media of lies and deceptions! Marrs explains that
the "Red Jewish *Mafiya are in firm control behind the scenes in Washington, D.
C.*" and I might add, Ottawa, Canada.

Citizens simply do not realize the extent of the police state fascist world
order being concocted around them. They fail to notice the symptoms of
the underlying Zionist control of our nations and how the masses have
been duped into staging criminal wars on the behalf of these global crime
syndicates. Afghanistan, Iraq and Libya were all wars based on intentional
public deception through the Zionist media, with blatant false flag events
like 9-11, the London and Spanish train bombings, and so on. These
wars had nothing to do with protecting America from radical Islam, but
everything to do with the religious fanaticism of the global elites, in their
quest for global dominance and what some people call a "Jew World Order."

Marrs provides a shocking view of the fanaticism of Talmudic Judaism.
Whereas most people consider the Old Testament as being the sacred book
of the Jews, with the Ten Commandments and the laws of normalcy-loving
Moses, it is really the Talmud that forms the deeper basis for Zionist thinking
and for their predatory behaviours and attitudes towards non-Jews, the
goyem. Marrs provides various disturbing examples of the "Antichrist nature
of Ju*daism's holy book, the Talmud ...:*"

> The Talmud is not only a diabolical volume recommending and
> justifying the most horrendous of sins and crimes, it also contains
> a blasphemous diatribe against Jesus Christ. Jesus is held up as
> a contemptible, loathing creature—a servant of Satan whose soul
> resides in Hell, wallowing in misery in boiling hot excrement. (p. 35)

... the Talmud commands: "The best of the Gentiles—kill." (p. 261)

Israelis frequently use words similar to the condescending slang world "nigger" to describe Christians and Gentiles—vulgar, Yiddish slur words like "shiksa," "schwarte," and "shegetsz."

Since the Jews are claimed to be the Master Race, whose souls are said by the Talmud to be on a far higher plane than the animalistic, "satanic souls" of Gentiles, it is common for Jewish authorities to brand all Gentiles by the derogatory Yiddish term "goy," a term akin to a curse word. Meanwhile, Arabs are deemed so inferior they are even lower than the goy." (p. 312)

... the hate-filled, Talmudic beliefs of the Rabbis and their Zionist followers ... include the teaching that Jesus was born a bastard and his mother, Mary, was a harlot *(Mishna Yebamoth, 4:13);* that Jesus was practiced black arts of magic *(Sanhedrin, 1076)*, and that Jesus is now suffering eternal punishment in a boiling vat of filthy excrement *(Mishna Sanhedrin X, 2)* These references come from the English translation of the Talmud known as *The Soncino Talmud.* (p. 313)

The famous Jewish rabbi, Maimonides, acclaimed by Christian apologists and defenders of Zionism as "a great man of God," encouraged Jews to kill all Christians. In the Talmud *(Hilkoth Akrum, X, 1)*, Maimonides says, "Do not have pity for *them., Show no mercy to them. Therefore, if you see on in difficulty of drowning, do not go to his help...it is right to kill him by your own hand by shoving him into a well or in some other way."*

... the Jew's own holy book, the Talmud, commands that heretics and traitors be killed without delay *(Abhodah Zarah, 266)* and that a Gentile taken prisoner may be killed, "even before he confesses...the sooner the better" *(Choschen Hammischpat, 388, 10)*.

The Talmud teaches that in the world to come, the New Earth, the wealth of the Gentiles will revert to the Jews. Gentiles who abandon the "idol" Jesus, whom the Jews hate, will be allowed to live, though only as servants of the Jews. Those who persist in their worship of Jesus shall be killed. The punishment, according to Talmud's Noahide Laws: death by beheading.

> In that glorious future world *(Tikkum Olam)* to come, possessing all the wealth of the Gentiles, the Jews shall be their own Messiah, indeed, their own "god." (p. 89)

> ... the Lubavitchers—and many other Jewish groups—are big advocates of the Noahide Laws. ... (which) require all Gentiles to be "righteous." Being righteous is defined as not worshipping idols. And Jesus is declared in the Talmud to be an idol! In summary, under the Noahide Laws, all Christians who worship Jesus Christ are idolaters and will be duly punished by beheading! (p. 180)[15]

These are obviously very disturbing claims about Talmudic teachings. Is there really such a subgroup of Jewish fanatics who have such hateful and Satanic feelings and beliefs? They do not value goyem life and think that they have an inherent right to use any means to establish their psychotic world disordered state centered in Jerusalem under the flag of the six pointed star. Are the US, Canada, Britain, countries of Europe and around the world, really controlled by such a cabal of Luciferians and Satanists with such evils in their heart controlling our politicians and bringing us into such an new world order as they scheme?[16]

---

[15] Internet sources since 2008 have reported on 20,000 guillotines being imported to the US from China, while FEMA camps dot the nation, and trains with shackles and leg irons have been stockpiled. Hundreds of thousands of coffins have been stored up in Georgia, prepared for the mass extermination of American citizens. Ordinary people cannot imagine such things and this makes them such perfect victims of the psychopathic elites, who of course want to 'save the Earth.'

[16] Personally, in my life, I have had varied Jewish friends and loves, especially during an earlier period of my life when I was a university professor at a largely Jewish University in Downsview, Ontario. I do not believe at all that the majority of Jews are subject to such attitudes and beliefs, nor were they even aware of such viewpoints as held by the terrorist fanatics within the Jewish community. Jewish people have been even more subject to the deceptions of the elites than most others. Unfortunately, most do not have the uprightness of heart to speak out, when they realize the massiveness and extent of the nightmare scenario being played out by such Zionist lunatics as have highjacked our nations. Of course, to face the real Beast of our times, we need Jews, Christians, Muslims, Hindus, Natives, and all others, upright of heart, to come together and turn back from this madness. The elites have long used religious difference to divide and conquer, and waged wars through deceptions. To colour all Jews with the offences of the Zionist elite, would be similar to condemning all Italians because of the mafia, or all Mexicans because of their drug gangs, or all Muslims because of Muslim extremism (which has mainly been financed and orchestrated by Zionists anyway).

Marrs provides a shocking list of all the deviant measures being introduced as part of the new world psychiatrically disordered society, which we are becoming:

21 Ways the Illuminati Are Smashing Americans' Resistance to the Globalist Agenda

1.
Immigration lawlessness and rising crime wave by illegal aliens.
2.
Government bankruptcy and indebtedness at an all-time high.
3.
Social Security swindle — Social Security Fund battered as Feds blow money on worthless spending scams.
4.
Veteran mistreatment and genocide. Most V. A. hospitals are deathtraps; Vets receive inferior medical care. Millions of Vets are dying from Agent Orange (Vietnam), Persian Gulf War sickness, and other service-related illnesses.
5.
Outsourcing of American jobs — to foreigners in Pakistan, India, Red China, Mexico, Indonesia, etc. America's manufacturing base declining rapidly and being shifted overseas.
6.
Foreign student takeover of America's colleges, universities, and public schools.
7.
Corporate globalism — Greedy U.S. corporations, as globalist entities, are unpatriotic and hostile to American interests.
8.
Harnessing of U.S. Military for global mercenary duties. Americans forced to pay for and fight Israel's wars and die for causes unrelated to U.S. defence.
9.
Hate Crime Laws — state, federal, and the U.N. — forbid free speech, prohibit criticism of Israel and prevent the Christian gospel being preached.
10.
Sexual barbarism and dehumanization accomplished by vulgar, crude, sexually explicit, physically degrading movies, television,

cartoons, books, video games, advertising and other media.
11.
Private property regularly seized and its uses restricted to
promote the Communist agenda of environmentalist and globalist
organizations.
12.
Unfair and unlawful tax system used to rob producers and transform
U.S. citizens into federalized serfs and wards of the state.
13.
Manipulation of water supplies and contrived water shortages used
to drive up water prices and control the citizenry.
14.
White race discriminated against and American culture savaged by
promotion of "cultural diversity."
15.
Two meaningless political parties whose real agenda are identical,
and corrupt, rigged elections which frustrate the will of the people.
16.
Satanization of society through occult influences and symbols which
permeate media, music, entertainment, and sports.
17.
Free Press replaced by propaganda ministries and elitist media
accomplices who work non-stop to psychologically hypnotize,
mesmerize, and control the minds of the population.
18.
"War on Terror" used as pretext to create an American police state
and remove the peoples' constitutional rights.
19.
Death culture promoted. Conditioning of minds. Desensitization of
the masses to the mass genocide to come, with abortion, euthanasia,
necrophilia, cannibalism, group death, and cruelty.
20.
Gulag concentration camps prepare for resisters and dissidents.
21.
Religious debasement. False religions promoted and encouraged.
Traditional Christianity portrayed as anti-Semitic, bigoted and
politically incorrect. (pp. 281-2)

What Marrs depicts as happening in America, is found also in Canada
and all the countries of the world under the control of this global crime

syndicate. M|arrs provides a horrifying picture of the degradation of human beings and society being systematically carried out from within. The true terrorists are within our own countries and they fund terrorism around the world, while intentionally deceive the masses through their propaganda and media.

Marrs regards America as already under Zionist control:

> Of course, the media, even as important as it is to our culture, is only a bit piece of the whole that is now, regrettably, under the big thumbs of the Jewish Zionist elite. Our educational establishment, Wall Street, the banks, the Federal Reserve, our Congress, the White House, and our judiciary—each and every one is infiltrated by Zionist radicals who put Israel and their own "Chosen People" first, to the detriment of everything sacred to honest, God-fearing, hard-working Americans. (p. 348)

> ... a great global superpower, the United States, has fallen into the hands of Zionist Jews who control its culture, media, education and medical systems, and government. (p. 384)

> ... the Pope ... and the Vatican are now, in the 21st century, joined hand in hand with Zionist Jewish rabbis and the treacherous criminality of Jewish politicians. (p. 385)

The manner in which the American public was deceived about 9-11 was only possible given such an insidious control of the media, publishing, the police and intelligence communities, and the governments. Fortunately, the massive public deceptions perpetrated against citizens around the world are beginning to be more broadly understood.

Marrs fills in many fascinating bits of history which are not normally related as part of orthodox education. Marrs argues that after the World Zionist Congress in 1897, the Zionists were behind Bolshevism and Communism, with such Rothschild's agents as Lenin and Trotsky, and that it was primarily Russian Christians who were slaughtered during the Russian Revolution—66 million of them according to Marrs! Quite a human carnage! The Illuminati were then behind the World Wars, and then the formation of the United Nations in 1945. Marrs writes: *"In 1945, a powerful group of Jewish cabalists set up the puppet United Nations. In 1948, they founded the state of Israel ... Their minions now oversee the media and Hollywood and are in charge of America's CIA, FBI, and Federal Reserve banking system."* (p. 331) Jewish Masonic billionaire dynasties and their lieutenants already control vast global banking, multinational corporations, the media, the pharmaceutical industry, and their political resources. Marrs foresees them as about to bring tragedy and chaos to Israel and the entire world, all in accord with the Book of Revelations. Marrs predicts: *"Bloodshed and turmoil shall infect and envelop the Middle East and Israel. The United States — controlled by the powerful magic and cabalistic Satanism of these Jewish plotters — shall not escape the disastrous days just ahead."* (p. 329)

Of course, the New Testament is not a popular read among Zionists. Marrs quotes Abe Foxman, head of the Jewish Anti-Defamation League, who states: "The New Testament is a lying, hateful, harmful book, ultimately responsible for the deaths of six million Jews." (Source: *Never Again? The Threat of the New Anti-Semitism*) Similarly, Talmudic text suggests: "Jews must destroy the books of the Christians, especially the New Testament." (Shabbath, 116a) In fact, it is a criminal offence in Israel for a person to proselytize by passing out a New Testament.

Marrs' *Conspiracy of the Six-Pointed Star* is a scary and disturbing book and provides a Christian interpretation and perspective on the chaotic world situation, relating it to the *Book of Revelations* and New Testament scripture. Certainly, at this time in human history, the threat does exist that a major World War will erupt within the Middle East, involving nuclear weapons, which could engage the larger world community. The world is certainly run by madmen:

> Babylon 21 — world domination of the Jews, assisted by Superpower America, presided over by a Jewish Messiah, incarnated by Satan, ruler of a desolate and decadent but rich global empire. The Bible prophesized it would come. (p. 326)

These books and movies certainly provide a shocking and disturbing overview of conspiracy theories from different perspectives and leaving innumerable unsolved enigmas and mysteries. However, it certainly seems that the time is late, as the agendas and crimes of the elites are being more broadly exposed around the world.

Policy Contributions to the
Canadian Action Party

In August of 2008, I attended the convention of the Canadian Action Party held at Carleton University in Ottawa. Although I had never previously been involved with any political or other groups, I thought that CAP could provide a means by which to work with others who were waking up to the dire situation that we are in as Canadian citizens. I submitted the following two policies to CAP and both were passed and currently form a portion of the CAP party platform.

> Under the existing policy:
> <u>Royal Commission to Investigate 9/11; NAU; Afghanistan</u>
>
> Whereas:
>
> The RCMP, CSIS and the Military Intelligence have all participated in the cover-up of the true causes of the 9-11 terrorist attacks and failed to fulfill their duties to the Canadian public and to serve honourably our police and military personnel.
>
> Therefore:
>
> The Canadian Action Party calls for the establishment of a citizens committee to conduct a thorough investigation of the police, intelligence and military communities in order to expose the systemic corruption which has infested these services; and to support a new generation of honourable men and women to assume the superior posts within these services.

This policy suggests that we need an open and honest public inquiry into the police services, the intelligence community and military leadership, all of whom have gone along with the public deception concerning 9-11 and subsequently of Canadian involvement in a criminal war in Afghanistan. Further, the RCMP have done nothing to truly enforce the Canadian anti-terrorism legislation but are colluding with their New World Order controllers. The senior officials in all of these services need to answer publicly for their betrayals of the Canadian people and face criminal prosecution under the Canadian anti-terrorism legislation.

The second policy which I submitted and which was passed concerned the issues of chemtrails, inoculations and the like:

Whereas:

There is a massive body of research suggesting that an intentional program of spreading diseases and health problems has been underway for many years in Canada, as elsewhere in the world; and further, that many pharmaceuticals being promoted have not been adequately researched, nor their effectiveness properly followed up. Serious health risks appear to be associated with chemtrail spraying, inoculations, the fluoridation of drinking water, the use of aspartame and other additives, and the introduction of irradiated and genetically modified foods, and a range of pharmaceuticals. The government appears to consistently support the corporate agenda while putting the health of Canadians at risk.

Therefore:

The Canadian Action Party calls for the establishment of a citizens committee to conduct a thorough investigation of these highly questionable programs and a review of the existing scientific literature on these practices and substances. In the interim, the Canadian Action Party demands an immediate cessation of chemtrail spraying, and any enforced inoculations.

This policy recognizes the control of our government by the corporate sector. This control by the elites extends into *Health Canada* and the medical establishment. Why do none of these agencies speak out against chemtrails or the quack science used to support the inoculation programs and GMO foods?

My involvement with CAP continued from 2008 into the spring of 2010. At the convention, I was elected as the chairman for Native and Aboriginal Affairs and I subsequently regularly attended the CAP executive meetings conducted by telephone conference calls. I also continued through 2009 to contribute to the Policy Committee and authored three additional policies which had been adopted as interim policies by the time of my withdrawing from party activities.

FIRST NATIONS CONCERNS

Whereas: The native community has historically suffered from incursions, abuses and destruction as a result of colonization, marginalization and the suppression of their people and culture. At the present time, native bands across the country are involved in disputes with the government and corporations over land claims and the ongoing corporate seizures of lands and resources. Further, the Canadian government has consistently failed to honour treaty obligations, to investigate serious crimes committed against the native communities (particularly the genocide against native communities), and to protect native rights and freedoms.

Whereas: The native community is further being assaulted by the same corporate practices and schemes as are currently threatening all Canadians — including the destruction of the environment through chemical spraying, the poisoning of the land, air, water and soil, the highly questionable practices of mass inoculation programs, the threats of biological terrorism, and the assault on Canadian sovereignty by the so-called 'new world order elite.' It is essential that CAP be recognized as a possible political instrument to support the changes that native communities seek within Canadian society. Further, it is essential to CAP to have the help, strength and wisdom within the native community to enable us to address the shared issues and dangers we face as Canadians in this period of international corporate-financial control and the increasing formation of a totalitarian and police state system.

Therefore: It is the intention of CAP to seek direct input from First Nations communities across Canada to work with us so that we can learn what policies best address native issues; and to search mutually for ways in which we can transform the corruption of the Canadian government and corporate sectors, the police services and judiciary, so as to restore justice and individual rights within Canada while enabling aboriginal communities to thrive. CAP will ideally have a native person as the Aboriginal Chairperson and we invite submissions from the native community to help shape our policies for the future.

BIOLOGICAL THREATS—
INCLUDING THE SWINE FLU, BIRD FLU,
THE H1N1 VIRUS & OTHER RECOMBINANTS

"At present the population of the world is increasing...
If a Black Death could be spread throughout the world once in every generation, survivors could procreate freely without making the world too full... the state of affairs might be somewhat unpleasant, but what of it? Really high-minded people are indifferent to suffering, especially that of others.... Gradually, by selective breeding, the congenital differences between rulers and ruled will increase until they become almost different species. A revolt of the plebs would become as unthinkable as an organized insurrection of sheep against the practice of eating mutton." Bertrand Russell, *The Impact of Science on Society*

Whereas: A global elitist network, allegedly including Henry Kissinger and David Rockefeller, the UN and other "think tanks" operated and/or influenced by the elites, propose population reduction as a means of preserving life on the planet and ensuring the use of the world's resources for the self-selected elite. Further, biology labs are used to create all kinds of new viruses and influenzas, using recombinant DNA methodologies and gene splicing. The threat of global pandemics is now very real as the elites perceive such flues/viruses as the means by which they might effect, in part, a population reduction. AIDS has now been proven (Dr. Len Horowitz *Emerging Viruses, Aids & Ebola: Nature, Accident or Intentional* 1996) to have been created and dispersed into the populations of sub-Sahara Africa and the homosexual communities as such a 'weapon of mass destruction.' The most recent H1N1 influenza is itself suspect as the product of the biological weapons industry.

Whereas: Not only are threats posed by such engineered biological bacteria/viruses, but further, the outbreak of such pandemics might also be used as a pretext to impose martial law, restrict population movements and to introduce programs of enforced inoculations. Such enforced inoculations may themselves constitute another *"weapon of mass destruction"* to be used against the civilian and non-civilian populations. These inoculations are introduced without adequate testing and research, and the corporate pharmaceutical companies obstruct the objective scientific evaluation of their inoculation products while consistently denying negative effects and research.

Therefore: CAP demands criminal investigations and open public inquiries into all eugenics programs of the global elite, the research being done in biological labs within Canada and the immediate investigation of all inoculation programs. We oppose any enforced inoculations and would ban any media propaganda used to influence and/or convince the populace into submitting to inoculations or other preventative methods which are not clearly and unequivocally documented scientifically to be safe and effective. CAP favours the use of voluntary home quarantines, natural medicines and detection test kits as the primary method of containing such outbreaks. We reject the use of any Canadian facilities to participate in designing and/or creating any biological weapons of mass destruction. CAP also calls for the removal of personnel and funding of joint ventures with non- Canadian companies and foreign countries engaged in such biological warfare activity. Lastly, we demand criminal investigations into the possible corruption of *Health Canada* and the inordinate influence and control exerted by the major pharmaceutical companies over our elected government officials and public agencies.

INTERNET FREEDOM

Whereas: The corporate media have a civic responsibility to truthfully inform the public as to both national and world events. Unfortunately, they have instead carried on a systematic program of propaganda and misled the public about the causes of 9-11 and the true nature of the so-called terrorist threats to our society. They have further failed to inform the public adequately about the Security and Prosperity Partnership, the Bilderberg meetings, and the corporate agenda being advanced within our society. They have failed to inform the public about chemtrails, the dangers of inoculation programs and water fluoridation, and the true causes of numerous terrorist activities within our society and the larger world community. The Media has essentially become a voice of double-talk, propaganda and public deception owned by the corporate elite.

Whereas: The internet has served the growth of the truth movement, in both exposing the crimes of the international corporate and elites and in providing a real alternative to the corrupted mainstream media. Members of the elites are now calling for the shutting down and/or restriction of the free flow of information through the internet as their crimes are being revealed, and the public is questioning the truthfulness of the mainstream media.

Therefore: The Canadian Action Party demands that internet freedom be maintained as an open source of world wide information, communication and means of petition.

These three policies were adopted by the Interim leader in 2009, although CAP members went on to later revise the Biological Threats policy.

My involvement with CAP demanded considerable time during some periods when there were leadership issues and numerous executive meetings. This put a great stress on my and Karen's relationship and it was during this time, that our home mysteriously caught on fire July 2, 2009. I barely escaped while only being slightly burnt while Karen was fortunately out of the house taking a morning bike ride to visit local horses. I still have regrets over my involvement with CAP and how this had come to adversely affect Karen and my lives and relationship. I withdrew from CAP after moving into a new house in Kemptville where the Zero Point Institute is now established. I felt that I had to focus on my other work, especially my mystical/spiritual studies, as these also represent elements essential to dealing with the modern crisis in the life of humankind.

Wake Up
Fellow Canadian Citizens

This is a warning letter to fellow citizens to wake you up to the threats being posed to you and your children, country and world by the rampant criminality established within the Canadian government and society, as it is in the United States and elsewhere.

There is now overwhelming criminal and scientific evidence that demonstrates that the 9-11 attacks on the Trade Towers of New York were not the actions of crazed Muslim or Arab terrorists hijacking airplanes, but instead *an inside job* carried out by the shadow government and elite groups which have high jacked our society, and who control both our government and media! The buildings were clearly brought down by controlled demolition and there is massive evidence questioning every aspect of the public story sold to you through the corporate media. In fact, the mainstream news media play an active role in staging such events. These facts are known by those in your government and media, who have intentionally deceived the public about these events and the wars being waged and the police-terrorist state being intentionally created within Canada.

Canadian society has been hijacked by these criminal psychopathic elements—within the corporate elites and financial community, the government, within the police and intelligence communities. Your police services do not serve you but instead the same corporate elite who select your government figures for you. The truth of the 9-11 attacks is known by those within the Conservative, Liberal and NDP parties, all of whom are complicit in covering up these crimes and the ongoing criminal activities of your government. The prime ministers of Canada are, or have been, members of the same elites—the Bilderbergs and CFR, and such. These criminals and traitors are selling out Canadian sovereignty and independence to the same corporate and financial elites to allow for the creation of what they like to call their New World Order—a fascist empire, which has woven a web of deceit and delusions among the 'sheeple,' the sheep people being led to slaughter.

The scope of this criminal conspiracy is quite freighting and poses a threat to all of us. These elite groups of financiers have infiltrated your society throughout and are carrying out all kinds of devious activities to cause death, disease and hardships for the populace and the environment. They are intentionally poisoning you through the fluoride in your water; the high altitude chemtrail spraying of heavy metals, viral and carcinogenic matter; aspartame in your sodas and foods, a known carcinogen; mercury and other poisons within the inoculations given to you and your children; through genetically modified and irradiated foods which introduce carcinogens into you and your environment while causing nutritional deficits; and through other means. These are the activities of an elite group intentionally trying to poison you, others and the world in order to reduce the world population to their ideal of five hundred million, while causing widespread food shortages and enslaving the masses of humankind in an Orwellian police state society. This is happening within your society and world now! And it is hidden from you through your mainstream media and enabled by your supposed government. J. Edgar Hoover, once head of the FBI once stated: "The individual is handicapped by coming face to face with a conspiracy so monstrous he cannot believe it exists." Most people are asleep to the whole Orwellian nightmare being imposed over Canadian society, and how the banksters, the banker gangsters, will take it all in their schemes. Search the internet and learn something of the 'real news' and the looming threats posed to us.

The Conservatives, Liberals, NDP and the Greens are all complicit in these schemes.

FABLED AIRPLA—
NES

The Role of the Corporate Media in Creating & Perpetuating the Mass Hypnosis of the American Public

An Investigative Psychological and Forensic Examination of the September Clues Video Series

Mrs Renaud:
Oh, yes, yes we did. As a matter of fact, we we
heard it and and cause I was just like standing
there, pretty much looking out the window,
I didn't see what caused it or if there was an
impact.

Host:
So you have no idea right now...

Mrs Renaud:
Oh, there's another one, another plane just
hit. Oh my God, another plane just has just hit
another building, flew right into the middle of it.
Explosion.

Abstract

This article is based upon an attempt to understand the criminal evidences presented within the *September Clues* video series of film maker Simon Shack www.septemberclues.info). The *September Clues* series clearly documents the fraud committed against the American peoples and indeed humankind by *the corporate media* in concocting fabricated images and stories concerning significant 9-11 events. The 9-11 crimes were not committed by Muslim extremists as the public was lead to believe; there were no high jacked airplanes, nor passenger airplanes hitting buildings and conveniently disappearing inside, *despite what you think you saw on your favourite TVs;* the Two Towers did not fall because of non-existent airplane crashes and an fanciful pancake effect, but due to a well-executed controlled demolitions; and the treasonous actions and inactions of the American military, police and intelligence communities at the highest levels have enabled these monstrous crimes and the 9-11 fraud to be perpetrated against the American peoples, as indeed to humankind upon this planet.

The *September Clues* is based upon the corporate news coverage as aired both live on September 11th and/or as subsequently broadcast. The *September Clues* series clearly documents the complicity of the corporate media throughout in creating, fabricating and perpetrating the mountain of lies upon which the official fraud story of 9-11 is based. Essentially, they have fostered a delusional (or false belief) system within the minds of the American public. In fact, there is clear, indisputable evidence that the corporate media intentional deceives the American public regarding all significant international events and national issues on a daily basis. This is a

---

[9] On completing this review, I mailed it to the filmmaker Simon Shack and received this encouraging letter in response. Simon was pleased that someone had made the effort to review his video work so carefully:

> "I found your article/forensic-analysis of *September Clues* most articulate and acute. By and large, it certainly meets with my full approval as to the overall interpretation of the many 'human', behavioural aspects I strived to highlight in my research-documentary. ....

> *I am, obviously, well pleased of your comprehensive analysis of my documentary, as it is just the sort of 'peer-review' I was hoping would emerge in support of*

consistent, clearly demonstrable ongoing criminal activity by the corporate media to maintain a delusional understanding of current events among the American public, so as to allow these criminal cabals to not only destroy the sovereignty of the United States of America, to impoverish and sicken the public, to carry out criminal wars, and to bring about a 'fascist world' system under the control of these psychopathic networks. However, the corporate media were particularly at their best on that day of infamy, September 11, 2001, when they actually got to help carry out a mass murder of their fellow countrymen and women, as well as of citizens from around the world.

In my view, the *September Clues* series is one of the most profound documentary real investigative video series ever produced in the history of humankind. This is despite the fact that the series is amateurish in ways and difficult to really understand. *September Clues* rates up there with such a masterpiece as *The Empire of the City* which gives a historical overview of the crimes of these cabals against humankind through modern and ancient history. The mass media of America perpetuates a form of mass hypnosis and fosters a 'false consciousness system' based upon all varied and ingenious usages of false witnesses, faked TV images and scenes, faked polls, surveys and call-ins, the misinterpretation and withholding of evidences, the use of fraudulent consultants and specialists from allied criminally oriented think-tanks, and all forms of the *obstruction of justice* used to conceal the true nature of news events from the American public. The media conglomerates within the US have indeed participated actively in perpetrating the greatest fraud in American history, as they continue to maintain all the frauds and crimes of the elites routinely being committed by these international globalist cabals.

There needs to be an open public criminal investigation of the 9-11 events and of the corporate media to bring to justice the true perpetrators of

---

my longstanding research. However, it would appear you have stopped short of looking into the full and updated research findings as published on my website www.septemberclues.info: in the last two years or so, and with the help of several researcher colleagues, we have determined beyond reasonable doubt that the alleged "3000" victims of the day were, by and large (if not all), fictitious identities 'generated' by a digital database. In all logic, there was no "added-value" for the perps (only massive, dire aggravation!) in murdering thousands of Wall street bankers, brokers or insurance agents in the twin towers - which were more likely kept empty, rigged for demolition, and brought down without any human loss. (see: THE MEMORIAL SCAMS http://www.septemberclues.info/vicsims_photo-analyses.htm.) **Simon Shack, 2011** these horrendous crimes against humanity and their many minions, and the application of the anti-terrorist legislation to seize the assets of these criminal cabals worldwide—including the corporate media.

If the true perpetrators of these horrendous 9-11 crimes were actually brought to justice worldwide, this would indeed restore the wealth and abundance of this Earth to humankind and re-establish morality, international law and justice within our societies. This is the major opportunity for humankind to transform this planet in a unified and spiritual way to awaken humankind to the multiple crimes against them being committed daily by these insidious cabals and as being consistently and very cleverly both hidden and perpetrated through the corporate media. 9-11 was simply a case of Hollywood creativity and good old American corporate media war propaganda used to intentionally foster the creation of a 9-11 fable and mythology—essentially a delusional system which has been accepted by the masses of the American public.

The September Clues Video Series

This series can be viewed on www.youtube.com and is posted on the website www.nodisinfo.com. The series is labelled as parts A through G and includes an epilogue. (In addition there are some other *youtube* videos which supposedly 'debunk' the series.) Each part of the series runs about ten minutes. The series is not verbally narrated and explanatory material is presented in text and diagrams. This format forces the viewer to actively attend to the video and to construct within oneself what is being explained and its implications. I have had personally to review this series repeatedly to grasp its content and still do not fully understand all the points being made or which could be made. Only by watching and listening to the series repeatedly, stopping and resuming the action, and note taking, was I able to assess the full impact of what is being demonstrated as to the fraudulent nature of the corporate media video coverage. Over time, I found additional unmentioned anomalies, which occur to me with my background in clinical and forensic psychology.

Parts of the corporate media coverage are so particularly peculiar, that one has to hear or see something over and over again to order to grasp what is actually being done and how ridiculous it is.

However, as one considers more and more of these 'oddities' and 'inexplicable elements' in the news coverage, not ten or twenty, but hundreds, one reaches a point when it all comes together and one realizes what a farcical hoax was intentionally concocted to deceive the public— particularly in regards to the issue of the fabled airplanes. Elements of the news coverage when really seen and grasped then appear *absurd*. This is similar to how it is *absurd* to consider that that the Towers fell at free-fall speed into their own footprints as supposedly due to airplane impacts, office fires and "structural damage;" or as absurd as a passenger airliner slamming into the Pentagon, folding up its wings to squeeze into an 18 foot wide hole and being missed by the hundreds of video cameras surrounding the Pentagon; or as absurd as the fact that none of the imaginary high jackers were caught on any videotapes boarding any of the supposed airplanes at airports with ongoing video surveillance; or as absurd that Building Seven, containing all the criminal file investigations of banksters and Wall Street financiers, fell down into its own footprints without even having to be hit by an airplane and without having been pre-wired and ready for 'the shoot,' as they like to call it.

The official fraud story of 9-11 is already patently absurd and I do not think that there is one shred of evidence to support anything of what the public, like sheep, were led to believe, again all through their favourite corporate media and TV. Almost every one of their viewers is absolutely sure that he or she personally 'saw' an 'airplane' crash into the second tower. Of course, *they saw it on their own favourite TV's,* and of course then, it must be so.

The whole of 9-11 was an obvious criminal concoction and fraud from start to finish, and there is such overwhelming evidence for this already, that in some ways, *the issue of planes or no planes* is incidental and so has not been taken up generally by the 9-11 movement—considered as a distraction, or at least, an issue that is not helpful towards making a public and scientific case against the official 9-11 story or waking up the brain damaged public. This logic and thinking is however completely wrong and ill-informed, as indeed, the issue of plane or no plane is tied into a larger issue of whether or not the corporate media coverage was *completely pre-scripted* with access to video lab technicians, sound studios, actresses to swoon and actors to bear false witnesses, and professional liars from think-tanks marched out to influence, persuade and deceive, as is their trade. *The corporate media actively staged this event!* This is the only possible explanation for all the peculiarities and anomalies, lies and deceits of their coverage, as will be presented in this article. In my view, this could be proven in any impartial court before any half competent judge, anywhere in the world, which unfortunately no longer exists.

The *September Clues* series is not only profoundly important so as to enable us to address the scientific issue of whether or not there were any planes at all used on 9-11, but further and even more importantly, it documents with *criminal evidence* that the major network news coverage was indeed completely pre-scripted and intentionally designed to deceive the public from beginning to end. Indeed, those within the corporate media are amongst those terrorists needing to be charged for these horrendous 9-11 events and indeed, according to existing anti-terrorist legislation, the assets of the corporate media should be seized by the government on behalf of the citizens of the United States of America. These resources would subsequently be used consciously and truthfully to awaken the American public to all the crimes perpetrated against them and peoples around the world over the past decades—all that has been covered up, distorted and obscured by their favourite TVs and media personalities.

While the American people were sleeping, they came and stole it all away—your country, your truth and constitution, the dignity of your dead, your houses, monies, pensions, jobs, health and lives. But let us return to that day of infamy, 9-11, and critically evaluate how your favourite corporate media helped to mass murder your countrymen, while traumatizing a nation and intentionally deceiving you—or at least, most of you.

The Corporate Media's Live Coverage of the Fabled AirplaneDisappearing into the South Tower

The September Clues series begins by presenting the only *five live coverage shots* of the supposed airplane hitting the second tower. This includes shots by the four major networks – CNN, CBS, FOX, NBC and Channel 5 WBII. These brief clips of news coverage supposedly document a passenger airliner slamming into the South Tower of the World Trade Center and setting off an explosion. Taken together, the corporate media initially provided under 15 seconds of visual evidence for such a fabled airplane.

As it happens, this fabled airplane is supposed to have entered so swiftly and completely into the South Tower that there was no subsequent external visual evidence of any airplane parts or sections whatsoever even though there was a fairly large hole in the building. The fact that there was a hole in the Towers is of course an agreed upon fact. The fabled airplane entered so smoothly and completely into the building that it left no evidence of this beyond that provided by the corporate media videos and then subsequently by a number of 'amateur videos' supposedly made by impartial witnesses, but which also appear to have been created simply in media studios by half competent technicians. In fact, the half-competent is an apt description of the secondary video sources, which like the corporate media shots, reveal varied and assorted types of video trickery and endless peculiarities.

Part A of the *September Clues* series opens with a rather shocking statement, noting:

"When criminals have unlimited access to instruments of mass persuasion, Solid proof of their crimes are hard to expose.
On September 21, 2001

Almost all pieces of evidence were quickly removed
In fact, all but ONE
It is spread all over America on tapes recorded by American families.
And Verifiable on Official TV Archives
www.archive.org/details/sept_11_tv_archive

As the film producer notes, these videos provide criminal evidences which are verifiable and which were not so easily removed by those involved to subvert criminal investigations. Although over time, other physical evidences have emerged, such as particulate matter containing weapons grade explosives used in controlled demolitions and some of the imaginary high jackers themselves, living and breathing, and wondering why they were blamed for such horrendous crimes. But the video evidences are here to stay, records of the criminal activities of the corporate media in deceiving the American public. Fortunately, their methods are sloppy, their stories inconsistent and absurd, their actresses and actors not believable. Although overall a good performance, these actors and actresses do not deserve Oscars but something else instead, such as criminal prosecution for their role in deceiving the American public while helping to mass murder their fellow countrymen.

CNN-The most trusted name in news

The first CNN coverage in Part A is only about a minute long and provides their original footage of the airplane which is in sight for approximately 2 seconds.

The CNN clip begins with the host and a guest witness, Winston Mitchell, who maintains that he is at the north side of the Towers. The camera is centred on a view of the North Tower, while the south Tower is obscured behind. When the 'supposed' airplane enters the scene, it enters from the right, crosses the screen and disappears behind the North Tower. A second or so later an explosion is visually evident. This video provides a view of the airplane passing behind the North Tower.

The two seconds of the fabled airplane occur while the host is engaged with this witness. This is a fairly accurate accounting of this conversation which is proceeding as the plane is seen moving across the screen:

Host: Winston can you see … are you on the north side there were the mi ,,, the plane made, er, contact?

Winston: Yea, I am. But I'd say the huge, the hole is, let me just go and get a better look, right now. (We then hear the sounds of Winston shuffling about as if going to have a look and some indistinguishable voice in the background.)

Host: Ok, go ahead.

Winston: The uh, I'd say, the hole takes about, (plane enters the screen here, crosses to the left and disappears behind the tower) it looks as though six or seven floors were taken out … and there's more explosions right now, hold on. People are running … , hold on

Host: Hold on just a, we have an explosion inside.

Winston: The building is exploding right now, you got people running up the street, I am going to go and see what is going on.

Host: Ok, er, just put Winston on pause there for just a moment.

Even in this 60 second clip, there are numerous anomalies. I will review each of these according to what I consider the most significant to the lesser so. Some of these are addressed in the video series, while others are my observations and comments. Further, some of these anomalies only arise when the live CNN coverage is compared with other coverage of the live recordings on network TV or to subsequent amateur video of the supposed same events.

1. Firstly and most significantly, the CNN coverage completely 'blacks out' for about a second at the moment of the supposed airplane impact—actually there are eight black frames. Such a 'black out' can be produced by a half-competent technician using a fade out lever and then it can be simply reversed a second later. Why, in the most important moment in a century of news, would CNN, the most trusted name in news, have such a momentary blackout right at the moment of supposed impact of the airplane? CNN, in fact, was not the only network to feature such a bizarre black out at this critical moment. This is a complete anomaly requiring explanation as the most parsimonious explanation is simply that these blackouts were produced by technicians involved somehow trying to obscure particular details of the unfolding scenes or to guard against something untoward, like tell-tale indicators cropping up on public TV.

Another peculiar element here concerns the fact that just an instant before the 'blackout' occurs and just briefly afterwards, other close up images of the North Tower are shown, but it is interesting how these scenes are flashed *subliminally* before the blackout and a moment afterwards, before the CNN switches back to its distant perspective on the North Tower. How and why were these momentary alternative perspectives inserted just at these instances surrounding their fade out and for what reason? The effect is to suggest that another big hole is being created in the second tower, as there was in the first tower. This scene is then displayed for only seconds before they return to first distant view of the North Tower. This is very clever

camera work! To jump to a totally different shot, flashed subliminally, then to a brief blackout and another subliminal shot, to convince us that something made a big hole in the Tower behind our line of sight obstructed by the North Tower.

2. The airplane portrayed in this video is quite dark, almost black, which is peculiar as these airplanes are not painted black or dark grey and it is a sunny day in New York City. The image is quite blurred and unnatural looking. Further, the unnatural background is whitened and discoloured, given the prevalent sunny weather conditions. This supposed airplane moves across the screen in an horizontal manner, which actually contrasts with another live broadcast which depicts *'a dive bombing'* airplane which descends from above and varied amateur videos showing an airplane banking sharply before entering the building.

3. The host, nor anyone else in the studio, where this event is being monitored live, ever mentions the appearance of a low flying airplane passing across the screen. The host is completely silent until a visual explosion is event, at which time he does not report another airplane, but only an explosion inside the building. This of course is what we would expect if these images were being concocted in a studio, as indeed no plane would be visible, because the image of a plane is being produced for public consumption, by your most trusted name in news.

4. Although we are listening to Winston on the telephone across the street from the Towers, supposedly, and we can hear ambient voices in the background and we can hear Winston 'shuffle about' when he says he is going to look outside at what is happening, we do not hear any explosions coming over the telephone from Winston, even though he is reporting hearing "more explosions." Why are these not heard on Winston's call, which of course they should be? In fact, the sounds of explosions were

missing from all of the eye-witness telephone calls, despite the callers reporting these on their phones!

5. It is interesting to note that the host almost says 'missile' instead of airplane in regards to what hit the first Tower but he corrects himself in time. (Alternatively, I think that this may be done deliberately to help create an anomaly, uncertainty and conflicting ideas about what happened or rather what was done.) If we can have people debating whether or not it was a big plane or a small plane, or a missile, then we can obscure the fact that there was nothing, other than some half-competent technicians imposing a video image over an ongoing scene.

These are all major issues! The momentary blackout, the discoloured artificial looking airplane and backdrop, the failure of the host to see an airplane, which must also have been visible for seconds before the two seconds on the screen, and the entirely suspect report of Winston that he is hearing massive explosions while his phone call shows him to be a liar and poor actor. His 'shuffling about' is overheard but not a peep out of his explosions.

In sum, the folk at CNN have some interesting explaining to do. This footage cannot conceivably be accepted as evidence of the existence of a passenger airliner hitting the second tower, no matter how much CNN proclaims to be – *the most trusted name in news*.

CBS

The second live network coverage on part A of this series involves the CBC. The CBS clip is a minute and 15 seconds long with about one to two seconds of video coverage of an airplane and it offers all kinds of bizarre elements and peculiarities.

There is just over one second of visual contact with this fabled airplane, which this time, instead of approaching the Tower parallel to the ground as CNN portrayed, this fable airplane drops down out of the sky from above and behind the Towers. The CBS camera angle is of both towers but it is taken from below the level of the Towers, as one cannot see their roofs. About six seconds before the explosion is visibly evident, this fabled airplane is well 'above' both towers and dropping down from above, first appearing at the top of the screen. This is called the 'dive bomber scenario.' Somehow, this airplane above the Towers descends into the tower within a few seconds. Of course, this is in total contradiction to the horizontal flight path displayed on CNN! One simply cannot have both a horizontal and vertical line of flight of the same airplane at the same time. There are other amateur videos which show over three seconds of the plane on its horizontal course, which are also completely contradictory to the CBS dive bomber footage.

The video once again is riddled with peculiarities, especially when considered in relationship to other evidences, or should I say fabricated evidences. The image of the plane is not distinct and instead is like a little blob although it does suggest the appearance of an airplane. Unfortunately, I don't have the necessary equipment and expertise to more closely examine details of these images. This time, the scene has a blue wash and a dark airplane.

195

In the CBS footage, the most outrageous elements of their studio work involve the conversation ongoing while this plane drops down out of the sky in the background. The host Bryant Gumbel has his producer's wife, Teresa Renaud, on the telephone live from Chelsey, a subdivisions of Manhattan north of Towers, past the other subdivisions of Tribeca, Greenwich Village and Soho. This is the conversation proceeding during the time that the fabled airplane strikes the second tower.

Host: I understand that Teresa Renaud is with us right now. Mrs Renaud, good morning.

Mrs. Renaud: Good morning. How are you?
Host: This is Bryant Gumbel, I am down at 59th and 5th, where are you?

Mrs. Renaud: I am in Chelsey and we are at, er, 8th and 16. We are the tallest building in the area and we, my window faces south. So it looks directly onto the World Trade Centre. And I would say, you know, approximately ten minutes ago, there was a major explosion from probably it looks like about the 80th floor, it looks like it has effected probably four to eight floors. Ur, major flames are coming out of the, lets see, the north side and also the east side of the building, yes.

Host: Yes, Um, you're over in Chelsey? Um, did you hear the explosion from your position?

Mrs. Renaud: Oh, yes, yes we did. As a matter of fact, we we heard it and and cause I was just like standing there, pretty much looking out the window, I didn't see what caused it or if there was an impact.

Host: So you have no idea right now ...

Mrs. Renaud: Oh, there's another one, another plane just hit. Oh my God, another plane just has just hit another building, flew right into the middle of it. Explosion.

If one listens to this segment several times over, one realizes how preposterous it is. Most significantly, this witness in one breath states *"I didn't see what caused it"* and then in the next breath, says *"Oh, there's another one, another plane just hit."* Of course, Mrs Renaud knew what the story was meant to be and she betrays her prior knowledge of this. She forgets in the moment and cannot keep her story straight from one moment to the next. Once again, no explosions are heard over her phone line, despite her report that she is hearing them.

The claim further that she witnessed this second plane hitting the building is a complete fabrication. Firstly, why does she not mention a plane until after the explosion and not before. It is only after the explosion that she reports 'another plane.' No media newscaster or cameraman sees the airplane before it hits the building or reacts to anything prior to when the explosions have already occurred, which it seems is what they take as their 'cues.' Further, the second plane hit the building on the opposite side from her line of sight, and the manner in which it dive bombed down from above, would not possibly have enabled her to see that it was a plane that set off the explosion. Simply take the police to Mrs Renaud's apartment and take photographs from there to document the possibility of these things.

Of course, there are other anomalies in the conversation. Firstly, why does she refer to 'we' as hearing the explosion and then to "I" as standing at the window? Does she have a multiple personality disorder or is there someone there to support her and guide her through her acting bit, but who is not to be mentioned? I personally think that someone indicated to her so as not to say we, or else she just remembered and shifted her usage. Consider her use of 'I' and 'we' in these segments: *"I am in Chelsey and we are at, er, 8th and 16. We are the tallest building in the area and we, my window faces south. ...* " This makes sense as she is likely referring to 'we' as to indicate she and her husband, TV producer Jack Renault of the *Early Show*, as people are apt to do in using 'we,' although it is curious how it is then *"my window."* When asked if she heard the explosion, Mrs Renault responds, *"Yes, yes we did,"* and then she continues on, *"As a matter of fact, we we heard it and and cause I was just like standing there, pretty much looking out the window."* (By the way, these are not typing errors, but her actual word usage. I am not used to such phrases as *"pretty much looking out the window."*) Likely, her producer husband is hiding away in Chelsey with her helping to support her through her acting ordeal and she is not supposed to refer to him, but she cannot help it due to her anxiety, uncertainty and the mechanical speech automaticity of referring to 'we.'

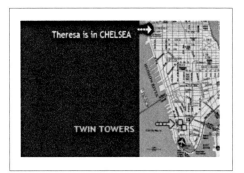

Other elements of her conversation suggest anxiety and deception. Why does she see 'major flames' coming out of the building. This is somewhat unusual description but one must wonder why she is seeing flames, while everyone else including the CBS live coverage is viewing primarily billowing black smoke from an oxygen starved fire. Further, consider how she adds on the word *"Explosion"* at the end of her last statement. I have never heard anyone in my life simply say 'explosion,' without it being in a sentence or something and she simply says it in a most ridiculous sounding way to add it on. She just sticks it on the end probably realizing that she had forgotten to say 'explosion' as it was written on a piece of paper before her. As a clinical psychologist, psychotherapist and having worked with criminal offenders for 12 years, this whole thing is an obvious hoax and she is a liar. Once again, one has to be almost brain dead, like the majority of the American public, not to question these things.

Another curious feature of this segment is the 'swooning' of some fine actresses in the studio produced to document the dramatic crashing of the fabled airplane into the second Tower. When I hear these swoons, they sound more feigned than real to me, as if part of a dramatization and produced on cue.

Of course, these are my comments simply on the conversation ongoing while the fabled airplane appears and disappears very quickly in the background. However, overall, I would have to consider that this CBS segment offers evidence of conspiracy to commit mass murder to ensure one's corporate media status, but no credible evidence to establish the existence of any fabled airplane.

In the *September Clues* series, at the end of the CBS coverage, the film maker has inserted a photo of an individual, David Handschuh, a witness who maintains, *"I didn't see the plane although I was right below the tower."* David is shown against a backdrop photo of an explosion outwards from the South Tower but no evidence of an airplane. Of course, David was below the Tower, truly on the scene — instead of a mile away in Chelsey wondering how WE did.

WNYW FOX 5

The third of the live shots analyzed in Part A of the *September Clues* series is provided by a feed from a helicopter, which seems to be located a mile or so from the Towers when a fabled airplane suddenly appears on the screen and then hits the second tower. This time the video image of an airplane is present on the screen for approximately 2 seconds. Of course, no one mentions seeing the airplane ahead of time even though the helicopter line of sight would have allowed the pilot, crew and cameraman and to see an airplane well before the impact. Of course, in none of the live clips does anyone ever mention an airplane until after the visual sight of an explosion. After the cue provided by the explosion, the media immediately begin to refer to this fabled airplane. Once again, there is an artificial wash to the screen. I would think it must be easier to fake these things if the visuals obscure the background which would allow for clearer differentiation of this fabled airplane.

Once again, the whole clip is less than a minute in length, but within this period, the half-competent technicians make such profound mistakes that it is almost ludicrous — demonstrating conclusively that the images being presented were being fashioned within a video studio and an image of an airplane has simply being superimposed over the background of the Towers. Of all evidences, this clip is the most damning evidence of the *media's fabrication of the airplane images*. Of course, if there was really an airplane, then there would be no need for such a fabrication.

This clip begins with the helicopter miles away from the Towers with a panoramic view of New York showing the skyline for miles to the right of the Tower, the direction the fable airplane is supposed to come from. However, in the opening panoramic view there is no airplane at six seconds before impact. The cameraman then zooms in on the Towers in three

steps, getting a closer and closer look. However, it is only after the cameraman has zoomed up the final time that suddenly an airplane appears on the screen as if from nowhere. No one noticed the airplane ahead of time, of course because there was nothing to see from the opening panoramic view.

What is most shocking in this video, beyond the sudden appearance of plane out of nowhere, is what is referred to as *the 'nose out shot.'* When the image of the airplane appears to enter the tower from one side, it appears to be completely unimpeded by its passage through the building and its 'nose' is then

seen projecting out from the other side of the Tower! The host even says afterwards *"the plane went right through the other tower,"* giving recognition that he also had seen this nose out shot. Of course, he shouldn't have reported that and no one claimed subsequently to see the nose of an airplane sticking out of the other side of the Tower, although that is shown in their video. At least, it is shown for just a moment before they go to their infamously clever black out.

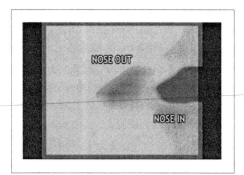

Not only does the plane appear to pass unimpeded right through this massive steel framed building until its nose sticks out on the other side, but the film producer then does a comparative analysis of the pixels of the images of the nose entering and existing the building, and the images are almost completely the same. This is patently absurd; firstly, that the plane would pass through the building unimpeded and at the same rate of speed, and further that the nose of the plane would still be completely intact. The only possible way to explain this is that the fabled airplane is not really a airplane, but an image superimposed over the background. However, this image, because of the drift of the helicopter to the left, is moved too far along the horizontal axis. The image of the plane needed to have stopped in its motion .28 seconds earlier. In Part A, the film producer shows how this likely happened. He also has shots which show how the plane image is a layering, as at one point, the image of the airplane bumps into its layered boundary, and its nose is cut off. In fact, one can also see the overlapping of layer edges as the plane enters into the Tower, as if a real plane can cause *pixel bleed*. One has to watch the video to see these things and how phoney they are.

Once again, we have a Fade to Black just after the moment of impact, or rather of the explosion. The fade out of the video feed is in three phases and lasts for 15 frames. There is then a three frame fade in. This is time enough to try to hide the nose out shot and resume a natural coverage of events. How ridiculous is this, to have such blackouts at these moments of impact or studio mischief.

This whole video clearly documents the fabrication of this fabled airplane. Such preposterous images cannot possibly be taken as serious evidence of this so-called fabled airplane. No airplane, largely of aluminium, can pass through a steel framed building without impedance and emerge intact on the other side. And then, it is not even visible to anyone afterwards as sticking out of the building! These shots alone of the fabled airplane reveal the farce of what the public came to accept.

Even more absurd in regards to the 'nose out' shot, concerns how this clip from Fox is then replayed by supposed rivals (and co-conspirators) at CNN within six minutes of being presented on Fox. However, when these images of the airplane entering and exiting the south tower are replayed on CNN, the banner at the bottom of the CNN screen is used to obscure all the critical images of the airplane including the *nose out shot*. However, the hosts on CNN actually say such things on air as: *"Well there you see it, a second airplane hitting the South Tower."* However, despite saying this, they are completely obscuring the actual image of the airplane by their banner, so that we don't actually see anything of any airplane! They are just telling us that we are seeing it, so that we will think that that is we saw.

As it happens, the original Fox videos *"have been remixed"* and the critical nose-out shot is now removed from their archives. Of course, this is just further evidence of the fraud they have helped to perpetrate, their fabrication of evidences, the obstruction of justice and the destruction of evidence—against themselves. Of course, these days, the US has become a completely lawless insane nation, a nation of double speak and mass lunacy.

Fox anchor, Jim Ryan offers the only truthful comment of the Fox coverage. He remarks, *"I think we have a terrorist act of proportions that we cannot begin to image at this juncture."* Yes, Mr Ryan was certainly right, as the mass of the American public had not even begun to imagine who the true terrorists really were. Instead the corporate media already had some patsies lined up—Mr. Osama Bin Laden and his unholy warriors, recovering from strip bars, alcohol and cocaine in the days before, but leaving Korans behind. Jim Ryan's coworkers then offer a chorus of *"Oh my God," "My goodness, a second plane has crashed into the other tower …"* My God, we had not imagined, although it seems that at least some of those within the corporate media had and knew full well what they were doing on that day when they sealed their fates.

NBC

Part B of the *September Clues* series begins with a live clip from NBC, which has the fabled airplane on screen for the longest period of time — approximately five seconds. This footage is shot from a helicopter which is above the towers, such that we can see their roofs. This airplane seems to descend down from above and behind the towers. The plane image is very blurry, appearing almost like a blob, white on top and dark underneath, and it is shown against an unnatural grey-washed skyline. The film editor refers to this image as *'the ball.'* The image does not feature distinct wings.

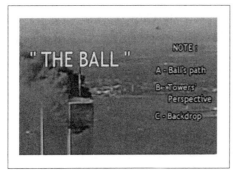

Just after the image of the plane blob descends and before impact (which is outside of the line of our sight), the screen switches to a close-up of the existing damage to the North Tower. This 'Ball' version is available in the NBC archives. We then witness synchronized explosions in the North Tower which occur as the fabled airplane is supposedly striking the South Tower behind! No one mentions these visible additional explosions occurring while the fabled airplane is supposedly causing such explosions in the building behind.

Once again, no host or commentator comments on an airplane before explosions in the South Tower are evident. Immediately then, a witness online with host Elliot Walker, the NBC news anchor, another news media person who claims to have witnessed the first impact and who has been silent in the background, suddenly pipes up: *"Oh, my goodness. Oh, another one just hit, something else just … a very large plane just flew directly over my building and there's been another collision. Can you see it? I can see it on this shot. Something else has just … and that looked like a 747."*

This is again most peculiar and unbelievable. She reports a very large plane as just flying directly over her building, which somehow she then knows to be a 747, although of course we do not hear any of this on her phone line, nor of the explosions which then occur. She then states that she can "see it on this shot," referring, I guess, to what she is witnessing on TV? But of course, none of the live TV shots show anything distinguishable as a 747, as she reports. Once again, this witness is an obvious fraud and her story unbelievable, another of the pathological liars assimilated into to the corporate media of America, that great country of liberty, truth and justice — what a joke.

Such false witnesses plant the seed ideas that constitute the story line being fabricated for public consumption — the high jacking of passenger airliners by Muslims. If there were no imaginary airplane story, then the public who is not brain dead, might wonder, what caused such fine Towers to explode and fall at near free fall speed all neat and dandy into their own footprint, in such a dramatic fashion. The passenger airliner fraud was to camouflage the fact that bombs or some forms of explosive devises and charges had simply blown out holes in the building, roughly designed to look like the damage that a airplane might inflict on a building, and then the whole building was brought down in a controlled demolition, all supposedly caused as a consequence of the fabled airplanes. What a remarkable fraud!

The *September Clues* series then features a short shot of a scene very similar to that shown on *NBC*, described as 'a private VHS tape" which shows the banner of *Live Chopper 4*. In this segment, the ball shown on the NBC video is not there, but instead, there is a very faint near invisible object which streaks across the screen, suggestive more of a missile. Further, this video has a series of line markers which keep appearing and disappearing on the side of the building where the explosion is to occur, and a final marker occurs just at the explosion site a moment before the explosion. These moving marker lines are somehow being coordinated by a lab technician and are not present on the same scenes of the NBC footage.

Of course, this is all quite ridiculous as we cannot have both of these videos as simultaneously valid depictions of what occurred. Why is the missile not on the 'the ball' video, or 'the ball' image on the missile scenario. Obviously, the most likely, simple and parsimonious explanation is that both are the products of media manipulation designed to fabricate misleading evidences and then further to mislead and confuse people. Could it have been a missile instead of an airplane? Or was it simply inconsistent and sloppy media work and pixelated images imposed on existing live coverage shots? Certainly, we still have no credible evidence for a fabled airplane hitting the South Tower, but we do have evidences of the half-competency of media personnel.

September Clues then compares video versions shown on the NBC live and on the Evening News. On these two videos taken from almost the same angle and perspective, the planes have different trajectories on the video. However, the evening news has a much clearer image of a plane and the background is now completely eliminated and there is a grey wash. Further, there is evidence on both videos of a 'black spot' appearing for an instant seen between the two Towers, as the airplane supposedly passes behind the first tower. Although both videos have this black spot suggestive of a airplane behind, both of the images look totally artificial and these spots are at different heights on the same buildings! Obviously, NBC has spruced up its evening news to provide a better image of a fabled airplane for a sleepwalking public—all of whom are absolutely convinced that there was an airplane, because of course, they personally saw it on their own favourite TV.

It is not as if any of these first four live shots, and variants latter released, which appear to be second efforts, offer any real evidence of any real airplane. If there was such a real airplane there would simply be no chance for such inconsistent, mutually exclusive shots and clips, and fraudulent witnesses!

WBII-Channel 5

The fifth of the live shots of the fabled airplane hitting the South Tower on that day is also from the same perspective as the different NBC shots, but a different airplane, different trajectory and with the black spot passing between the buildings at again another height. In this live shot, the background is completely obscured with a hazy discoloured sky. Again, the fabled airplane enters the screen from the left and is in view for about three seconds. This airplane is a streaky black blob moving across the screen, but at least is has partly discernable wings in several frames.

Just as the fabled airplane hits the building, one of the female new hosts is stating, *"I believe that could be a police helicopter that is, OH, WOW...,"* while a second female anchor then comes quickly online to correct this, stating, *"We just saw another of what I believe was a plane."* It is of course useful to have such clarifying statements from our media personnel to inform us of what "we" just saw.

This concludes the opening analysis of the live shots of the 9-11 fabled airplane hitting the South Tower. This material covered here thus far is only about 15 minutes in length of the hour and a half of the *September Clues* series and we are still only on part B of the series. The results of our analysis thus far must, by any sane logic, be supportive of what the film editor concludes on screen:

9/11 TV was one big lie.

It is simply not the case that there are one or two oddities, peculiarities or anomalies in the live coverage shots of the fabled second airplane, and in the variants of these shots later inserted into the news coverage. Instead, every one of the five clips presents numerous inexplicable elements in the depictions of the airplane and in the conversations ongoing within the studios, and with supposed eye-witnesses. Further, the different shots are even inconsistent with each other.

This concludes what I have most wanted to focus upon in my presentation on this *September Clues* series—the original live coverage of a fabled airplane hitting the South Tower. In the days, weeks and years after, other amateur videos emerged, supposedly turned in by objective witnesses at the scenes but these also show all kinds of other anomalies. What appears to be most likely is that the news networks simply had individuals ready to film the second explosion in the South Tower from different perspectives when it happened, so that airplanes could subsequently be inserted or overlaid onto their videos which captured the actual events—which were the interior explosions.

Pentagon and Shanksville Absurdities

September Clues series, Part B, then shifts the focus to the events at the Pentagon and West Virginia, where we had other fabled airplanes. *September Clues* features some amusing footage as related to the airplane that disappeared into a hole less than twenty feet wide in the Pentagon and of another airplane that disappeared into a fifteen foot hole in a field out in Shanksville. Both planes disappeared with no signs of any major clearly identifiable airplane parts, although it seems possible that a missile might have struck the Pentagon.

Part C has the most ludicrous video coverage another news media personality, Mike Walter. Mike's early report, on that fateful day, concerned what happened at the Pentagon. He states in the first clip:

> "I saw this plane, a jet, an American Airliner jet, coming, and I thought this doesn't add up. It's really low, and and I saw it, it just went, I mean, it was like er, a cruise missile with wings."

This in itself is already peculiar. Why does Mike say in one line that it is an American Airliner jet and then in the next line, describe it as being like a 'cruise missile with wings?' This is patently absurd.[10] However, Mike later does another interview to explain again what he witnessed.

> I looked up and I saw the jet banking, and er clearly, you see the AA on the side and I knew it was American Airlines jet, and er, it went

---

[10] Actually, this is not too absurd, but it is Walter's later statements which are absurd. The Citizen's Investigative Committee (December 2010) has produced a film documentary which seems to establish that there was indeed a passenger type aircraft which passed north of the route usually depicted as the flight path of the fabled airplane, and which approached the Pentagon extremely low but then veered off and ascended. This is a different flight path than that depicted where the light poles on the highways were knocked over, which was staged. So the fact that people may have been witness to a large passenger plane at the Pentagon is still consistent with the thesis that there were no airplanes actually destroyed on that ill-fated day, when the elites sealed their fate. Also, Walters might have been confused as having legitimately seen both, although not in the way he describes.

into a steep decline and accelerated. Boom, right into the Pentagon, the side of the Pentagon. And, and the wings on the jet just folded back and it just kind of crumbled, it kind of came together like an accordion and just pierced the wall of the Pentagon. There was this huge … Boom.

Now there is no mention of the cruise missile with wings, but Mike has now fabricated that he witnessed how the airplane on impact with the Pentagon was able to *"fold its wings back"* — enabling it to fit into the under 20 foot hole in the side of the Pentagon. To anyone with any semblance of intelligence, this is a complete affront to you.

Mike is then shown repeating his tale once again and trying to discredit all the questions and rumours circulating concerning his report. He wants then to *"set the record straight."* Now he works for WUSA- TV 9 NEWS NOW in Washington and he feels compelled to explain his story once more to fellow television employees.

One of the things that really bothers me, is the fact that er, people constantly are calling me, and emailing me, and want information about this, and I am happy to talk to them. But a lot of them say that, er, well, you know, physics just says that this is impossible, what happened. But what happened is pretty obvious. The force of this jet hitting the Pentagon at about 500 miles an hour. When something hits a concrete structure like that, you know, this belief that the wings would go in is just ridiculous. What I saw was the actual jet going in but the wings folded back like this (demonstrating with his hands). So that's why, when you look at the hole, you say its not big enough, but that why, the wings were not strong enough to withstand the impact, they folded back, and that's why the jet went in, and that's why the hole that you see isn't as large as you might imagine in another structure.

Basically, the only reason that I am doing this, is because (visible gulp) over the last five years, I have been getting a lot of phone calls, emails and, and my words have been twisted, and I figure that if you are going to the internet for information, then go and find the right information. One other suggestion, keep an open mind, but always try to get the facts.

Mike Walter's explanations are absolutely ludicrous maintaining that this airplane folded its wings back on impact with the Pentagon within some split second and his appearance on this video is most revealing. His eyes  are continually shifting to the right indicating that he is lying and try to recall what he should be saying. He provides only an absurd explanation of his reports and acts as if he has adequately addressed the facts of the matter. Anyone who gives any type of credence to such an obviously dishonest and invented speech is really quite mentally and emotionally limited themselves. We see in the invented stories of these media personalities, how their descriptions are so non-sensible, disjointed and deliberately evasive: Like Mrs Renaud, who was "pretty much looking out the window." Personally, I have never pretty much looked out a window in my life. Nor have I ever heard of an airplane folding up its wings in an instant, denying all laws of mechanical motion and of inertia. Of course, the Hollywood of news services in America can really concoct almost any imaginary tale, and they have enough pathological liars on staff that it is no problem to produce any kind of witness one might want.

In the *September Clues* series, while Mike is talking, the film director shows on screen the fabled airplane entering into the South Tower with its wings conveniently disappearing inside. This is at the same moments that Mike is explaining, *"When something hits a concrete structure like that, you know, this belief that the wings would go in is just ridiculous."* Of course, this is exactly what is shown as occurring with the South Tower on the faked amateur video. Mike's explanation of how he saw the wings fold back in the instant of hitting the Pentagon is far more absurd and ridiculous even than this. Did the five ton engines also fold back! This man is such a pathetic hypocrite and liar no matter where he works.

The *September Clues* series then follows Mike with what I regard as an honest reporting by the CNN News anchor, Jamie Mc Intrye on scene at the Pentagon. This individual has not yet been scripted and in his naivety actually reports the truth! In response to a query concerning the 'fabled airplane,' Jamie responds:

You know, it might have appeared that way, but from my close up inspection, there is no evidence of a plane having crashed anywhere near the Pentagon. The only site is the actual side of the building that has crashed in. And as I said, the only pieces left, that you can see, are small enough that you can pick them up in your hand. There are no large tail sections, wing sections, er, fuselage, nothing like that anywhere around that would indicate that the entire plane crashed into the side of the Pentagon.

Of course, poor Jamie had latter to recant. How had this massive airliner which had been able to fold up its wings and fit into a small hole, now been able to leave no substantive evidence of its existence?

Of course, Jamie had to subsequently make his reparations for having actually been honest on the TV News. His latter testimony on the CNN News has the banner overlaid, *"CNN's Jamie Mc Intrye confirms the plane at the Pentagon."* Oh, yes, the most trusted

name in news is at it once again. Jamie is asked about the release of some new videos by the Pentagon to supposedly show the fabled airplane striking the Pentagon. Very handy of the Pentagon to obstruct justice by withholding the thirty plus videos of the whole affair, but they do now manage to produce two brief and edited videos from one particular perspective. The hostess asks Jamie about *this breaking news*:

This is again a more complete version of the six still frame images that CNN obtained unofficially back in March of 2002 and broadcast then. The full tape has been something that the government has been holding, er, as evidence in the trial of Z. M., but now that that trial is over, they have released the full video, er, and the video, which runs for a minute or so, shows what happens just before the impact, and also the plane coming into the building. It is from two separate, ah, cameras, both at the same location, at a Pentagon checkpoint entrance and it is hard to see as we are playing it here. It is sort of stop action video. Again, very similar to the still frames that we saw before. But when you run the video back and stop it, at one point, you see what appears to be the nose of the plane just entering the frame. The very next frame, there is an explosion. And then in the second angle which is taken from another camera, a little bit lower down, er, you can see, er, what appears to be a white flash, that also looks like the plane. But again, its not going to be distinct enough to convince conspiracy theorists, but for anyone with any common sense, and er, given all the other evidence we have, there is really no doubt that a plane hit the Pentagon.

Jamie has recanted and his future is assured. And while Jamie is giving these shallow descriptions of one frame that *"appears to be the nose of an airplane"* and of another frame in this *"stop action video,"* a euphemism for an edited version, *"a white flash that also looks like the plane."*

Neither of these images provides any evidence of an airplane! He then

appeals to our *"common sense"* to accept such ridiculous concocted, edited and spliced videos and stills as conclusive evidence of the existence of a fabled airplane. Even the video which we are being shown is highly suspect and shows no evidence of an airplane! It is as if the public is supposed to believe his words rather than what they are actually being shown visually. If American citizens had any common sense they would begin to demand the arrest of these Pentagon officials and the seizure of the tapes in total, along with all these fraudulent media personalities willing to help mass murder their fellow countrymen and obstruct the true processes of justice and criminal prosecution. I wonder what the going price for souls is on that ill-fated planet Earth.

September Clues then provides some coverage of the 'fabled airplanes' which supposedly crashed or was blown up in Shanksville. This material begins with a copy of a photograph depicting a mid sized mushroom type cloud which is quite symmetrical in form rising from the background. It simply looks like a bomb had exploded and created a cloud over the hole in the field. It certainly does not look like an explosion caused by an airplane

the "CRASH SITE"

crash landing with momentum and impacting the ground to spread debris and fire over an area of land. The crash site itself looks like a 20 foot hole with some garbage in it. Of course, officials happened somewhere to find an Arabian passport and bandana, and a fabled victim's licence, which had expired in 1998. This fabled airplane, Flight 93, also managed to disappear so completely that its remnants were gathered up in a few paltry buckets and containers. Once again, there was no credible evidence of any fabled airplane crashing in Shanksville, but only evidence of more deception and lies.

Amateur Videos of the Fabled Airplane Striking the South Tower

Part C of *September Clues* is entitled *'Flying* Elephants' and deals with a first sample of the amateur videos of the second fabled airplane. (Part F of the series later deals more extensively with the amateur videos, see *Forged Out*.) These are reportedly shot by *"the man on the street."* In all, there are now at least 36 of such efforts. However, as pointed out by the film editor, *"A back-to-back comparison shows how they all disqualify each other."* He then documents obvious inconsistencies and absurdities.

The first amateur video is called the "Al-Quaeda shot," reportedly found by the FBI on the Al-Quaeda website—or should we say the CIA-aeda website. This tape shows a dark charcoal coloured airplane on a horizontal path for about three seconds before striking the South Tower. This is then directly compared with the 'dive bomber scenario' which shows a breathtakingly steep descent with a G-force levelling within the last seconds. These trajectories cannot both be true.

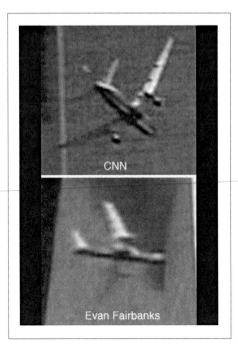

The filmmaker then examines the image of a dark charcoal airplane. These planes are a silver grey colour and it was a bright sunny day on 9-11. So how one would have such a phoney black plane on this horizontal flight path is of course an anomaly in itself, but then especially so, when there are other videos of the supposed same event which show the plane as almost white. In fact, the video of the fabled airplane entering the Tower as shot from below the South Tower, shows clearly the almost white wings of an airplane. Once again, the fabled airplane cannot be both

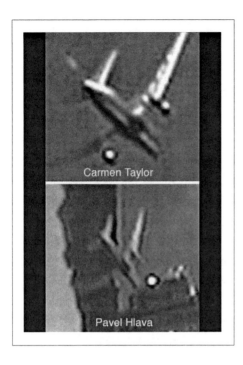

Carmen Taylor

Pavel Hlava

dark charcoal and bright white at the same time under the same lighting conditions, although of course, one can do almost anything one wants within a media studio. Of course, this makes it complicated if different studios are producing different versions and effects to create the *TV media's image pool* of these events. Of course, none of this would have been necessary if there had been a real airplane.

There are all kinds of other anomalies in different videos. One dramatic video showing the plane entering the Tower as shot from below is really most peculiar. The videographer has the South Tower in view but is including a picture of man who seconds before the explosion looks up in coordination with the sound track of an airplane and then down again. Who would normally frame a video of the Towers in this way to portray this whole event? More likely, it is being staged with a scripted actor, or assembled as a composite in a lab. Another video features an older Jewish man who is describing the plane impact on the first Tower, when the second explosion happens in the background. Yet the scene behind him is actually being produced by some type of virtual reality software, which produces the most peculiar frames of a type of 'glass man' who walks behind the scene and half of his head disappears. It's like a game boy or computer graphic scene. This is all preposterous. These witness and events are staged and fabricated. Further, in this clip there is no sound of an incoming airplane.

There is yet no credible evidence for these airplanes but all kinds of criminal evidence for the fabrication of evidence by media personnel, news reporters, actors and actresses, sound effects produced in sound studios, and so much more. It is all a house of cards, touch it and it crumbles under any kind of serious investigative examination.

And if so many of these evidences of a second plane are fraudulent, the simplest explanation is that there must not have been an airplane at all, as  then there would not have been any need to fabricate such evidences. If one is presenting the truth, it is all so simple. Creating and maintaining a delusional system is more complex and requires such video labs, software and computer expertise, half-competent technicians, Hollywood whores and the pathological liars of the corporate media. The methods of the news media and Hollywood itself can easily produce such image files and deceptions, and do it routinely.

Part C of the *September Clues* series concludes: *"Various techniques were used to produce the 9/11 image pool."* At least, they might have better co-ordinated their efforts to make their videos consistent with each other. Of course, none of this would have been necessary if there had been a real airplane, real witnesses and sounds. One of the amateur videos even contained the same *"Oh, my God,"* sound track element as on one of the TV productions, and other feigned swoons and such!

In one of the amateur videos released in 2006, the *"Bob and Bri"* clip, the people had an excellent view of the two Towers moments before the second strike. However, at the moments of impact, the camera jumps around and several frames have been edited out, even though the sound track is continuous. However, on the last frame before the impact, there is no evidence of a plane whatsoever. But why were frames edited out of this clip? The *September Clues* editor suggests that perhaps it was to edit out a frame of a missile, although I would suspect it was designed to create a reason to believe that something had been edited out, such as a missile, when really there was nothing there, which would have been evident if the video had not been tampered with. The way the video is edited leaves it unclear what happened.

What a joke. The only way to explain all the anomalies on the amateur videos, the most simple and parsimonious way, is to conclude that they are all simply fabricated evidences intentionally created to deceive and confuse the public and to mix with other authentic pictures. (We will examine more of these amateur videos and who produced them in a later section, *Forged Out*, as presented in part E of the series.)

The Supernatural Physics of Disappearing Airplanes

As it happens, fabled airplanes are not like quantum particles, which could be here, there and everywhere at the same time, exploring all possibilities simultaneously. An airplane cannot simultaneously be charcoal and white, grey, a blob or ball, a distinct jet, a small plane and a large plane, descending horizontally and vertically, all rolled up into one in imaginary space-time. The numerous amateur and corporate media images of the planes present a hodgepodge of possibilities and inconsistencies. Of course, if there was simply an airplane, such inconsistencies would not exist and there would be no need to fabricate clearly artificial images. The studio offers a world of visual effects and possibilities. Of course, in the real world, these amateur videos can't all be true as airplanes are not like quantum particles.

Part C of *September Clues* also raises the important issue of how a supposedly real airplane with wings and a tail of aluminium was able to seamlessly enter right into the steel framed South Tower, so completely and without obstruction, such that it then completely disappeared from view. There are no photos of the hole in South Tower as showing any evidence of an airplane inside. Further, no parts of the airplane broke off and fell to the ground upon impact, as one would certainly expect of the weaker aluminium wing and tail structures. In fact, the motion of the airplane into the building shows no obstruction to its flight path at all! The 'nose out shot' discussed earlier showed the motion of the plane right through the whole building in a jiffy in a completely unobstructed manner. These are

217

either instances of Divine Intervention, new methods of dematerializing material entities or more simply, half-competent video technicians.

Most peculiar is one of the amateur videos depicting an airplane directly entering into the South Tower. On one frame of the video, the left wing has completely disappeared and yet there still is no hole there in the Tower. The timing is slightly off. This same video also shows synchronized explosions both above and below the right wing as it enters the building. These explosions could not be caused by the wings but are obviously evidence of planted charges, which were not obscured by the superimposed image of the airplane. Of course, it is much simpler to fake an airplane entering right into a building, than it is to show a non-uniform crash with parts breaking off upon impact. The fabled airplane just slips into the building so nicely and tidy, simply vanishing! Isn't that clever and cunning of them.

People sometimes wonder why the South Tower was blown up first, before the North Tower, since the latter had burned for longer. As it happens, recordings of the emergency firemen transmissions included a fireman on scene who states that the fire was now confined to only a few floors and that with two more hoses, they would likely be able to get it under control. Of course, it would have been embarrassing to have had the fireman arriving on scene at the hole and finding no airplane! The demolition of the South Tower had to be first as the firemen in their bravery and selflessness were about to deal with the first emergency. Of course, they had no idea that the whole building was pre-wired for a controlled demolition and that to the likes of Kissinger, they are nothing more than the soldiers, *"stupid, dumb animals"* to be used as pawns in the game plans and strategies of the criminal psychopaths who high-jacked America.

The *Architects and Engineers for 9-11 Truth* should attempt to model impacts of such aluminium airplanes passing into steel frame buildings and determine how such an impact would really unfold. This scenario of the airplane entering into the building without obstruction and then disappearing completely from view is another of those jokes in this whole

9-11 fraud. The fact that these things are given any credence documents the naivety and lack of common sense within the American and world public. It is as if people are so used to the techniques of the road runner, cartoon characters, the Simpsons and impossible things, that they no longer have the intelligence to question the most obvious of frauds. Even the sizes of the holes left in the Towers barely accommodate the massive planes which are supposed to have slipped inside so cleverly and cleanly. Of course, all the planes on 9-11 vanished in one way or another.

Eye-Witnesses to the First Fabled Airplane

Part D of the *September Clues* series then presents some of the original eyewitnesses on the five major news networks. All five networks had first hand eye-witnesses of the first 'fabled airplane' handily on the phone with four minutes of the first explosion — *"virtually all of whom were news media professionals."*

CNN live featured Sean Murtagh, the vice president of finance and a CNN producer, online at 8:50 am after the explosion at 8:46.

> "I just witnessed a plane that appeared to be cruising er slightly lower than normal altitude over New York City and it appeared to crash into, I don't know which Tower it is, but it hit directly in the middle of one of the World Trade Centre Towers. ... It was a jet, er, it looked like a two engine jet, er, maybe a 737. ... a large passenger commercial jet ... "

Notice that Sean was unsure of which Tower this fabled airplane has crashed into but he describes where it hit in the tower — in the middle. Was Sean unaware of which tower was which even though living in New York?

Fox News, a few minutes after the first strike, had on-line one of the producers of *"Fox Report,"* Owen Moogan, on the scene:

I am on the roof of my building which is about five blocks to the south of the world trade centre and I am looking right now at the World Trade Center. There is a massive gaping hole, er on the second Tower. It's unbelievable to look at, there's a massive hole

Host: It looks something like out of a movie. There is a huge hole in the side of Tower number One, (the host correcting Owen as to what Tower has been hit.)

Owen: Tower One. (as if repeating to himself so as to remember)

Host: Owen, your apartment is just a few blocks from it. Did you hear anything?

Owen: I was lying in bed, ah, and all of a sudden I heard what sounded like, er, a plane or something coming extremely low and then we just heard this shattering explosion, I came to the roof and … (cut off)

Owen is supposedly looking at the towers from his rooftop, but makes a mistake as to what Tower has been hit. Could he really live five blocks away from the Towers and not know how to distinguish the two even when he is supposedly looking at them? Further, when the host corrects him, Owen repeats it to himself out loud — I would say so as to remember what he had forgotten.

The next clip is of Senior ABC Producer Mark Obenhaus, of the *"Seeing is believing"* show, who has apparently seen 'the incident.'

Um, well I was leaving my house to go to work and I walked down the street to go to the subway. I was at the corner of Franklin and West Broadway, and as I was approaching the subway, a tremendous roar, er, went over my head and I looked up immediately, and it was a plane, um, and much, lower than I have ever seen a plane in lower Manhattan. And it was a large plane, I couldn't (cough) identify it as anything specific, except that it was a commercial jet certainly. Um and it, it, my eyes followed it because this is approximately fifteen blocks from the world trade centre and it, it just slammed right into it and it was completely engulfed by the building. It was extraordinary. No wings flew off. Nothing like that. It just went directly in creating this cavern like hole. It reminds you of the worst kinds of effects in movies, but you are reassured that you are watching a movie … that it's an effect, but this is not.

Mark then leaves shortly to 'work the story.' Don't worry Mark the plane was an illusion too, although the explosion and hole were not. It is interesting that Mark describes the airplane, noting that *"It just went directly in creating this cavern like hole. "* It certainly was peculiar how that plane was so completely engulfed as Mark notes, as if produced by movie effects and he is seeing this from fifteen blocks away unobstructed by the buildings of the city! Such a witness is vital to immediately beginning to create the myth of how an airplane actually went *into* the building, lock, stock and barrel, like a movie effect and it conveniently disappears from view.

Back then to CNN, where Dr. Jay Adlersberg is online, a medical reporter for ABC's *Eyewitness News*, who was also downtown at the time.

> I am actually uptown at 86th and Riverside. I can see the World Trade Centre from about half the building up to the top, and about five minutes ago, as I was watching the smoke, er, a small plane, I, it looked like a propeller plane came in from the west, and um, about twenty or twenty five stories below the top of the centre, it disappeared for a second and then exploded, um, behind a water tower so I couldn't tell whether it hit the building or not. But it was very visible that a plane had come in at a low altitude and appeared to crash into the World Trade Centre.

Now we have a small plane, perhaps a propeller plane. Again we find such unusual wording, as *"it was very visible that a plane had come in … and appeared to crash. "*

Another first hand witness was Mark D. Birnbach, a FOX TV employee. The Host opens by asking Mark if he was able to see any markings on the airplane:

> Yea, there was um, there was definitely a blue logo, it was like a circular logo on the front of the plane, towards the, definitely towards the front. Um. It definitely did not look like a commercial plane. I didn't see any windows on the sides and, as far as I knew, when I saw it coming down, I was like, well LaGuardia (the airport) is pretty far

221

away and that plane is really slow, and er definitely it looked very low, and um, I am completely panicked. I am freaking out. I can't believe what I just saw.

Most of these so-called first hand witnesses have peculiar elements in their comments, not only the er's and um's, disjointed sentence structure and repeating elements. Mark says the logo was *"on the front of the plane, towards the, definitely towards the front."* Mark is describing something different from the last witness, *"definitely not a commercial plane."* Note also he describes not seeing *"any windows on the sides,"* as though one could see both sides at once! He does not say that he couldn't see any windows on the side of the airplane, but on the 'sides.'

The problem for such scripted witnesses, in my view, is that they were trying to describe what they haven't really seen but they know approximately what they were supposed to have seen or to report.

Further, it is fine for the news networks to air somewhat conflicting stories and then to resolve the cognitive dissonance produced in viewers over time, by coming to a mutual agreement and story line. However, even in these first hand eyewitness accounts, we have conflicting comments: that this fabled airplane was *"a large passenger commercial jet," "a commercial jet certainly," "a small plane… like a propeller plane"* and *"definitely did not look like a commercial plane."*

To me, none of these are credible witnesses. Although I do think that Mark was freaking out and panicked and couldn't stay on the line, as he was realizing the nature of what he had become involved in and its seriousness. Within the media itself, many witnesses so-called and others are only partially aware of what is unfolding, as part of the necessary compartmentalization and 'need-to-know' strategies routinely used in such staged false flag events.

The *September Clues* series then shifts focus and offers a clip from 41 seconds after the second fabled airplane strike. The news anchor is explaining that "key suspects" come to mind, Osama boogie man Bin Laden and *"who knows what."* This host then has on air another firsthand witness, Eric Shawn, a FOX *TV terror expert and war correspondent,* with connections inside the FBI.

Eric Shawn: I was walking down Fifth Avenue, er, which is close to our studios and I heard a jet, perhaps a 737 or a small airbus, er, flying low, unusually low over Fifth Avenue, making a right. I am not going to er say, I don't know, I don't have any reports on what kind of plane hit the world trade centre. But people looked up and it made a right toward the, toward the building. John, what we just saw though, was obviously if that would be was a second aircraft that hit the,er, the, er southern Tower of the World Trade Centre. That obviously raises the spectre of an intentional terrorist attack, here, if that is indeed what we are looking at. Er, I don't know what the reports say, what type of plane hit the, the Tower, but I did see a er a jet airliner that was fairly low.

This is again peculiar. Eric reports hearing a jet, although he doesn't say he saw it, and then he seems to hear it go right. He describes it as 'making

a right,' as if it were an automobile which can make a turn in seconds. Of course, the fact of a second airplane raised the *'spectre of an intentional terrorist attack'* and Eric was certainly the right man to have *on live as an eye-witness.* As he is giving his report, Fox is listing some of Eric's areas of involvement in covering stories, including the 93 WTC bombings (involving the FBI), the Waco siege, TWA flight 800, the Anthrax Treat, and lastly, but most importantly the *"hunt for Bin Laden."*

O, how clever and cunning. Of course, almost 10 years after 9-11 the FBI still have not issued an arrest warrant for Bin Laden, as no direct evidence of his involvement has ever been produced. (Other than videos of Bin Laden's confession later proven to have been faked by the media with a poor look alike!) But there was Eric Shawn conveniently witnessing the plane somehow, or at least seeing people look up and then summing up that there must be a terrorist attack going on. Eric is a "specialist" probably from a Rockefeller think-tank, who happens to specialize in the *"hunt for Bin Laden."* This is all so phoney and obviously pre-scripted and staged.

September Clues then features additional clips of witnesses of the fabled airplanes, including:

Stewart Nurick- a younger upcoming Jewish waiter/intern at CBS *Early Show*, who states: *"I was literally, I was waiting a table, and I literally saw a, it seemed to me to be a small plane, I just heard a couple of noises, it looked like it bounced off the building. Then I heard, a, I saw a huge like ball of fire on top, and then the smoke seemed to simmer down, and it just um, you know, a lot of smoke was coming out, and then, that's pretty much the extent of what I saw."*

Stewart was 'literally' waiting on a table and then he 'literally saw' a plane. Is Stewart seeing these things on paper or in real life? Then he sees a 'small plane' which 'bounced off the building' and he seems not to see the gaping hole. Stewart is mistaken in numerous elements of his report. When one sees an airplane supposedly at fairly close view, why would it *"seem to be a small plane?"*

Don Dahler, ABC Reporter and War correspondent, on *Good Morning America*, reports:

> *I am about four or five blocks, just North of the World Trade Centre, and, er, about ten, I would say ten minutes ago, fifteen minutes ago, there was a loud sound, that, I can only describe it, it sound like a missile, not an airplane. Then there was a loud explosion and immediately lots of screaming out on the streets. Er, And I don't want to er, cause any speculation, but that's the only way I could describe the sound. …*

This eye-witness suggests the possibility of a missile attack, instead of an airplane attack.

Jim Friedl, an unidentified unknown individual, provides a key element to the creation of the disappearing airplane myth. He is more definite in what he says and saw, especially how the plane *"went directly inside the building."* Jim is featured on CNN on *Good Day America* and left unidentified:

> It was pretty heavily banked, er, maybe 45 degrees, I mean, hard to tell. It was kind of unremarkable because you do see planes fly through here. It was just a large plane, like a 727, and, er, that's the only reason that I kept looking and it went directly right into the building. I thought, you thought, it was going to keep following the river and keep on going, but it didn't.

The Host then questions:

> Now, after the plane struck the building, from your vantage point, it apparently went directly inside.

Jim responds immediately and with authority:

> That's correct.

This is obviously scripted and peculiar, not possibly believable. Was there really nothing remarkable about a large airplane banking so sharply in downtown New York. And then, Jim describes it as just entering *"directly right inside the building"* as if there is nothing remarkable about that, but he is more concerned with his prior expectation, which had been that it would just fly up the river. Obviously, Jim was playing a role and planting the seed idea of the plane just popping handily into the building. He was more authoritative and professional than poor old Mark who was freaking out.

Dick Oliver, a reporter from the street, is on line with *NY Good Day* and provides another angle on the day's events for Fox.

> Jim, I don't know if we have confirmed it, if this was an aircraft, or, to be more specific some people said they *thought they saw a missile. But I don't know how people could differentiate but we might leave open the possibility that this was a missile attack on these buildings.*

Yes, Dick is playing this exact role—to *"leave open the possibility that this was a missile attack."* That is why Dick reports people saying it sounded like a missile, to leave open this possibility, just as the waiter, who was literally waiting, kept open the possibility of a small plane bouncing off the building. It is fine for initial reports of an event to have such incongruities and such, which creates cognitive dissonance and uncertainty in the public's mind about what is happening. The TV media can then present its final formative conclusions and people gloss over all the inconsistencies and absurdities of what they were actually being told along the way. The conspiracy theorists can debate over whether it was an airplane or a missile, instead of layered images in TV video studios and a pool of scripted witnesses. Yes, a passenger airplane flew directly right into the building and disappeared from view. The formative conclusions of the media can resolve the dissonance in viewers, as when our terrorism expert pops up 15 seconds after the second fabled airplane to start planting the seeds or *memes* in the public's mind that they are under attack by Muslim extremists. And Eric is an authority of course, an expert on *"the hunt for Bin Laden."*

In the next moment, Dick is immediately corrected by news anchor, Jim Ryan, who explains:

> All, I must say that, er, we have an eyewitness who said it was a large plane, that crashed first, and, then, as we were watching the live picture here at the studio, we *saw* a plane crash into, crash into the other Tower of the World Trade Centre. And again, let's, er, just to be sure, "There it is. The plane went right through the other tower of the World Trade Centre.

While Jim Ryan is saying this, CNN is replaying the original clip of the 'nose out shot,' but it is obscured by their banner so that you can't see anything to confirm an airplane. Your news media can tell you what you are seeing without even showing it!

The next clip is of Jane Derenowski, an MSNBC producer, who claims to have seen the first plane, which she describes:

> Well, it looked, it wasn't a Cesnna or anything like that. It was a larger plane, a mid-sized plane and we could hear it very low, and, er … (trails off on *September Clues*)

Next, is Elliot Walker, an NBC News Producer, a term most appropriate—a news *producer,* and several others—as witnesses to one or both of the airplane crashes.

The *September Clues* series then provides a listing of those eye-witnesses who reported hearing and/or seeing one or more of the fabled airplane crashes and who told their tall tales *live* on TV. These included:

> Sean Murtagh — CNN Vice President of Finance
> Mark Obenhaus, -- ABC Senior Producer
> Owen Moogan — Fox Senior Producer
> Sid Bedingfield — CNN Executive Vice President
> Richard Davis — CNN Executive Vice President new Standards and Practices

Rose Arce – CNN Producer
Jeanne Yurman – CNN reporter
Winston Mitchell – ABC/CNN Producer
Eric Shawn – FOX TV Senior Correspondent
Jennifer Oberstein – Ritz-Carleton Hotels/NBC tour operator
Jane Derenowski – MSNBC Producer
Dr. Jay Adlersberg – ABC medical reporter
Elliot Walker – NBC NEWS reporter
Theresa Renaud – wife of CBS producer Jack Renaud
(the Early Show)
Mark D. Birnbach — FOX TV employee
Mike Walter — USA Today Reporter
Joel Sucherman – USA Today.com Editor
Steve Anderson – USA Today, dir. of communications
Fred Gaskins – USA Today national editor
Jim Friedl (unidentified)

This is quite a listing of corporate media executives, producers and reporters. The only exceptions are Jennifer Oberstein, who worked for a Hotel associated with NBC tours, and Jim Friedl, an unknown, a defining witness to the fabled airplane disappearing into the building.

Of course, the *September Clues* series is only presenting brief samples of material from media coverage and it is most certain that if we could access and analyze all the clips and tall tales of the day, we would likely find all kinds of additional anomalies. Every witness seems fraudulent one way or another in what they are reporting, in their language and details. Certainly, the 'fabled airplanes' were eye-witnessed *live on-line* that fateful day of 9-11 by quite a clan of primarily *media insiders*, news reporters and producers, some on the way up we might say.

The eye-witness testimony to the quantum airplanes, which are large, midsized, small and like a missile and entering directly into the building, while bouncing off it, and all such non-sense, simply cannot stand as credible documentation for a fabled airplane. It is much more likely that it is all contrived, intentionally deceptive so as to create conflicting stories, but then to arrive at the official account to be illustrated over and over again with the best bits of the video image pools. The witnesses are simply not credible in their descriptions, their speech and stories. Of course, the media's attitude is likely that all the uncertainties will simply be forgotten and left for the conspiracy theorists, who can argue over missiles, airplanes or what type of craft it was.

17 Seconds

Part E of the *September Clues* series (which begins at 41.45 seconds into the 1.31 hours) is entitled *17 Seconds* and it features an analysis of strange bleeps and sound markers on different network sound tracts, which suggest co-ordinated timing between studios. There are several instances of this.

The 17 seconds refers to the time between the official 9/11 commission time of the second explosion established at 9:03:11 and the seismic data which recorded the explosion at 9:02:54. The film editor suggests that the TV airing time was thus delayed by 17 seconds compared with the real events—a 'safeguard buffer' between the actual events and the TV airing.

All five networks had synchronized audio clues which occurred 17 seconds before the moment of the explosion in the South Tower.

The first of these shown occurs during the ABC coverage with guest Dan Dahler online. It occurs just as Dahler is saying "we're seeing," which is 17 seconds before the visible explosion in the South Tower. Don is 'on scene' and describing the fire and smoke from the first explosion in the North Tower. One wonders why there is no background noise from Don's phone or evidence of the explosion in the South Tower. After the explosion, the TV host states, "That looks like a second plane," which the audience has just seen on the video. However, Dan Dahler actually states, *"I did not see a plane go in, that just exploded."* Of course, Dan did not likely know what was unfolding and naively described his actual ongoing perception of the scene. He was there and he did not see an airplane, but only an explosion. The staff at the ABC network were able to see an airplane however, along with the viewing audience.

The film editor then compares the ABC video of the 17 seconds before the explosion with the FOX TV footage. Fox has a 'audio surge' which matches

the ABC's Twin Beep in synch, duration and spacing. He then compares
ABC & CBS, which are sharing at times, offset camera feeds, and the CBC
audio surge again matches the ABC twin beep in synch, duration and
spacing. However, the video streams are off about 3.6 seconds. Next, the
ABC coverage is compared with CNN, where again the images and cues are
offset by 2.5 seconds, but both again have audio clues at the beginning and
end of a 17 second timeframe. In this case, there are synchronized 'snap
sounds' at the ends of these clips. NBC then has 'a glitch' at the beginning
of the 17 seconds, which glitch is caused by sloppy video editing. ABC and
NBC then have identical 'slam' sounds at the end of the seventeen second
period.

To explain these peculiar observations and the coincidental sound surges
or sound markers at the beginning and ends of these clips, the film editor
asks if indeed ABC, CBS, FOX, CNN AND NBC were all five linked up. Or,
of course, these could be multiple coincidences for the coincident theorists,
but it suggests something far more sinister. The film editor asks, *"Was the
9/11 TV coverage run from a single Command Center?"* Certainly, given the
complexity of the hoax perpetrated on 9-11, this was likely so.

Part E of *September Clues* then notes that the reason given for the BLACK
OUT of all the local TV stations was because the antennae were on the
World Trade Centre. This knocked all local live TV coverage off the
air. The editor concludes: *"No airplanes were highjacked on 9/11, ONLY
AIRWAYS." September Clues* then plays a *"curious audio incident on Fox TV."*
While the show is ongoing, a side communication is clearly heard. A man's
voice asks, *"Grade 9, Chopper 5, anyone on?"* Chopper 5 refers to the Fox
News Helicopter 5. The Grade E-9 is a US Navy ranking of a "Master-Chief
Petty Officer." This segment ends with the editor's comment: *"Let's leave it
at that."*

9/11's COLOURFUL TV broadcasts and Mask Edges

Part E next illustrates the multicoloured backgrounds and videos broadcast on TV that day in New York, which was a bright sunny day. The corporate media TV images differed in tones as the white balance and colour settings were so varied. High-end equipment can maintain the natural colours of scenes, however not on that fateful day. Instead, the scenes range from yellowed, to grey, purple, and blue hazes. The TV networks had different colours despite having similar vantage points. Five different networks, five or more different colours.

The ABC *"international shot"* of the second fabled airplane, shown to international audiences, clearly presents phoney images. Firstly, the edge of the Tower about to be impacted is artificial and unnatural looking, with a partial visible edge extending along the length of the building. The airplane image is somewhat distinct in shape, showing basic structures, but it is a most unnatural solid dark object with no markings or differentiations. It is

really quite a ridiculous image of an artificial airplane. Further, it is on a blue and grey hazy background with no resolution of the city or skyline behind. When this image of the airplane meets the artificial edge of the Tower, on particular frames there is still a slight line of light between the Tower and the airplane, even though the plane is supposed to simply be going into the Tower. At one point, the nose of the plane is cut off when it meets these edges. This is an obvious fake. The airplane image and the Tower images are somehow on different portions of the screen or on different layers. This is a ridiculously phoney image of a fabled airplane. Another version of the same shot has a dark border along the edge of the towers, perhaps to obscure the details noted above. However, this other version of the international shot has the airplane causing pixel bleed on the Tower as it is supposedly passing behind. These are not even good fakes.

Of course, why would there be any need for any fakery if there were indeed real airplanes. Also, if we have an image of a fake airplane hitting the South Tower, we do not see any other evidence of a real airplane on that video, or a missile. How anyone could believe that the ABC international shot is not phoney is beyond me. Of course, most people don't care for evidences anymore, as they simply parrot what they are told on their favourite TV's. An international audience of 200 million views were shown this ABC international shot through *EuroNews*. The film editor notes, *"Overall however, most shots betray unmistakable signs of tampering."* Of course, none of this would have been necessary if there had been a legitimate airplane. Further, some of the unusual effects of the masked edges may have been used to obscure the explosions going off within the building, or according to the film editor, to mask a possible missile. One way or another, the images are clearly doctored with unusual features needing to be accounted for.

The film editor then illustrates one of his own productions of a bat-mobile, with Bat Man and Robin passing behind the Tower, just as the plane was shown to do in the corporate media footage. He actually does a better job than the former, with no pixel bleed.

Part E ends on the note, *Turn it Off*, referring of course to your own favourite TV. The images of both the planes and the Towers are doctored in multiple ways.

Forged Out—
The Amateur Videos

Part F of the *September Clues* series then examines additional 'amateur videos' and provides some information about the people who submitted these to the authorities. The film editor suggests that the 'live shots' were likely not to be replayed too frequently, all 15 seconds worth, but afterwards, the media released other versions of their own shots in addition to a rash of amateur videos which emerged after the event. These provided the most dramatic views of "the airplane crash." However, these show all kinds of media manipulation and anomalies.

The first EVAN FAIRBANKS shot is taken from below the South Tower, framed with the upper profile of a passer-by in the foreground, who looks up towards the Tower in the clip just after the explosion. The airplane is more naturally coloured, light and grey and fairly distinct. The airplane slides ever so nicely into the building without any seeming resistance or evidence of breaking apart. This clip produced a dramatic *"shock and awe"* TV experience.

The film editor then begins to examine the possibility of there having been a missile and how it might have been edited out and a plane inserted. However, personally, although I do not consider the 'missile possibility' completely disproved, I consider it highly unlikely and unnecessary. What is simplest is simply to have explosions and create the varied airplane images over recordings of the actual explosions from different angles. Anyway, the editor suggests this first clip could have been created in a four step process: 1. Tower shot with real missile strike is filmed from a suitable location; 2. foreground street scenery is composed; 3. Tower shot is inserted with a reacting man to add some 'life' to the scene. *September Clues* shows the layered edges existing between the foreground and the

Tower background, wherein the hues and lighting effects betray tampering; and 4. the superposition of an airplane image over the supposed missile. It is then shown how the plane enters the building so smoothly with no deceleration on impact.

The producer of this video was amateur Evan Fairbanks of KSK Studios, whose vita describes his talents as *"Creative programming solutions for television, interactive and multimedia;"* certainly, a lucky man to have on the spot.

The second amateur video is credited to Luc Courchesne, a Canadian 3D artist. This is another dramatic video from right underneath the airplane and the image of the plane is quite distinct, although its wings appear to be at impossible angles. By the time this plane hits the building, it is almost completely upside down and then one of its wings disappears from view even before there is yet a hole in the Tower. Then it seems to have a quarter wing section as it slips inside. The left wing then disappears inside, but still no hole and no wing! Mr Luc Courchesne happens to be the inventor of the *"Panoscope 3E"*, a virtual reality program. Somehow, Mr Courchesne's program must allow for such quantum tunnelling effects, whereby an airplane wing can disappear into a building without obstruction. This is all quite clever but again quite ridiculous.

The next *"Hezarkhani shot"* has another dramatic shot of the fabled airplane, again with a fairly distinct airplane image, although its left wing also

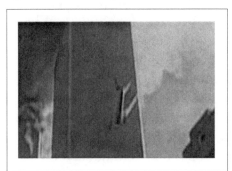

disappears before impact. Frames of this picture also show synchronized explosions occurring above and below the right wing as the plane enters into the building. In fact, there is evidence of multiple charges synched with the strike on both Towers.

The series then reviews additional 'amateur videos' and the 'alleged authors.' The first was filmed by Clifton Cloud of Scharff Weisberg' audio-video services; then by Scott Myers, a video/software engineer for ABC TV-US Navy; Naka Nathaniel, of the New York Times, a multimedia journalist; Devin Clark, a motion graphics animator at MTV/Comedy Central; Sean Adair, of Adair Film & Video Productions, a *"consultant in the arcane arts of digital media and visual effects;"* Kelly Guenther, a Pulitzer-winning NYT photojournalist; Robert Clark, a photographer for National Geographic; Jennifer Spell, a director/producer at SPELLBOUND pictures; Gulnara Samoilova, Associated Press photo retoucher, shown with Mayor Guiliani; and Thomas Nilsson, photojournalist for Norweigian populist tabloid "Yerdens Gang," All of these shots, each of which is shown, are credited to professionals in the photo/video/newsmedia industry! All contributed to the image pool to be drawn upon by the TV and printed media sources.

Dr. K. Kahleel, in his article *Brainwashed: Proof of No Airplanes on 9-11,* provides interesting notes on some of these *'men on the street'* who were the sources for some of the so-called amateur videos. Dr. K. notes:

> When videographer and Israeli diamond dealer and Zionist mole Michael Hezakhani was asked how he could have possibly created a plane video and where and when he took it, he said, *"Call my lawyer."*

> When videographer Scott Freeman was asked repeatedly about the nature of his video, he said, essentially, *"I don't want to talk about it anymore."*

> When the pro-Zionist documentary film maker, Scott Meyers, who makes videos which demonize Muslims, was asked about his incriminating video, he responded, *"A guy gave it to me, can't remember his name."*

> When videographer Evan Fairbanks was asked about the nature of his supposed video, he said it looked *"surreal,"* like a fame made in Hollywood."

What more can one say. The corporate media and Hollywood do indeed have all kinds of resources to perpetrate exactly the public deception of such 'fabled airplanes.'

234

Part E then examines three different shots all variations of a "common matrix," by three different authors: Wolfgang Staehle, Robert Clark and Tina Cart. These three shots are from the same perspective, but in each case, the first provides the widest angle view, then the second, and third, but all from the same perspective but framed differently!

The film editor then includes these comments on screen: *All alleged authors of the "AMATEUR" shots would be suitable scapegoats in the event that any of those forgeries were exposed. All could credibly be blamed for having sought fame or fortune Ð and the case would be closed. In fairness, there was one exception to the rule. His name is PAVEL HLAYA, a construction worker from Czechoslovakia."* A clip then shows Pavel on an ABC news show on September 11, 2003. He is introduced as an individual who happened to film both airplanes striking the Towers on that day, although he had not realized it for over six months. The first shot was a distant view of an object in the sky before the first strike and the second of his shots was from close under the Towers. However, as it happens, in this strange universe, his 2nd shot is a re-edit of the Hezarkhani shot, although with different foreground buildings! Again, the Towers have the same unusual frame edges on them.

The editor then provides a quotation from the site www.mediacen.navy:mil/vi/comcam.htm. *"Totally imagery control of any terrain is a primary sector of modern warfare."* Of course, most common folk could not imagine anything so monstrous and deceptive. But the editor points out that *"Fake broadcasting for war propaganda has several historical precedents. Its purpose is to generate popular support for waging mean and unpalatable wars."* Of course, there were many reasons why the targets for 9-11 were as selected. Not only was this a false flag terrorist event to whip up the frenzy and patriotic fervour of the public, but it was also to get rid of those monstrous buildings. Previous applications for controlled demolitions of the Two Towers had been rejected and the city was demanding the removal of the asbestos from the buildings, a massive and expensive project. 9-11 events were also staged to destroy evidences at the at the Navel Accounting unit in the Pentagon and as held in Building 7 by the Securities and Exchange Commission, the FBI and CIA, on Wall Street crimes and racketeering. There were diverse and multiple reasons why 9-11 unfolded as it did and how the media shaped the minds of the sleeping public as to the course of events. Few people realize that the corporate media play active roles in staging, scripting and covering over the crimes of their masters.

Hoax for Export

Part G begins at 1:01 and is ten minutes in length. It includes varied subject matter and clips under the rubric of *hoax for export*.

The film editor opens section G with the comment: "*We have seen how missiles were most likely used on 9/11*" and that this raises two questions. I would like to comment here again, that I do not agree with this suggestion and it is not established by the *September Clues* video and media analysis. Certainly, there is more of a possibility of a missile than there was of an airplane, but neither are required if you have some video technicians, supportive actors and actresses, and planted charges.

Anyway, the first question is: What happened to the 4 airplanes and their passengers? In fact, according to the Federal Aviation Association, Flight 93, which supposedly was downed in a hole in Shanksville, and Flight 175, which supposedly hit the South Tower, were only deregistered on September 28th of 2005. Of course, we have reviewed over a dozen of the varied videos of something, a quantum airplane exploring different flight paths, colours, shapes and sounds, simultaneously, and then hitting the South Tower. And now, we find out that this fabled airplane was not decommissioned until four years latter. Further, it turns out that no airport logs exist for the other 2 airplanes, Flight 11 which was supposed to have flown into the North Tower to disappear inside, so nice and cozy; and Flight 77 which was the flight to *'fold back it wings'* before disappearing into the hole at the Pentagon. These flights are not even recorded in the airport logs of the day! This is a somewhat remarkable fact. The film then questions, what happened to their passengers, but if none of the planes were high jacked, then something else must have been done or arrangements made.

The film doesn't explore this issue but moves on to ask: *Didn't people see a large plane from street level?* The answer provided is that *"SOME DID (a small minority"* and a web address at www.checktheevidence.com (911/ NYT9-11AccountsAnalysis). There is some video evidence of fly-by jets in the area and several witnesses reported a missile.

The international shot shown most around the world originated from the *Live ABC* broadcast. This is a ridiculously phoney shot of an airplane and it has the anomalies along the edges of the Towers — the *mask edges*, as they are called. This forgery came in varied versions and on one, there was a pitch black band running the full length of the Tower, which is most unnatural. When the airplane image hits this band, you see pixel bleed caused by the airplane image on the edge of the Tower. This is quite absurd. This black mask edge version was actually shown in Japan on the day of 9-11.

September Clues then critically examines the Naudet brothers' videos. These two French Canadian videographers, Jules and Gedeon, managed to capture both impacts of the fabled airplanes. In fact, it is the only video of the first impact, other than the very distant image which turned up years later on Pavel's camera. Their most famous shot of the first airplane is shown briefly but without much discussion. A number of features of this video are somewhat peculiar. Firstly, the fireman walking across the scene looks up towards the sky as if hearing something, but then he simply looks back down again. Of course, in a real life emergency situation, such a dramatic airplane spotting in downtown New York is bound to engage an observer's attention. Secondly, it is very odd how the film maker is able to zoom in on the plane and follow it into the Tower, as though he knew all along what its path was supposed to be. Of course, the airplane in this video is also of very poor quality and it also enters swiftly into the building with no obvious obstruction or break up.

The Naudet brothers' video of the second impact caught only an instant of a dark shape moving towards the South Tower on the opposite side of the building from their vantage point. This is a very disjointed clip as the camera dances around before and after the impact. Further, there are 3 unexplained cuts in the footage of the dramatic moments. By comparing their video with other sequences of the event, the film editor is able to determine that almost 30 frames are deleted. Further, their video shows the north face of the South Tower as completely white, on the shaded side of the building, as it is seen in other clips. This is clearly a fraud.

> These video fabrications were the very core of the 9/11 TV hoax. The corporate news media has proactively supported this global scam bred in rogue power circles. Beyond the clear evidence of video doctoring, a close scrutiny of the 9/11 TV archives reveals a consistent pattern of FOREKNOWLEDGE and SCRIPTED NEWSCASTS.

Part E then looks as some of the foreign footage which suggests such foreknowledge and scripted newscasts. The first on BBC world has a newscaster lecturing Great Britain on the physics of the buildings collapse, claiming wrongly that the exterior walls of this building supported its weight, instead of interior columns. The airplane crashes were thus able to weaken the buildings enough to cause their collapse.

Next is the most famous video of the BBC Live broadcast where the collapse of Building 7 is being reported, while the building itself is still visible and standing in the background. Of course, Building 7 was not even hit by an airplane and no steel framed building in the history of humanity had ever previously fallen in under 6 seconds into its own footprint, due to 'fires' in this case. Reporter Jane Standley is describing the collapse of the building even before it has occurred—of course, because she was scripted as were all the fine actors and actresses in this tragic-comedy. In fact, this was 20 minutes before its collapse—a feat for which of course, BBC has never had to account. This is similar to how other reporters describe the second Tower as collapsing before it showed any evidence of such. The Tower is described as in a state *"of near collapse,"* before anything like this is visible. Another reporter describes the Second Tower as *"almost collapsing there"* while it is still standing perfectly erect.

The film script reminds us that *"we live in an Orwellian world."*

Part H (1:11) begins with a collage of 9/11 shots with all the discoloured backdrops and artificial scenes put to music. It then shows varied shots of the Towers against different backdrops, but where the backdrops seem to move with respect to the building. Obviously, different kinds of image layering have being used. Such is evident in varied shots, where parts of the surrounds are whitened out, while others maintain some realistic details. It is as if the scenes were composed with different foregrounds and backgrounds being added as layers in the final results.

They then demonstrate how even the collapse sequences appear to have been tampered with. The editor notes: *"The variety of the video trickery was designed to bewilder any comparative analysis of it."* This certainly applies to some of what were supposed to have been helicopter shots, which show numerous kinds of anomalies, suggesting even the use of digitally simulated buildings. All quite a hodgepodge to be sure.

The Epilogue

Finally, the *Epilogue,* addresses five major questions. The first concerns the eyewitnesses on the streets of Manhattan. As it happens, the vast majority of witnesses did not report a large passenger plane. *September Clues* then plays a sampling of such witnesses claiming to have seen the plane—all seemingly quite contrived and questionable, and then clips where the witnesses claimed to see a missile.

The second question asks: *"What if someone had snapped a clear picture of a missile hitting the WTC?"* It is then noted that *"all New York cell-phones blacked out on 9/11."* The official cause given was network overload. No digital pictures then. Secondly, as reported on Italian TV, police officer Michael Pappas recounted that during his call on duty within the first hours of 9/11, they entered a store which had developed films with people's names on in alphabetical order. A sign they viewed, read *"Pick up at September 11 at 10:00 AM."* The New York Police had been collecting people's film rolls in the early hours of the attack! How clever of them.

The third frequently asked question concerns what caused those wide airplane shaped holes in the Towers? The answer is suggested by varied videos which show synchronized explosions within the Towers. This is evident in the clip of the first strike and in a number of clips of the second.

The forth frequently asked question, concerns where are the airplanes? The video shows then parts of planes, supposedly, held at the Smithsonian Institute or as scattered on the street—but nothing substantive from any of the four sites.

Lastly, what about the families of the passengers? Apparently 3 of the 4 flights were bound for the LAX, Los Angeles airport, but *"It is a FACT that grieving families and friend never showed up at the LAX."* This could have included the friends and family of 221 passengers. A reporter on scene at the LAX reports that such survivors were "beginning to trickle in," just at this moment, but none are evident within the newscast. The announcer then notes that LAX was being evacuated and shut down except for emergency services. Of course, there was no need to accommodate grieving families and friends.

Evidence for Airplanes or a Criminal Media?

The more closely one examines the evidences for airplanes, the evidences slip away like sand in a sieve, to leave nothing substantive or conclusive. Instead, one finds massive evidences for fraud, staged witnesses and soundtracks, half-competent image layering techniques, and for conspiracies to commit mass murder. The corporate media has intentionally helped to *'stage'* these events while deceiving the world's public.

The corporate media of America helped to create the mythology of high jacked airplanes causing the explosions within the Two Towers, and subsequently of causing the buildings to blow up and collapse. The fabled airplanes were just another link in the whole series of absurdities expounded as part of the 9-11 mythology.

There are many within the corporate media willing to mass murder their countrymen if it will advance their careers, earn them sexual favours, or line those fancy pants with lots of that American blood money.

Concerning the criminal evidence against the corporate news media for their involvement in staging 9-11, the *September Clues* series clearly documents that the corporate media of America actually helped to carry out the 9-11 false flag terrorist event. They actually conspired together and co-ordinated it all with an army of media men and women, and elements through the corrupted intelligence, police and military communities of America. What a sad state of affairs and this criminally corrupted media daily spins its propaganda and deceptions.

Who Owns the Media?

To address this issue, I will quote portions of an article published by Texe Marrs, dated May 5, 2009 and entitled: *Do the Jews Own Hollywood and the Media?* Marrs is most direct in getting to the core of the issue, although he does not go into much detail concerning all of the specifics of who these individuals and companies are that constitute the corporate media. (For individuals who are interested in this issue, there are numerous internet research articles addressing this issue.) However, Marrs gets to the crux of the matter in his notes. He begins by asking:

> Do the Zionist Jews own Hollywood and the media? Are they using the media to mold and shape American opinion by constantly injecting Zionist propaganda and bias into news programs, movies, television shows, even children's cartoons and entertainment?

In a subsection entitled, *What do Knowledgeable Jews Say?*, he notes:

> How about going to top Jews in the media themselves and see what they say? Take Joel Stein, for example, columnist for the Los Angeles Times newspaper and regular contributor to Time magazine. In his column in the LA Times (Dec. 19, 2008), Stein says that Americans who think the Jews do not control Hollywood and the media are just plain "dumb."

> *"Jews totally run Hollywood."* Stein proudly admits. He then goes on to provide a long, long list of Hollywood/media chieftains—all Jews!—to prove his point. On his list, Fox ... Paramount Pictures ... "Walt Disney ... Sony Pictures ... Warner Brothers ... CBS ... MGM ...NBC/Universal Studios ... (I have excluded the specific names from Marrs's listing, but these were the company associations).

> *"As a proud Jew,"* says Joel Stein, *"I want America to know of our accomplishment. Yes, we control Hollywood."*

> Stein says he then called Abe Foxman, Chairman of the Jewish ADL, to ask him, why don't more Jews just come out and boast at this great accomplishment? Foxman responded by admitting that yes, it's

true that most of the top execs *"happen to be Jewish."* In fact, Foxman told Stein, *"all eight major film studios are run by men who happen to be Jewish."*

Ben Stein ... the well-known Jewish actor, economic and writer, when asked *"Do Jews run Hollywood?"* stared blankly at the questioner, then retorted, *"You bet they do—and what of it?"*

Shahar Ilan, writing in haaretz.com, the internet division of Israel's top daily newspaper, commented, *"The Jews do control the American media. This is very clear, and claiming otherwise is an insult to common knowledge."* ...

So powerful is the Jewish control over the media that Nathanael Kapner, a rare Jew who converted to Christianity and now is adept at reporting these things, asserts that no longer can we trust our local daily newspaper. Zionist Jews have taken over the 'local newspaper' in America," Kapner writes.

However, the problem is not simply that Jews have come to dominate the media throughout North America, as elsewhere, but further, as Marrs notes in his next section, *Jewish Media Spew Out Pro-Zionist Propaganda:*

The fact that Zionists control virtually every media outlet in America is no doubt why the American citizenry hears only one version of events in the Middle East—the pro Jew, pro-Israel side. This led Dr. Kevin MacDonald, professor at California State University to write:

"In the contemporary world, organized American Jewish lobbying groups and deeply committed Jews in the media are behind the pro-Israel U. S. foreign policy that is leading to war against virtually the entire Arab world."

This Zionist bias and propaganda spin by the Jewish-owned American media is not new. ...

... Time magazine, Newsweek, NBC, ABC, CBS, CNN, FOX—and many more are all owned or run by Jews and operated solely to further the aims of the traitorous, anti-American, ever growing Zionist World Empire.

All America is in the Grip of the Hidden, Red Iron Fist of Zionism

Of course, the media, even as important as it is to our culture, is
only a bit piece of the whole that is now, regrettably, under the big
thumbs of the Jewish Zionist elite. Our educational establishment,
Wall Street, the banks, the Federal Reserve, our Congress, the White
House …, and our judiciary—each and every one is infiltrated by
Zionist radicals who put Israel and their own "Chosen People" first,
to the detriment of everything sacred to honest, God-fearing, hard-
working Americans.

The news media owned by primarily Jewish or Zionist New World Order
folk, on that day of 9-11, helped to stage the mass murders of fellow
planetary citizens, all while blaming it on radical Muslims, and as a pretext
for waging imperialist wars against the sovereign nations of Afghanistan and
then Iraq.

This same Zionist media is even now *pimping* their next war—against Iran,
justifying it all as a question of self-defence, with fabricated evidences
and all kinds of experts to talk of the threat to civilization posed by radical
Islam. What a joke this would be, if it were not all so tragic: After almost
two million murdered, millions more injured, orphaned and desolate, and
a land desecrated by war crimes and depleted uranium, and robbed of its
wealth. And all based on lies—the lies of fabled airplanes slipping ever so
swiftly into buildings and disappearing from view. What a world of deceit,
hatefulness and madness these Zionists have concocted for human kind.
And, who could possibly be more radical, more homicidal and genocidal,
than those Zionist Jews wanting to create their new world nightmare for
humankind upon this planet. However, as the motto of the Israeli Mossad
suggests: *"By means of deception, we wage war."* Oh, how cunning and
clever of the corporate media to aid in the scripting, illustrating and staging
of 9-11.

Do the Media do their Job?

I often hear people comment that they don't think that the media *'do their job.'* This would make me laugh if it were not all so tragic, because, of course the media do *'do their job.'* The problem is simply that people don't understand what the actual role of the corporate media is—what their job is. Their job is not to enlighten or inform the American public, but to deceive and mislead them, to brainwash them with propaganda and lies, and to hide all the crimes of the elites being committed daily against the citizenry of the US, and indeed, against peoples around the world. And the media do a very good job doing just this—deceiving the public, as they did on that fateful day of 9-11.

The corporate media is well designed to deceive the American public concerning all major national and international events on a daily basis, to enable the war crimes of the American people against other nations around the world over the past fifty years; to enable the elites to poison the population through inoculations, GM foods, chemtrails and psychotronic weapons, while the masses remain completely unaware; and to sell such things as financial bailouts so that the financial elites can impoverish America in their game of madman Monopoly.

Because of the media, we have a nation asleep, a nation of sleepwalkers, of sheep, of hypnotized soul-less creatures, controlled by psychopathic elites willing to deceive their fellow countrymen, bear false witness and commit mass murders—and all while making it appear so noble and good.

Reclaiming America: Application of the Anti-Terrorist Legislation to the Corporate Media

Since 9-11, the countries of the world have enacted anti-terrorist legislation allowing any country to seize the assets of any individuals involved in terrorist activities. 9-11 was a terrorist act. The people behind it have conspired to mass murder their countryman, to deceive the public and then to engage in horrendous war crimes against foreign peoples and nations. Imagine if America were ever able to really enforce its own laws and bring about true justice to those who perpetrated the 9-11 events; the same so-called elites who daily commit other criminal and terrorist activities against both American and world citizens. To seize the assets of the perpetrators of the 9-11 crimes and their networks would likely resolve the debt of the United States of America and bring about a new age of health, wealth, human rights and justice. The crimes of the elites will someday be documented by that same media which they have fashioned for the destruction of American society and of all spiritual values on this sacred planet Earth. How cunning of them, to concoct such fabled airplanes!

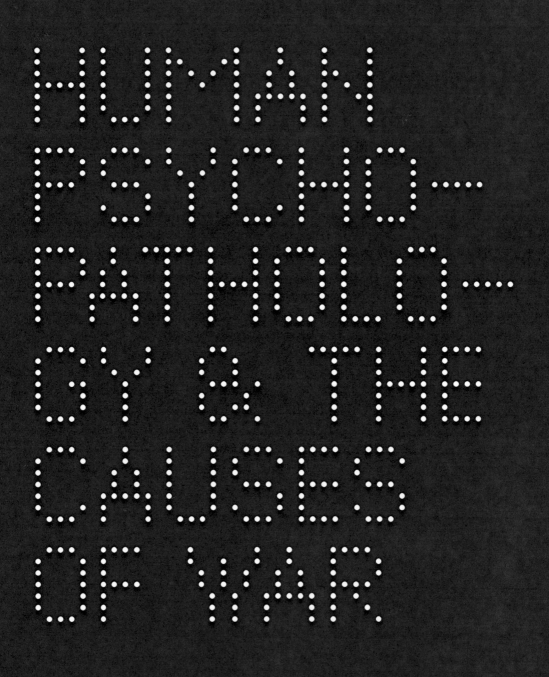

HUMAN PSYCHO-
PATHOLO-
GY & THE
CAUSES
OF WAR

"I must tell you that the chief particularity of the psyche of your favorites, namely, the 'periodic-need-to-destroy-the-existence-of-others-like-oneself,' interested me more and more with every succeeding century of theirs, and side by side with it the irresistible desire increased in me to find out the exact causes of a particularity so phenomenal for three-brained beings."

G. I. Gurdjieff, Beelzebub's Tales to His Grandson, 1950, (p. 318)

The Strange Psyche[11]
& Psychopathology of Your Favorites

This selection of material on human psychopathology and the causes of war is from *The Slugs*, an exposition of the masterful story of mystic G. I. Gurdjieff, *Beelzebub's Tales to His Grandson* (1950).

At the turn of the century, G. I. Gurdjieff (1872-1949) and a group of individuals, who called themselves the *"seekers after truth,"* attempted to piece together a system of ancient, esoteric knowledge about the origins, nature and purpose of life on Earth. As a result of his search, Gurdjieff came into contact with the fourth way, an esoteric teaching which he dates to *pre-Egyptian times*. Gurdjieff once responded to a student's inquiry

---

[11] The opening illustration, *Guernica* is by Pablo Picasso, hangs at the United Nations building in New York City, U. S. A. An interesting historic note is provided online:

> "In an act with extraordinary historical resonance, United Nations officials covered up a tapestry reproduction of Pablo Picasso's anti-war mural *"Guernica"* during US Secretary of State Colin Powell's February 5 presentation of the American case for war against Iraq.

> Picasso's painting commemorates a small Basque village bombed by German forces in April 1937 during the Spanish Civil War. The painter, in desolate black, white and grey, depicts a nightmarish scene of men, women, children and animals under bombardment. The twisted, writhing forms include images of a screaming mother holding a dead child, a corpse with wide-open eyes and a gored horse. Art historian Herbert Read described the work as "a cry of outrage and horror amplified by a great genius."

> The reproduction has hung outside the Security Council chamber at UN headquarters in New York since its donation by the estate of Nelson A. Rockefeller in 1985. As the council gathered to hear Powell on Wednesday, workers placed a blue curtain and flags of the council's member countries in front of the tapestry. (http://www.wsws.org/articles/2003/feb2003/guer-f08.shtml)

It is interesting to note the all-seeing eye of the Illuminati portrayed in Picasso's masterpiece, hanging over the war scene. Wars are the human sacrifices of the Illuminati and such Hasnamusses as the plutocrats, the power-possessing beings and the 'stock jugglers.'

concerning the origins of the fourth way by stating that: *"if you like, this is esoteric Christianity."* (1949, p. 102) However, Gurdjieff then explained that Christian forms of worship and teachings were themselves borrowed from earlier pre-Egyptian times: *"... only not from the Egypt that we know but from one which we do not know. This Egypt was in the same place as the other but it existed much earlier. Only small bits of it survived in historical times, and these bits have been preserved in secret and so well that we do not even know where they have been preserved."* (1949, p. 02) [12]

Beelzebub's Tales are written in an extremely strange and challenging fashion—a remarkable work that defies easy reading, classification or understanding. Even the setting of the *Tales* is out of the ordinary as the story is told from a cosmic, extraterrestrial perspective—as befits a work of such otherworldly aspirations and dimensions. The central figure and narrator, Beelzebub, is traveling through the cosmos on the spaceship Karnak. To pass the time and to fulfill his *"being obligations"* to his grandson Hassein, Beelzebub takes the opportunity to educate Hassein concerning the laws of the cosmos and the strange psyche of the three-brained beings on planet Earth— all while recounting his six visits to the planet earth while Beelzebub and his kinsmen had taken up residence on the planet Mars. Beelzebub explains the abnormalities of the Earth's inhabitants, those strange *"three-brained beings on planet Earth,"* while portraying in great detail the peculiarities of the human psyche and the history of their ill-fated solar system *"Ors."*

According to Beelzebub, the three-brained beings on planet earth had developed quite abnormally, due to varied cosmic catastrophes. They had actually come to *"perceive reality topsy-turvy"* and to be totally conditioned by *"sensations of 'pleasure' and 'enjoyment.'"* Beelzebub describes this *"perceiving reality topsy-turvy"* as taking the *"ephemeral for the real,"* as contemporary three-brained beings have *"most artistically mechanized themselves to see nothing real."* (p. 85) The strange psyche of those unfortunate beings has become dual, with what should be their real consciousness, which includes

---

[12] A recent news item, reported by *The Associated Press*, announced *"Archaeologists discover 2,500-year-old lost cities."* The report states that archaeologists had found "an intact city" submerged in water only six to nine metres deep off the northern coast of Egypt. The ruins are theorized to have been build during the waning days of the pharaohs in the 7th or 6th century B.C.. The secretary general of the Supreme Council of Antiquities, Egypt's top archaeology body, describes the find as *"the most exciting find in the history of marine archaeology."* (*Ottawa Citizen*, 2001)

the "Divine being-impulse of objective conscience," passing into what they call their "subconsciousness," and an artificial 'egoism' has become crystallized in their common presences:

> "This exclusively particular property … has passed to the contemporary beings as a certain lawful and inseparable part of their general psyche, and this particular property of their psyche is called by themselves 'egoism.' (p. 376)

> "… this 'Unique-particular' being impulse egoism and … now secondary strange being-impulses … usurped the place of the 'Unique-All-Autocratic-Ruler' in their general organization; then, … every manifestation … of such a Divine being-impulse became a hindrance to the actions of this 'All-Autocratic-Ruler.'

Instead of having a real I as a Unique-All-Autocratic-Ruler, the strange lopsided beings have a false egoism formed within them:

> "… which localization is always predominant during their waking existence, and which localization is nothing else but only the result of the accidental perceptions of impressions coming from without, and engendered by their abnormal environment, which perceptions in totality are called by them their 'consciousness;' (p. 377)

This said 'egoism' gives rise further to all kinds of other being impulses which are also peculiar and unbecoming to three-brained beings, but which came to dominate the life of humankind. Beelzebub provides varied listings of such characteristics among your favorites:

> "From the time when the said egoism had become completely 'inoculated' in the presences of your favorites, this particular being-property became, in its turn, the fundamental contributory factor in the gradual crystallization in their general psyche of the data for the arising of still several other quite exclusively — particular being-impulses now existing there under the names of 'cunning,' 'envy,' 'hate,' 'hypocrisy,' 'contempt,' 'haughtiness,' 'servility,' 'slyness,' 'ambition,' 'double-facedness,' and so on and so forth. (p. 379)

The strange three-brained beings living on planet earth perceive reality "topsy-turvy" in that a false consciousness system is established within them as a result of accidental things, such as the so-called education and conditioning experiences determined by the abnormal conditions of life. The true consciousness of humankind thus passed into their so-called 'subconscious,' or was *'driven back inside.'* A false egoism is crystallized in humans and manifests in all sorts of ways unbecoming to three-centered beings. Beelzebub often lists their charming qualities:

> *"... there are completely crystallized in them and* there unfailingly become a part of their common presence—regardless of where they may arise and exist—functions which exist under the names 'egoism,' 'self-love,' 'vanity,' 'pride,' 'self-conceit,' 'credulity,' 'suggestibility,' and many other properties quite abnormal and unbecoming to the essence of any three-brained beings whatsoever. (p. 107)

In terms of *"perceive reality topsy-turvy,"* the three-brained beings' knowledge of reality is no longer based upon their own being-experience, the fulfilling of their being obligations and *"being-Partkdolg-duty,"* nor is it based upon their own *"sane or active deliberations,"* or upon the *"instinctual sensing of reality."* Instead, Beelzebub describes people as ready to believe any old tale and as imaging that they understand themselves and all those things about which they talk, profess and write their books. Beelzebub refers distastefully to *"the scientists of new formation"* with their invented sciences and philosophies, and the *"disease of lying,"* by which people imagine that they know all kinds of things—none of which they have directly experienced or arrived at through their own 'sane deliberations.' The lopsided three-brained beings breeding on planet earth no longer *"instinctually sense reality"* or "instinctually sense cosmic truths," but came to perceive reality *"topsy-turvy."*

A second major abnormality of humankind is also quite odd, as explained by Beelzebub: *"that every repeated impression from outside should crystallize in them data which would engender factors for evoking in them sensations of 'pleasure' and 'enjoyment."* (p. 88) Humankind came to be conditioned by sense pleasure and enjoyment. Beelzebub consistently describes the laziness and self indulgence of human beings, their imaginary concerns, vanity and egoism, the itching of the stomach and their multiform sexual vices. Most importantly however, Beelzebub portrays humans as continually misusing their sexual substances, *"only for the satisfaction of the said impulse"*—of pleasure. Humans do not understand the role that these sacred sexual substances play in the psychology of their possible evolution and the possible coating of their *"higher being-bodies."*

Beelzebub's Tales also describe the roles of various Sacred Individuals, 'actualized from Above,' who were born on the Earth in order to serve HIS ENDLESSNESS, by helping to restore sanity to those disturbed three-brained beings breeding there through the awakening of various *sacred being-impulses* still dormant in the unconscious. Unfortunately, the 'spiritual part' of humans has passed into their subconscious and a 'false consciousness' system has become crystallized in their presences and maintained by the abnormal conditions of being-existence established on Earth.

Beelzebub's tales are rich in surrealistic humour and portray most vividly the horror of the situation and the strangeness of the human psyche evident on that ill-fated planet Earth. Serious undesirable qualities have became crystallized in humans, who are no longer capable of sincere and active mentation or the instinctual sensing of reality, but are controlled by their 'egoism,' the reflexes of the stomach, greed and material interests, sexual vices, self-calming and other 'Hasnamussian' traits. The complex psychopathology of humankind gave rise to that unique 'particularity' of their psyche, the propensity to engage in war and such unbecoming activities as currently dominate the life of humankind.

The Dual Consciousness

With reference to consciousness, Beelzebub explains that the *"genuine being-consciousness"* of those strange three-brained beings on planet Earth has passed into their *"subconsciousness."* In consequence, a *"fictitious consciousness"* system has become dominant. The distinction between the *"genuine being-consciousness"* and the false consciousness system is between consciousness rooted within the essence of the individual and that structured around the false personality—acquired through the processes of conditioning, education and the like.

While elaborating upon the phenomenon of hypnosis, Beelzebub explains to his grandson, how a *"two-system-Zoostat"* or *"two independent consciousnesses"* formed within the strange psyches of those three-centered beings. Beelzebub emphasizes the destructive roles of education and socialization in forming this false consciousness system:

"... ensuing from the abnormal conditions of the being-existence of your favourites ... from the beginning of the arising of their offspring, they intentionally try by every kind of means, for the purpose of making them respond to these abnormal conditions round them, to fix in their 'logicnestarian-localizations' as many impressions as possible obtained again due to the results of their abnormal existence—which maleficent action of theirs towards their offspring they call 'education'—then the totality of all such artificial perceptions gradually segregates itself in their common presences and acquires its own independent functioning, connected only as much with the functioning of their planetary body as is necessary merely for its automatic manifestation, and the totality of these artificial perceptions is then perceived by them, owing to their naiveté, as their real 'consciousness.'" (p. 565)

Education and socialization impresses *"artificial perceptions"* upon the centers (the logicnestarian-localizations), which come to dominate within the false personality. This system is based upon the formation of habit structures which allow for the automatic functioning of the individual. This artificial, fictitious or "false" consciousness is then unknowingly taken to be the real consciousness of the individual! Certainly, this would be a sad state of affairs.

The fictitious consciousness is formed from the perception of accidental and mechanical impressions and the sounds of words which are described as *"empty,"* having meanings not connected to genuine being data, direct experience or to sane deliberations. Mr. G. describes the formation of this false consciousness:

> "... when these children grow up and become responsible beings, they already automatically produce their manifestations and their acts; just as during their formation they were 'taught,' just as they were 'suggested to,' and just as they were 'wound up;' in a word, just as they were 'educated.'" (p. 378)

Beelzebub explains what happens to the consciousness based on essence, which should be the predominant system:

> "But as for the sacred data for genuine being—consciousness put into them by Great Nature—which consciousness ought to be possessed by them from the very beginning of their preparation for responsible existence together with the properties inherent in them which engender in them the genuine sacred being-impulses of 'faith,' 'hope,' 'love,' and 'conscience'—these data, becoming gradually also isolated and being left to themselves, evolve independently of the intentions of the responsible beings, and of course also independently of the bearers of them themselves, and come to be regarded as what is called the 'subconsciousness.'"
> (p. 565)

Hence all the *"sacred data"* inherent within humans, which could allow for responsible life, become isolated from their general functioning and remain in a primitive state; while the *"false consciousness"* predominates in their automatic functioning. This is how Beelzebub explains to Hassein the formation of the strange psyches of those three-brained beings breeding on planet Earth, who perceive reality topsy-turvy and are so conditioned by egotism, the impulses of pleasure, the wandering of nerves and the sexual organs.

In recounting his work as a hypnotist while visiting the Earth, Beelzebub explains that the functioning of these two consciousness systems is related to differences in the blood flow within the human organism. In particular, he explains that the *"centre-of-gravity-of-the-blood-pressure"* in their presences will sometimes predominate within one part of the general system of blood vessels, and at other times within another part of the blood vessels. These differences are related to differences between the waking and sleeping states and used to explain the phenomena of hypnosis. Beelzebub functioned as a hypnotist putting humans into such a state by altering the particularities of their blood flow, primarily through the use of his own Handbledzoin (or blood of the Kesdjan, or astral body)—which he labels as "animal magnetism," in accord with the terminology of Mesmer's day. However, Beelzebub explains that even the ordinary waking existence of humans flows under the influence of such a hypnotic state.

Humans subsequently no longer instinctually sense reality and cosmic truths, nor acquire genuine being-Reason, as is proper to three-centered beings, nor do they experience the sacred being-impulses. A false "egoism" has been formed and is the root of many other peculiar being impulses— which Beelzebub describes as *"existing under the names of 'cunning,' 'envy,' 'hate,' 'hypocrisy,' 'contempt,' 'haughtiness,' 'servility,' 'slyness,' 'ambition,' 'double-facedness,' and so on and so forth."* (p. 379) Beelzebub emphasizes that those "slugs" are really not at all what they imagine themselves to be:

> "With such an already quite 'automated consciousness,' and completely 'nonsensical feelings,' they feel themselves to be immeasurably superior to what they really are." (p. 513)

The true consciousness, now in the subconscious, requires for its growth, the fulfilment of individual *"being-partkdolg duty,"* of *conscious labours* and *intentional suffering*, which would help to accumulate the data necessary for the development of the faculties of genuine being-Reason and to accumulate the substances required for the coating of the higher being-bodies.

Beelzebub describes the activities of various sacred individuals or messengers who visited the Earth attempting to awaken the genuine being impulses within humankind—as these are still latent within the so-called *"subconscious."* Particularly, Beelzebub emphasizes the importance of the awakening of objective conscience, which from a person's early life, has been *"driven-back-within."* The lot of humankind, the slugs on that ill-fated planet Earth, has been to become crystallized within a false consciousness system. One of the few sources of hope for humanity still lies in the awakening to the deeper dimensions of self latent within the subconscious, in the deeper emotional nature.[13]

---

[13] In the terminology of the Ouspensky version of the fourth way teaching, the only hope is through the dissolution of the false personality and the attainment of true self-consciousness, based upon the growth of the essence and the awakening of the higher emotional center.

The Awakening of Conscience: the remaining Sacred and Divine Being-Impulse in the Subconscious

"Objective-Conscience, is not yet atrophied in them, but remains in their presences almost in its primordial state." (p. 359)

Gurdjieff explains that a human soul is given by Mother Nature but only as a possibility for growth. The awakening of conscience is ascribed a central role in determining a human's fate:

"Nature only give possibility for soul, not give soul. Must acquire soul through work. But, unlike tree, man have many possibilities. As man now exist he have also possibility grow by accident—grow wrong way. Man can become many things, not just fertilizer, not just real man: can become what you call 'good' or 'evil,' not proper things for man. Real man not good or evil—real man only conscious, only wish acquire soul for proper development."

"... Think of good and evil like right hand and left hand. Man always have two hands-two sides of self-good and evil. One can destroy other. Must have aim to make both hands work together, must acquire third thing: thing that make peace between two hands, between impulse for good and impulse for evil. Man who all 'good' or man who all 'bad' is not whole man, is one-sided. Third thing is conscience; possibility to acquire conscience is already in man when born; this possibility given-free-by Nature. But is only possibility. Real conscience can only be acquired by work, by learning to understand self first. ... (In Peters, 1964, pp. 42-3)

Gurdjieff assigns a central role to the awakening of conscience in the alchemy of transformation. Conscience is a state in which a human *"feels all at once everything that he in general feels and can feel."* (Ouspensky, 1949) This form of feeling together serves to unify an individual's presence, overcoming the inner inconsistencies and contradictions maintained by "buffers" or defences. Buffers prevent an individual from realizing their falsities and inner "nullity."

According to the *Tales,* the impact of the organ Kundabuffer and its crystallized ill-effects is to isolate the "Divine being-impulse of objective conscience" in the "subconsciousness." At least, this helped to avoid the final degradation of this sacred being-impulse, as happened to the other sacred being-impulses. Beelzebub particularly regarded the infamous 'education' as fostering the formation of a dual consciousness system within your favorites, rendering them incapable of being 'sincere' and encouraging only 'deceitfulness.' Beelzebub comments upon the maleficent side effects of education and how it effects the emotional nature of children:

> "To teach and to suggest to their children how to be insincere with others and deceitful in everything, has become so ingrained in the beings of the planet Earth of the present time, that it has even become their conception of their duty towards their children; and this kind of conduct towards their children they call by the famous word 'education.'

> "They 'educate' their children never to be able and never to dare to do as the 'conscience' present in them instinctually directs, but only that which is prescribed in the manuals of 'bon ton' usually drawn up there by various candidates for 'Hasnamusses.'

> "And of course when these children grow up and become responsible beings, they already automatically produce their manifestations and their acts; just as during their formation they

were 'taught,' just as they were 'suggested to,' and just as they were 'wound up'; in a word, just as they were 'educated.'

"Thanks to all this, the conscience which might be in the consciousness of the beings of that planet is, from their earliest infancy, gradually 'driven-back-within,' so that by the time they are grown up the said conscience is already found only in what they call their subconsciousness.

"In consequence, the functioning of the mentioned data for engendering in the presences this said Divine impulse conscience, gradually ceased long ago to participate in that consciousness of theirs by means of which their waking-existence flows.   (p. 378)

Beelzebub describes the effects of parents and educators in cultivating insincerity and deceit, all according to the good manners or *bon ton* of Hasnamussian influences. Recall that Hasnamusses are those who lack the Divine being-impulse of conscience, as we shall explore currently. The child does not learn to act in accordance with their own conscience, which is instead 'driven back inside.'

Contemporary education and culture encourages the formation of *"egoism"* in those strange three-brained beings; a false consciousness system which is the basis for an array of other abnormal and unbecoming 'being-impulses.' Beelzebub frequently lists some of these unbecoming qualities; including such things as 'cunning,' 'envy,' 'ambition,' 'hypocrisy,' 'contempt' and so on. Beelzebub refers to the central 'egoism' itself as involving a "'Unique-particular' being-impulse" which results in an "exclusive regard for *their own personal welfare.*" However, this sacred being impulse did not simply disappear. Beelzebub explains:

"... in that consciousness of theirs, which they call their subconsciousness, even in the beings of the present time, the said data for the acquisition in their presences of this fundamental Divine impulse conscience does indeed still continue to be crystallized and, hence, to be present during the whole of their existence." (p. 381)

According to Beelzebub, the awakening of conscience is one of the few avenues remaining to change the sorry state of those unfortunate three-brained beings. The data necessary for the awakening of the sacred being impulse conscience have not undergone the more complete *"degeneration to which all the other sacred being-impulses were subject"* — those sacred impulses of *Faith, Love and Hope.*

The need for the awakening of conscience is a primary theme of *Beelzebub's Tales*, especially given the horrors of the situation, with humankind engaging in the processes of reciprocal destruction, war and animal slaughter, and producing an increasingly inferior quality of Askokin vibrations. Whereas human beings asleep are governed by the push and pulls of the good and bad, *"real man only conscious"* — and he has acquired *"conscience."* Beelzebub states that this objective conscience has to be acquired by work and the fulfilling of one's being duties and obligations.

Beelzebub describes conscience as a *"fundamental Divine impulse."* Unfortunately, he explains that there is *"... a total absence of the participation of the impulse of sacred conscience in their waking-consciousness."* Humankind came instead to *"strive to arrange their welfare during the process of their ordinary existence, exclusively for themselves."* Beelzebub provides shocking insights into how mechanical human beings usually deal with what he calls, so humorously, the arising of *the prick of conscience*:

> "... these favorites of yours (humankind), particularly the contemporary ones, become ideally expert in not allowing this inner impulse of theirs, called Remorse-of-Conscience, to linger long in their common presences.
>
> "No sooner do they begin to sense the beginning, or even only, so to say, the 'prick' of the arising of the functioning in them of such a being-impulse, than they immediately, as it is said 'squash' it, whereupon this impulse, not quite formed in them, at once calms down.
>
> "For this 'squashing' of the beginning of any Remorse-of-Conscience in themselves, they have even invented some very efficient special means, which now exist there under the names of 'alcoholism,' 'cocainism,' 'morphinism,' 'nicotinism,' 'onanism,' 'monkism,' 'Athenianism,' and others with names also ending in 'ism.'" (p. 382)

Beelzebub's tales are full of subtle and rich humour, portraying so simply the follies, weakness and stupidities of humankind. There are many ways of squashing the pricks of conscience, part of what Beelzebub labels the 'Evil-God' of *'Self-Calming.'* It is because of this egoism and *"self-calming"* used to squash any *prick* of conscience that the sacred being impulse of conscience remains within the subconsciousness.

The remorse of conscience brings about a form of conscious suffering, compared to the unconscious sufferings based on desires and attachments of the planetary body. Beelzebub provides a cosmic perspective of the origins of the sacred being impulses of conscience, while recounting the insights of Ashiata Shiemash:

> "The factors for the being-impulse conscience arise in the presences of the three-brained beings from the localization of the particles of the "emanations-of-the-sorrow" of our OMNI-LOVING AND LONG-SUFFERING-ENDLESS-CREATOR; that is why the source of the manifestation of genuine conscience in three-centered beings is sometimes called the REPRESENTATIVE OF THE CREATOR." (p. 372)

Beelzebub explains that human beings can actually assume a role in bearing the *"Sorrow of our Endlessness"* through the remorse of conscience and that this faculty is still present within those strange beings of planet Earth:

> "My later detailed researches and investigations very definitely and clearly showed me that, in that consciousness of theirs, which they call their subconsciousness, even in the beings of the present time, the said data for the acquisition in their presences of this fundamental Divine impulse conscience does indeed still continue to be crystallized and, hence, to be present during the whole of their existence. (p. 381)

Morality, as humans commonly understand it, is very different from the moral sense awakened with the remorse of conscience and the attainment of consciousness. Ordinary *"subjective morality"* is an accidental thing based on conditioning, imitation and rote learning, indoctrination, education, external rewards and punishment. Subjective morality differs from one individual, time and country to another. Recall that Beelzebub described your favorites morality as dependent upon the four sources of action of the local officials, which were "'mother-in-law,' 'digestion,' 'John Thomas,' and 'cash.'" In contrast, *"objective morality"* is the same everywhere and involves a consciousness of the objective nature of self and the realities of life and the cosmos. Objective morality and conscience are based upon a deeper consciousness than people ordinarily know and the *"instinctual sensing of reality"* and cosmic truths.

Beelzebub explains that humans can work in order to have the Divine function of conscience in their presence by *"transubstantiating"* in themselves their being obligations or duties. These being obligations are elements of an objective morality. Beelzebub explains that after the teachings of Ashiata Shiemash concerning the importance of conscience were spread throughout Asia, it had a major effect upon the people and brought about the cessation of war and a normalization of life on Earth:

> "All the beings of this planet then began to work in order to have in their consciousness this Divine function of genuine conscience, and for this purpose, as everywhere in the Universe, they transubstantiated in themselves what are called the 'being-obligolnian-strivings' which consist of the following five, namely:

> "The first striving: to have in their ordinary being-existence everything satisfying and really necessary for their planetary body.

> "The second striving: to have a constant and unflagging instinctive need for self-perfection in the sense of being.

> "The third: the conscious striving to know ever more and more concerning the laws of World-creation and World-maintenance.

> "The fourth: the striving from the beginning of their existence to pay for their arising and their individuality as quickly as possible, in order afterwards to be free to lighten as much as possible the Sorrow of our COMMON FATHER.

> "And the fifth: the striving always to assist the most rapid perfecting of other beings, both those similar to oneself and those of other forms, up to the degree of the sacred 'Martfotai,' that is, up to the degree of self-individuality.   (p.386)

The first being-obligation refers to maintaining the physical body and not being overly indulgent and conditioned by physical desires, the stomach and sex organs. The second involves striving for one's self-perfection, the attainment of real "I," one's individuality. The third involves seeking after truth about self and the nature of the world, striving to understand the fundamental cosmic laws which create and sustain life. The fourth involves paying for our arising in order to help lighten the Sorrow of our Common Father, overcoming egoism and striving to lessen the suffering and madness within the world. The final striving, or being obligation, is to help others towards their self-perfection, to attaining real "I."

Beelzebub explains that if it were not for the cosmic catastrophes which occurred, it would be natural for humankind as three-centered beings to strive in these directions. The degradation of humankind has led humans to forget their sacred *being-Partkdolg-duties* and their *'being-obligolnian-strivings,'* and to strive instead only for their own welfare—their own pleasuring, egoism, self-love and vanity, all through insincerity and cunning. The sacred being obligations and duties form an "objective morality" serving to connect humans to deeper cosmic processes, the sacred and divine.

Beelzebub describes humans *"as beings bearing in themselves particles of the emanation of the Sorrow of our COMMON FATHER CREATOR."* (p. 385) The awakening of conscience is thus a profoundly important stage in the transformation of the emotional life, leading to the awakening of the higher emotional center and connection with the life of the Common Father.

The possibility for remorse of conscience also prevents the *"final degradation"* in humankind of the other sacred being impulses of *"Faith, Love, and Hope."* The experience of the remorse of conscience and the bearing of the sorrow of the Common Father are steps to awakening and transformation. Fortunately, the data are still present within the strange human beings for such *"sacred being impulses,"* although they have passed into the subconsciousness. Meanwhile, humans invent ever new mean for their Evil-God of self-calming.

Hasnamuss-Individuals & the *'Naloo-osnian-spectrum-of-impulses'*

Throughout *The Tales*, Beelzebub uses the terms *Hasnamuss* and *Hasnamusses* to refer in a negative way to certain individuals or a class of people whose actions, manifestations and abnormal being-impulses embody the worst psychopathology of humankind and who cause the most sufferings, degeneracy, falsity and misunderstanding among the strange three-brained beings on Earth. On one occasion, Hassein turns to his grandfather Beelzebub and asks:

> "My dear Grandfather, during your tales you have already many times used the expression Hasnamuss. I have until now understood only from the intonation of your voice and from the consonance of the word itself, that by this expression you defined those three-brained beings whom you always set apart from others as if they deserved 'Objective-Contempt.'

> "Be so kind as always and explain to me the real meaning and exact sense of this word."

> "Whereupon Beelzebub, with a smile inherent to him, said as follows:

> "Concerning the 'typicality' of the three-brained beings for whom I have adapted this verbal definition, I shall explain to you at the proper time, but meanwhile know that this word designates every already 'definitized' common presence of a three-brained being, both those consisting only of the single planetary body as well as those whose higher being-bodies are already coated in them, and in which for some reason or other, data have not been crystallized for the Divine impulse of 'Objective-Conscience.' (pp. 234-5)

Beelzebub explains that the word Hasnamuss refers to those with an *"already 'definitized' common presences ... in which ... data have not been crystallized for the Divine impulse of 'Objective Conscience.'"* A fixed character or egoic complex dominates their 'common presence.' The fact that data for the Divine impulse of Objective Conscience are not crystallized in them suggests that this egoism is in full sway and the real consciousness has passed into the subconsciousness. Such individuals are primarily concerned for themselves and their multiform vices, and care little how much suffering and misfortune they cause others.[14] Beelzebub explains that some Hasnamusses consist of a planetary body alone, while others also have higher being-bodies coated in them.

Beelzebub describes seven *"Naloo-osnian-spectrum-of-impulses"* which form a *"certain something"* within the Hasnamuss-individuals. There are various kinds of Hasnamusses according to which of the seven impulses they are most subject. These include:

(1) Every kind of depravity, conscious as well as unconscious
(2) The feeling of self-satisfaction from leading others astray
(3) The irresistible inclination to destroy the existence of other breathing creatures
(4) The urge to become free from the necessity of actualizing the being-efforts demanded by Nature
(5) The attempt by every kind of artificiality to conceal from others what in their opinion are one's physical defects
(6) The calm self-contentment in the use of what is not personally deserved
(7) The striving to be not what one is. (p. 406)

Certainly, Beelzebub does not outline a very charming list of impulses. *The Tales* are full of stories where individuals embody such Hasnamussian characteristics and qualities. Such impulses are formed within the crystallized "egoism," so prominent among the strange psyches of those three-brained beings on planet Earth. The Hasnamuss individual no longer experiences the impulses of *"being-self-shame"* or of Objective Conscience and the history of humanity testifies to the horrors caused by these *"terrestrial nullities."*

---

[14] Ouspensky (1957) defined the Hasnamuss individual: *"... he never hesitates to sacrifice people or to create an enormous amount of suffering, just for his own personal ambitions."* (p. 300)

Different Hasnamuss-Individuals embody different elements from the spectrum of the Naloo-osnian-impulses. The third 'Naloo-osnian impulse'——the *'irresistible inclination to destroy the existence of other breathing creatures'* and the first impulse—towards every kind of depravity are most clearly embodied by those who bring about processes of destruction around the world—the wars, including conquering and rebellions, domination, violence and torture, animal sacrifice and slaughterhouses, and abortions. Recall that on hearing of the horrors of war from his Grandfather, Hassein was shocked as this *"need for periodically occupying themselves with the destruction of each other's existence"* ran *"like a crimson thread through all your tales."* (pp. 1055-6) Beelzebub describes such phenomenally strange behaviour, where: *"... they would suddenly, without rhyme or reason, begin destroying one another's existence,"* as otherwise unknown in the Universe. Further, he describes *"the periodic arising in them of what is called the 'urgent need to destroy everything outside of themselves.'* Beelzebub's observations of the Earth from Mars and his visits to the Earth were partly to understand how such atrocities could be possible. What happened within these men-beings such that their *"essence is gradually brought to such a phenomenal being-ableness to destroy, for no rhyme or reason, the existence of other beings similar to themselves?"* (p. 526) Hasnamuss-individuals have also destroyed and persecuted various sacred Messengers and their followers, and obscured the genuine religious teachings which might have changed human history and brought more normal conditions of being-existence to the planet.

Beelzebub's uses the term Hasnamuss in his impartial observations of the community of France and in his comments upon the fashion world of Paris. Writing in the 1920's in Paris and Southern France, Gurdjieff provides an amusing critique of the culture and society around him. In the *Tales*, it is during his sixth and final visit to the Earth that Beelzebub visited France, *"the contemporary 'chief-center-of-culture' for the whole of that ill-fated planet."* (p. 688) Beelzebub explains to Hassein how those beings who *"rush and flock from the whole planet"* to Paris the center of culture were particularly those who had:

> "... completely given themselves up to the 'evil-God' reigning there already without limit inside each of them, namely to that 'evil-God' who became their Ideal, and the conception of whom is very well expressed in the words: to-attain-to-a-complete-absence-of-the-need-for-being-effort-and-for-every-essence-anxiety-of-whatever-kind-it-might-be"; and coming to France, they must of course have,

consciously or unconsciously, a corresponding harmful influence
on the beings of the whole community.   ... when beings from
the whole planet ... flock to this chief center of culture, then these
beings ... occupy themselves with 'new-forms-of-manifestations-of-
their-Hasnamussianing,' or as is said there, with 'new fashions,' and
spread them from there over the whole of the planet. (p. 688)

These beings who flock to Paris manifest the fourth Naloo-osnian-impulse:
*"The urge to be free from the necessity of actualizing the being-efforts demanded
by Nature."* Further, they have given themselves over to what Beelzebub
calls the 'evil-God' of 'self-calming,' for which they invented such 'ism's'
as mentioned: *'alcoholism,' 'cocainism,' 'morphinism,' 'nicotinism,' 'onanism,'
'monkism,' 'Athenianism,' and so on.* Anyway, such Hasnamussian-individuals
flocked to Paris, as today to Hollywood, and the fashions, arts and dramas
became some of their chief occupations.

Beelzebub defines 'fashion' as consisting in this: *"... the beings devise various
new means of being-manifestation in ordinary existence, and means for changing
and disguising the reality of one's appearance."* (p. 689)

> *"... These said contemporary customs or fashions of theirs are,
> firstly, only temporary and thus serve for the satisfaction only of the
> personal insignificant aims of these present and future Hasnamusses,
> which become phenomenally abnormal and trivially egoistic; and
> secondly, they are neither more nor less than the results of automatic
> Reason based on that relative understanding ...*

Another of the 'inventions' of "several of these Hasnamussian candidates"
was that women cut their hair. This practice was not adopted widely in
France outside of Paris because of the stronger "feelings of morality and
patriarchality," but spread to England and America. Such a Hasnamussian
invention encouraged the appearance of 'Amazons,' lesbians, as well as
'suffragettes,' female illnesses and divorces. Beelzebub describes Paris as
the "collecting place for the beings with Hasnamussian properties from
other countries who continue to persist in this maleficent invention."

The fifth Naloo-osnian-impulse to artificially conceal from others one's
defects and the seventh, the *"striving to be not what one is,"* are both
illustrated in Beelzebub's depictions of the fashion world in particular and
of modern culture more generally. Beelzebub defines fashion as: *"This*

maleficent custom for them is that they periodically change the external form of what is called 'the-covering-of-their-nullity.'" (p. 501)

Beelzebub also portrays the Hasnamussian characteristics of artists and actors—with their *"'illusorily inflated' maleficent idea of their famous art."* Beelzebub describes such players, actors, comedians and artists among 'your favorites' as 'imitators of the mysteries.'

> "You must know that those beings who are assumed to be the adepts of this contemporary art which is adorned with a false halo are not only put on their own level by the other three-brained beings there of the contemporary civilization, particularly during the several latter decades, and imitated by them in their exterior manifestations, but they are always and everywhere undeservingly encouraged and exalted by them; and in these contemporary representatives of art themselves, who really in point of their genuine essence are almost nonentities, there is formed of itself without any of their being-consciousness a false assurance that they are not like all the rest but, as they entitle themselves, of a 'higher order,' with the result that in the common presences of these types the crystallization of the consequences of the properties of the organ Kundabuffer proceeds more intensively than in the presences of all the other three-brained beings there. (p. 512)

> "Every one of them really being in respect of genuine essence almost what is called a nonentity, that is, something utterly empty but enveloped in a certain visibility, they have gradually acquired such an opinion of themselves, by means of favorite exclamations always and everywhere repeated by them themselves like 'genius,' 'talent,' 'gift,' and still a number of other words empty also like themselves, that it is as if, among similar beings around them, only they have 'divine origin,' only *they* are almost 'God.'" (p. 514)

Beelzebub portrays the "terrestrial nullities" as concealing their inner emptiness and appearing as something that they are not. Unfortunately, they are idolized and imitated by other beings. Modern culture, the arts, literature and the sciences are portrayed as based upon the qualities of such Hasnamussian-individuals. Beelzebub describes them as having *"an already quite automatized 'consciousness,' and completely 'nonsensical feelings,'"* and further, *"they feel themselves to be immeasurably superior to what they really are.*" (p. 513) Any observation of an evening of contemporary television, movies or dramas, among your favorites, would convince any impartial, alien intelligence of the nullity of modern culture with its infamous artists and actors.

Beelzebub describes the contemporary actors "during their '*swaggerings*' in these theatres," as subject to the strange illness of 'dramatizacring.' Beelzebub fancifully relates this illness of dramatizacring to the carelessness of drunken midwives, who at their births, declare, "Eh, you, what a mess you've made." The histrionics of its caretakers destine the being:

> "If such a three-brained being there who has acquired at his first appearance the said predisposition to the illness of dramatizacring should by the time he reaches the age of a responsible being, know how to write and should wish to write something, then he suddenly gets this illness and begins wiseacring on paper, or, as it is said there, 'composing' various what are called 'dramas.'

> "The contents for these works of theirs are usually various events which are supposed to have occurred or which might occur in the future, or finally, events of their own contemporary 'unreality.' (p. 502)

> "It usually then further happens there that if the sick being has an uncle who is a member of one or other of their 'parliaments,' or if he himself gets acquainted with the widow of a 'former-business-man,' or if the period of his preparation for becoming a responsible being has for some reason or other been spent in such an environment or under such conditions that he has automatically acquired the property called 'slipping-in-without-soap,' then what is called the 'producer,' or as he is also called, the 'owner-of-the-lambs,' takes this work of his and orders the mentioned contemporary actors to 'reproduce' it exactly as it was wiseacred by this being who has fallen ill with this strange illness of dramatizacring. (p. 504)

And so the unrealities of sick wiseacres and Hasnamusses are reproduced, lauded and imitated among the contemporary beings—all leading to the further degradation of the 'arts' and of the common psyche. Beelzebub explains:

"Although indeed these contemporary theatres with all that proceeds in them happen to be in this way—but of course only 'for today'—an excellent means for the better sleep of your favorites, nevertheless the objectively evil consequences of these theatres for beings, and particularly for the rising generation, are incalculable.

"The chief harm for them from these theatres is that they are an additional factor for the complete destruction in them of all possibilities of ever possessing the need, proper to three-brained beings, called the 'need-for-real-perceptions. (p. 507)

Whereas in ancient times, the arts and drama were for the *'conscious reproductions of perceptions'* and to convey objective knowledge of the mysteries, by Beelzebub's last visit, the arts, literature, drama and the theatre were dominated by Hasnamusses of varied types. The Hasnamusses fashion worlds in which there is no place for such 'need-for-real-perceptions,' but provide instead titillating fictions.

The second 'Naloo-osnian-impulse' of 'the feeling of self-satisfaction from leading others astray' also plays a role in the modern Hasnamussian corporate media and the antics of Hollywood. In fact, the modern arts and culture provide, as Beelzebub explains, "every kind of data for Hasnamussian properties." Many Hasnamusses came to be employed with the media and academia of modern times, within the think-tanks and round tables of the power-possessing beings, and have so deceived the human race as to the true causes of historic events and their arch-criminal machinations. When Beelzebub visits America, he comments on the media and journalism of the time, noting: "… the sacred being-function of 'conscience' is completely atrophied among contemporary terrestrial what are called 'journalists' and 'reporters' …." (p. 942)

Throughout human history, Hasnamusses have distorted genuine religious teachings for their own purposes or invented theistic philosophies with fantastic fictions, which has lead to mass confusion and the further degeneration of *"sane mentation"* among their followers. The 'wiseacring' of Hasnamusses obscured the teachings and messages of the Sacred Individuals 'actualized from above.' The philosopher Atarnakh was such a Hasnamuss, who led the councils astray with false teachings and misunderstanding, which served to undermine the work of Ashiata Shiemash.

Varied religious teachings were invented by Hasnamusses who began to change and 'wiseacre' about everything that the sacred Messengers had taught. Beelzebub describes the arising of "their peculiar" religions based upon the "inventions" of certain individuals—with the germs of Hasnamussian traits already acquired in their presences:

> "... such beings began, as is proper to them for their egoistic aims, to invent for the 'confusion' of surrounding beings similar to themselves, various fictions, among which were also every kind of fantastic, what are called 'religious teachings' ... (p. 694)

'Your favorites' thus *"lost their 'sane mentation'"* and a large number of 'Havatvernoni' or 'religions' arose having *"nothing in common with each other."* Particularly, the *"maleficent idea"* of *"Good"* and *"Evil"* was introduced leading to further 'dilution' of their psyches; as well as their infamous notions of paradise and hell; and such images of Mr. God as an old Jew, or with a comb sticking out of his pocket.

At the time of ancient Babylon, when the issue of the day was whether or not man had a soul, another *"terrestrial Hasnamussian candidates of that time"* propounded the *"atheistic teachings of that period."* Beelzebub explains that according to this teaching, "there is no God in the world, and moreover no soul in man," everything follows a special law of mechanics and 'supernatural phenomena' are nothing but the "deliriums of sick visionaries." Such Hasnamussian theories are the mainstay of modern psychology, philosophy and science—which deny the soul in humans, the validity of 'super-natural phenomena' and the existence of God or Divinity in the World. Instead, everything is imagined to have followed mechanically from earlier causes, such as evolution by fortunate random mutations and happenstance.

Beelzebub recounts that when these ideas caught on in Babylon and due to *"their collective wiseacrings,"* it was gradually transformed into *"a veritable mill of nonsense."* The three-brained beings thus had *"a further mass of data for Hasnamussian manifestations"* and when they returned to their homelands, they began to *"propagate like contagious bacilli"* all the wrong notions about the soul, God and the World. These false teachings, along with the false religious doctrines, ultimately destroyed the last remnants of the holy labors of Saintly Ashiata Shiemash, as has been done with the teachings of the other Sacred Individuals actualized from Above.

Beelzebub offers a remarkable view of Hasnamusses and the spectrum of their perverse impulses. The Hasnamuss-individuals have the most disturbed and crystallized forms of egoism, with some special 'something' in their character, and most significantly, lacking the Divine or sacred being-impulse of objective conscience. Human history is littered with the names of Hasnamusses and stained with their blood crimes. Unfortunately, contemporary society and culture are today dominated by their degenerative influences and egotistic values, their invented theories and religions, and sciences. Today as throughout history, there is indeed a wide spectrum of Hasnamusses, without objective conscience, power-possessing beings, media shrills, masters of war and 'stock jugglers,' with 'special societies' for 'important' people. The Hasnamusses promote every type of depravity, sexual obsession, random and fortuitous violence, perversion and superficiality.

Hasnamusses come in different colors and manifest a spectrum of malificent impulses.

The Horrific Processes of Reciprocal Self Destruction

"... on that strange planet alone in the whole of the Universe does that horrible process occur among three-brained beings which is called the 'process of reciprocal destruction of each other's existence,' or, as it is called on that ill-fated planet, 'war.'" (p.107)

THE CHIEF PARTICULARITY OF THEIR STRANGE PSYCHE

In a sense, Beelzebub and Gurdjieff are characters from a higher dimension and time, and they provide a shocking portrayal of human psychopathology or insanity from an extraterrestrial and cosmic perspective. Gurdjieff's mastery of language empowers Beelzebub to depict most succinctly the strangeness of the psyche of those three-brained beings on planet Earth and the horrors of warfare.

At various times, Beelzebub discusses the *"process of reciprocal destruction"* and he attempts to elaborate upon the causes of warfare to a somewhat disbelieving Hassein, who simply cannot imagine such terrors. Beelzebub explains that by the end of his investigations, he concluded that there is a "periodic arising in them of what is called the 'urgent need to destroy everything outside of *themselves.*'" This periodic urgent need is one aspect of "the chief particularity of their strange psyche" and is described as now "completely crystallized and an inseparable part of their common presences."

Beelzebub briefly elaborates upon such archcriminal processes:

"The point is that when, during the apogee of the development of such a peculiarity—terrifying to every Reason—of the psyche of the three-brained beings, they begin to manifest outside of themselves this phenomenal peculiarity of their common presences, that is to say, when they begin to carry out on some part of the surface of their planet the process of reciprocal destruction, then, at the same time, without any deliberate aim, and even without what is called 'organic need,' they also destroy everything which chances to come within the sphere of the perception of their organ of sight. During the periods of this 'phenomenal psychopathic apogee,' they destroy also all the objects in the given place and at the given time which these same beings themselves, between whom this terrifying process proceeds, have intentionally produced as well as the productions which have chanced to survive and to reach them from the beings of previous epochs. (pp. 312-3)

Beelzebub depicts human madness so succinctly, as the strange three-brained not only destroy each others' existences but also everything that they see. He quotes the saintly Ashiata Shiemash, who refers to the *"degree of that psychosis of theirs called the 'destruction-of-everything-existing-within-the-sphere-of-the-perception-of-visibility,"* which accompanies their process of reciprocal destruction. (p. 519) Elsewhere, Beelzebub describes these processes as "such an unimaginable horror and such a hideousness that no name can even be found for it." (p. 1057)

In explaining the nature of a 'revolution' to Hassein, Beelzebub notes how these processes not only result in the destruction of each other's existence, but also in the destruction of properties, artefacts of earlier ages, as well as of accumulated knowledge, and especially, the destruction of those three-brained beings who happen to be freer of the consequences of the organ Kundabuffer:

> "... during their later revolutions of this kind, almost all the three-brained beings there or at least the overwhelming majority who begin to fall into such a 'psychosis,' always destroy for some reason or other the existence of just such other beings like themselves, as have, for some reason or other, chanced to find themselves more or less on the track of the means of becoming free from the crystallizations in themselves of the consequences of the properties of that maleficent organ Kundabuffer which unfortunately their ancestors possessed. (p. 119)

Such processes have recurred throughout of human history while the psyche of the three-brained beings degenerated further along with their religions. The only progress humankind apparently makes is to devise ever new inventions to apply during such wars, revolutions and the like.

The history of such processes of reciprocal destruction has also led to the murder of genuine initiates, the loss of their manuscripts and artefacts, and a loss of human history. Beelzebub explains:

> "… during the processes of reciprocal destruction, that is during what are called 'wars' and 'popular risings,' a great number of initiated beings of all degrees are for some reason or other invariably destroyed, and, together with them, there are also destroyed forever very many Legominisms through which alone various information about former real events on Earth is transmitted and continues to be transmitted from generation to generation. (pp. 455-456) [15]

The history of the planet Earth has been marred by these most horrific processes, involving such mass deaths, violence and terror, pillaging and destruction, the murder of genuine initiates and the loss of their knowledge.

Another of Beelzebub's interests in his studies of the strange human psyche concerns how their means for producing such horrific processes of reciprocal destruction changed through the centuries. Before Beelzebub's sixth and final descent to the Earth, he had been observing your favorite from the planet Mars, when he noticed something quite new to him: That, "without moving from their place, they did with a certain thing something which resulted in a tiny puff of smoke, whereupon a being from the opposite side immediately fell down either totally destroyed or with one or other part of his planetary body mutilated or destroyed forever. … "Such a means of reciprocal destruction I had never seen before...." (pp. 525-526) Beelzebub is depicting the invention of fire-arms and his comments illustrate horror of it allDthat someone over here does a little something with a finger and a man over there falls down dead or mutilated. Hasnamussian scientists on Earth in fact are always manufacturing new means to enable their processes of self-destruction, so that they can proceed most simply and with the least sweat or effort.

---

[15] In response to Hassein's inquiry regarding the meaning of this unusual term, Beelzebub explains: "This word *Legominism … is given to one of the means existing there of transmitting from generation to generation information about certain events of long-past ages, through just those three-brained beings who are thought worthy to be and who are called initiates … devised by the beings of the continent Atlantis."* (p. 349)

On another occasion, Beelzebub is describing his observation of a chemical experiment where red copper was produced and spread through a substance. Beelzebub compared this chemical reaction to his observations of the accumulation of 'corpses' among your favorites:

> "A rough parallel can be drawn between the occasional proceedings on your planet and the proceedings then in that small fragment of copper, if you imagine yourself high up and looking down upon a large public square, where thousands of your favorites, seized with the most intense form of their chief psychoses, are destroying each other's existence by all kinds of means invented by them themselves, and that in their places there immediately appear what are called their 'corpses,' which owing to the outrages done to them by the beings who are not yet destroyed, change color very perceptively, as a result of which the general visibility of the surface of the said large square is gradually changed. (p. 174)

When talking about the Hasnamussian sciences in Germany and their studies of 'chemical substances,' Beelzebub mentions the use of 'neutralizing gases,' described as 'ind*iscriminate-destroyers-of-the-already-arisen.*'

> "… there was then proceeding in the presences of the beings of their community, consequently in them themselves, what is called 'the-most-intense-experiencing' of the chief particularity of the psyche of the three-brained being of your planet, namely, 'the-urgent-need-destroy-the-existence-of-others-like-themselves'—and indeed, the beings of that community were then fully absorbed in their process of reciprocal destruction with the beings of neighboring communities—these others thereupon at once 'enthusiastically' decided to devote themselves entirely to finding ways to employ the special properties of that gas for the speedy mass destruction of the existence of the beings of other communities. (pp. 427-8)

Beelzebub explains to Hassein how at the same time in the community of England, the beings who had become "expert in inventing and distributing to the beings existing over the whole surface of your planet, vast quantities of every kind of metalwares called there locks, razors, mousetraps, revolvers, scythes, machine guns, saucepans, hinges, guns, penknives, cartridges, pens, mines, needles and many other things of the same kind," were able to use their talents for inventing and distributing 'metalwares' to enable these processes of reciprocal destruction to proceed more easily.'

Beelzebub explains how both of these maleficent inventions were both used in what your favorites called the "World War:"

> "It was plainly owing to the fact that during the said process what is called 'poison gas' was invented by beings called 'Germans,' and what are called special 'rapid-fire machine guns' by beings called 'Englishmen,' that the amount of Rascooarnos or deaths unforeseen by Nature took place on this occasion and in a far greater quantity than was then required by Her, or, as the candidates for Hasnamuss there, namely, the commercial businessmen, would say, 'overproduction' occurred in respect of the deaths of the three-brained beings required there. (p. 1115)

A primary result of the fantastic sciences and inventions was the increasing ease with which your favorites could manifest that monstrous particularity of their psyche.

Beelzebub describes the English as having become not only the inventors of such machine guns, but also as being "expert … in distributing" their metalwares. In fact, in the topsy-turvy reality of modern times, the 'philanthropic aid' of community of England to other communities largely consists in distributing the means to enable such processes of warfare and reciprocal self-destruction:

> "The beings of that contemporary community have been the benefactors of the other contemporary beings of your planet, offering them, as they say there, 'philanthropic aid,' especially as regards their first being-duty, namely, the duty of carrying out from time to time the process of 'reciprocal destruction.'

> "Thanks to them, the discharge of that being-duty of theirs has gradually become for your contemporary favorites, the 'merest trifle.'

> "In the absence of those inventions it used to be exceedingly arduous for these poor favorites of yours to fulfill that being-duty, because they were formerly forced to spend a great deal of sweat for it.

"But thanks to the adaptations of every kind invented by those contemporary beings, it is now as again our esteemed Mullah Nassr Eddin says, 'just roses, roses.'

"The contemporary beings now scarcely need to make any effort whatsoever in order to destroy completely the existence of beings like themselves.

"Sometimes sitting quietly in what they call their 'smoking rooms' they can destroy, just as a pastime, as it were, ten and sometimes even hundreds of others like themselves. (p. 433)

Imagine what Beelzebub would think of modern warfare with its arsenals of weapons for remote mass murder at the hands of the 'power-possessing beings' among us; all while the masses periodically feel such "urgent needs" to destroy the existence of other breathing creatures by one means or another. Further, the powerful nations of the world give exactly such 'philanthropic aid' to lesser or third world countries to enable the power-possessing beings there to more simply carry out their Hasnamussian aims on local citizenry or against other communities.[16]

---

[16] In modern times, the United States and England, like China, Russia and others, have given just such 'philanthropic aid' around the world to create quite a contemporary cacophony of madness and terror. In modern times, such weapons of mass destruction are even more varied and horrific than Beelzebub portrayed. Now for instance, Bill Gates and fellow 'philanthropists' fund such mass extermination and population reduction within third world countries through their 'inoculation programs.' Gates boasts of being able to help reduce the emerging African population through such means and he works to devise ever more devious and cunning ways of delivering such poisons—including the Hasnamussian invention of modified mosquitoes. In modern times, the Hasnamusses have further devised ways to use the being-foods themselves as weapons, through genetically modified foods, poisonous additives and chemical water, and the poisoning of the air through chemtrail spaying and radiation. Even weather modification and earth upheavals can now be used as weapons to enable such processes of mass extermination and enslavement. It is possible to create famines, hurricanes and storms, earthquakes and tsunamis. The powerful nations and plutocrats take such roles in arming other power-possessing beings militarily or otherwise, so as to enable such processes of reciprocal self-destruction and mass exterminations. Hasnamusses devises offer ever more 'cunning' means for aiding Lucifer himself in the arch-criminal scheme to enslave humanity through their networks of criminal gangs and special societies.

COWARDICE AND FEAR

Beelzebub wanted to understand how those men-beings' *"essence is gradually brought to such a phenomenal being-ableness to destroy, for no rhyme or reason, the existence of other beings similar to themselves."* (p. 526) He concludes that this *"terrifying periodic being-need"* to destroy each others' existence had been acquired over centuries due to the abnormal conditions of existence established there by past generations and which are perpetuated through the falsity of the educational system and within a society preoccupied with Hasnamussian sciences and inventions. Beelzebub explores also the role of the moon, planetary influences, the role of Hasnamusses and power-possessing beings, and more, as all play some role in the perpetration of such horrors of warfare through the life of humankind.

When it comes to the role of psychological factors, Beelzebub elucidates the role of their dual consciousness system and crystallized egoism, with its associated cunning, envy, greed, haughtiness, servility, and all such unbecoming being-impulses. However, Beelzebub also emphasizes the role of cowardice and fear:

> "… during these processes, they usually instinctively at first refrain from such an unnatural manifestation, but later when every one of them already in the environment of the process itself willy-nilly sees and becomes convinced that the destruction of the existence of those similar to themselves proceeds so simply, and that the number of the destroyed always grows — well then, each of them involuntarily begins instinctively to feel and automatically to value his own existence. And having become persuaded by his own eyes that the possibility of loosing his own existence depends, at the given moment, absolutely only on the number of beings of the enemy side not destroyed, then in consequence of the … impulse called 'cowardice,' and on account of the impossibility at each moment of reasonable deliberation by his being-mentation, weakened already without this, he begins from a natural feeling of self preservation to strive with all his Being to destroy as many as possible of the existences of the beings of the enemy side in order to have the greater chance of saving his own existence. And gradually progressing in this feeling of self-

preservation of theirs, they then reach that state, as they themselves say, of 'bestiality.' (p. 527)

The barbarous processes of reciprocal destruction are perpetuated through the instinctive fears and cowardice of the masses and a psychosis will spread through the population as they "eye that possibility of loosing their own existence.'

Elsewhere, Beelzebub comments on the 'cowardice' within your favorites, even in their dealings with other one and two-brained beings:

> "... your favorites, thanks always to the same abnormal conditions of existence, have gradually become, as they themselves say, 'cowardly' from head to foot, and because at the same time the need of destroying the existence of others has been inculcated in them, also from head to foot. And so, when they being already cowards 'of the highest degree,' are about to destroy the existence of the beings of these other forms, or when they chance to meet such beings ... then they become 'afraid,' as they say there in such case, 'to the point of wetness.'

> "At the same time, thanks to the inherent need in their presences to destroy the existence of other beings breeding on their planet, they at such moments contrive with their whole Being how to destroy the existence of these beings of other forms. (pp. 877-8)

Certainly there are a variety of unbecoming being-impulses formed within your favorites, destroying not only each others' existence, but also that of the one and two brained beings.

Power-Possessing Beings, Special Societies & the *League of Nations*

On hearing of the horrors of war from his grandfather, Hassein is shocked that this *"need for periodically occupying themselves with the destruction of each other's existence"* ran *"like a crimson thread through all your tales."* Hassein wonders:

> "Don't they really see that these processes of theirs are the most terrible of all the horrors which can possibly exist in the whole of the Universe, and don't they ever ponder on this matter, so that they might become aware of this horror and find a means of eradicating it? (p. 1056)

Beelzebub answers Hassein by elaborating upon why nothing is ever accomplished either by individuals or through their 'special societies' to eradicate warfare. Beelzebub explains that partly nothing is ever attained due to "the absence there, as is usual, of one common-planetary organization for a single line of action." (p. 1056) However, Beelzebub then characterizes the psychological development of those *"power possessing beings,"* who might assume a role in eradicating such horrific processes of reciprocal destruction and the nature of the 'special societies' which they form. Beelzebub draws this portrait of the power-possessing beings among your favorites:

> "... I must tell you that thanks to the abnormally established conditions of being-existence there, the 'waking psyche' as it is expressed there, of each one of them gradually becomes from the very beginning of responsible existence such that he can 'think sincerely' and see things in the true light exclusively only if his stomach is so full of the first being-food that it is impossible for what are called 'wandering nerves' in it to move, or, as they themselves say, he is 'stuffed quite full;' and besides, all his needs already inherent in him which are unbecoming to three-brained beings and which

had become the dominant factors for the whole of his presence, are fully satisfied, of course, only for that given moment. ...

"When these three-brained beings of your planet, particularly of the present time, who have the means of gorging to satiety and of fully satisfying all their other needs and who perhaps could do something for the struggle against this phenomenal evil prevailing on their planet, are satiated, and their mentioned needs are satisfied, and they are seated on what are called their 'soft English divans' in order, as is said there, 'to digest it all'Dthey do not profit, even during this time so suitable for sincere thinking ... but indulge instead in the maleficent self-calming. ...

"For instance, when after gorging and satisfying themselves these important and power-possessing beings of the Earth are seated on their said divans, the associative thoughts which ought inevitably to flow in them receives shocks from the reflexes of their stomach and sex organs and wander freely in all directions, as they say there, 'to their hearts content,' and so pleasantly free and easy, as if they, that is these thoughts of theirs, were 'strolling of an evening in Paris along the Boulevard des Capucinus.'

"When these power-possessing beings of your planet are seated on their soft divans, subjects like the following a-think in them.

"For instance, how to get his revenge on that acquaintance of his, John Smith, who a few days before looked at a woman he 'liked,' not with his right eye but with his left.

"Or this 'digesting' terrestrial power-possessing or important being thinks: 'Why did not my horse come in first yesterday at the races as I expected, but some other?'

"Or, 'Why do those stocks which are in fact quite worthless, go up every day on the market, higher and higher?'

"Or, finally, he thinks something of this kind: 'If I were in John Smith's shoes who invented a new method of breeding flies for making ivory from their skeletons, then from the profits obtained I would do this, that, and the other, and not as that fool, who, like a dog in the manger, will neither himself eat nor let others eat,' and so on in the same strain.

"Still, it does occasionally happen there, that some power-possessing or important being of the Earth suddenly chances to think not under the influences of the reflexes of his stomach and sex organs, but thinks sincerely and quite seriously about these or other questions, with particular regard to this terrifying terrestrial question. (pp. 1057-61)

This vignette illustrates how when such 'power-possessing beings' ponder on such issues, "their thoughts flow in all directions without any intentional exertion of any part whatsoever of their presence."

The next step in this cosmic tragedy is the complete degradation of the objectives of these individual as they find their way back to their self interest and greed: Beelzebub continues:

"… no sooner do the stomachs of these sincere agitated beings become empty or no sooner do they recover a little from these externally arisen impressions which had dejected them, than they not only instantly forget their vow, but even they themselves again begin consciously and unconsciously to do precisely everything which is generally the cause of the outbreak of these processes between communities. …

"Such a monstrous need arises in their abnormal psyche because they expect certain egoistic profits from these processes … and with their degenerated mentation they even hope that the greater the scale of the next process, the greater the extent of the said profits to be obtained, either personally for themselves or for their nearest.

"It even happens there, my boy, that certain of the power-possessing and important beings among your favourites unite and form a special society with the aim of jointly finding out and actualizing in practice some possible means for the abolition of this archcriminal property of theirs. (pp. 1061-2)

Power-possessing and important beings have united at times to form "special societies" for the eradication of warfare. Beelzebub briefly summarizes the results of one such historical society:

"But owing to their various personal egoistic and vain-glorious aims, the ordinary terrestrial important and power-possessing beings who had then assembled, very soon quarrelled among themselves and went their ways home without accomplishing anything." (p. 1063)

Beelzebub reports to Hassein that during his last visit to Earth, such a new society was being talked of, called the 'League of Nations' (the precursor to United Nations). According to Beelzebub, the problem is that "the beings with objective Reason do not happen to be in these societies," because they are not 'important.' And what does it mean to be 'important'? Beelzebub explains:

"In the course of observations during my last sojourn there I cleared up, among other things, that the beings with objective Reason do not happen to be in these societies for the following reasons:

"The point is that in order to participate in any society whatsoever, a being must always of necessity be important and such a being there among them, thanks once again to the abnormally established conditions of being-existence, can only be one who either has a great deal of money or who becomes what is called 'famous' among the other beings there.

"And since especially during recent times only those beings can become famous and important among them in whom the mentioned sacred function, namely 'being-conscience,' is entirely absent, then in consequence of the fact that this sacred function in the presences of beings is in general always associated with everything that represents and is Objective Reason, then, of course, those three-brained beings with Objective Reason always have conscience as well, and consequently such a being with conscience, will never be 'important' among the other beings.

"That is why the beings with Pure Reason there never have had and never will have the possibility of taking part in the societies of beings who are formed of important and power-possessing beings. (pp. 1069-70)

No one with Objective Reason or 'conscience' would ever be 'important' among the other power possessing beings on that ill-fated planet, and hence, they would have no chance of ever taking part in such 'special societies.' Instead, Beelzebub characterizes the emotional development of the power possessing beings, who "in respect of *Being are only perfected to the degree ... defined by the notion expressed in the following words: 'Look! Look! He already begins to distinguish mama from papa.'* " (p. 1066)

In reference to the meetings of the League of Nations, Beelzebub predicts that "nothing effective will come of it." Instead, he suggests that the members of the society:

"... will achieve personally for themselves by this new contrivance of theirs one 'most formidable' and 'most useful' result, namely, thanks to this 'official society' of theirs, they will have still another as it is said very plausible excuse for drawing wool over the eyes of their what are called 'proprietresses,' who are for these terrestrial contemporary power-possessing beings either their 'wife,' 'mistress,' 'mother-in-law,' or finally, the 'assistant' in some large store, and so on.

"Whereupon, thanks to this new official society of theirs, they will have the opportunity of passing the time tranquilly among their friends, important and power-possessing beings like themselves, and at these official 'five o'clocks' which without doubt will be very often arranged ostensibly for affairs connected as it were with the aims of this important official society of theirs, they will be able to pass the time without the silent though terrifying glances and watchfulness on the part of their 'proprietresses.' (pp. 1066-1067)

In addition to escaping the watchful eye of their proprietresses, enjoying 'five o'clocks' and 'Don-*Quixoting,*' and the advantages of being with other power possessing beings, Beelzebub suggests that such a society will also offer other advantages:

> "From this contrivance of your contemporary favorites some advantage might be derived, even quite a great one, but only for their inevitable newspaper, for drawing-room conversations, and, of course, for the various Hasnamussian manipulations of the terrestrial as they are called 'stock-jugglers.' (p. 1070)

Beelzebub explains that such societies may begin with some individuals who actually do feel some 'resurrected conscience' over previous wars, particularly when they happen to have suffered personal loses, but then very soon, the society has to involve new members:

> "These latter enter and take part in the tasks of such societies not because their conscience also begins to speak—far from it. They join only because, according to all those same abnormally established conditions of ordinary being-existence, they, being important and power possessing, must as a matter of course be members of and participate in every 'important' society.

> "When these other terrestrial important and power-possessing beings enter such societies and also begin to participate in their affairs, then they, with their personal egoistic and vainglorious aims, as a rule not only very soon send all the tasks of the society and everything that has been done by the beings with 'resurrected consciences' as is said 'flying up the chimney,' but as a rule, they also very soon, as it is also said there, 'put genuine spokes into the wheels of the first founders of these societies.'

> "And therefore, these societies of beings which are formed there for common-planetary welfare always quickly die—and die, as I already

told you, even without 'death agony.' (p. 1068)

Beelzebub's tales are rich in such surrealistic humour and portray most vividly the horror of the situation and the strangeness of the human psyche as evident on that ill-fated planet Earth. Serious undesirable qualities have become crystallized in humans, who are no longer capable of sincere and active mentation but controlled by the reflexes of the stomach, sexual itching, self-calming, greed and the need to escape the watchful eye of their proprietresses.

Gurdjieff, as Beelzebub, provides a dismal view of the psychopathology of humankind, the causes of war and your favorites' inability to eradicate it. Beelzebub explains simply that any three-brained being who had attained Objective Reason and experienced Objective conscience, "will never be 'important' among the other beings" and hence such societies are doomed to failure. [16]

Beelzebub explains to Hassein that in former times on Earth there had existed special societies of genuine initiates, who had acquired in their presences "objective data" —as a result of their own conscious labors and intentional suffering, and which could be sensed by those around. However, during the last two centuries, the term 'initiate' came to mean something quite different:

> "... those beings call each other by this name who belong to those what are called there 'criminal gangs' which in the said period have greatly multiplied there and whose members have as their chief aim to 'steal' from those around them only 'essence-values.'

---

[16] In modern times, this same sentiment motivates the arch-cunning Lucifer with his 'special societies' to seek population reduction and to maintain the world under the financial control of certain 'important' and 'power-possessing beings.' The United Nations was proposed as such a special society to eradicate war and restore world order, but it was controlled from the outset by Hasnamusses, stock jugglers and important power-possessing beings emboldened with "Hasnamussian sciences" and seeking world domination and control. The UN produces good press and fancy words, but no results and does nothing even to expose all the lies and deceits upon which the wars are based. The UN now proposes to have its own supply of nuclear weapons, a means by which it might provide some 'philanthropic aid' to some of the 'useless eaters' and 'breeders' upon the planet— the goyem.

"Under the pretence of following 'supernatural' or 'mystic' sciences, these criminal gangs there are really occupied, and very successfully, with this kind of plunder.

"And so, any and every genuine member of such a gang there is called an initiate.

"There are even 'great-initiates' among these terrestrial initiates, and these great-initiates especially at the present time, are made out of those ordinary initiates of new formation who in their 'virtuoso-affairs' pass, as is said there, through 'fire-water-copper-pipes-and-even-through-all-the-roulette-halls-of-Monte-Carlo.' (p. 350)

Beelzebub's remarks suggest that the special and secret societies devolve into criminal gangs, robbing the common peoples of 'essence-values' while plundering them. Beelzebub's final cryptic references to the 'great-initiates,' their 'virtuoso-affairs' and the roulette halls of Monte-Carlo, would seem to be in reference to the Rothschild dynasty of European bankers, infamous for just such affairs, for owning many such halls and for concocting innumerable wars and rebellions, while deceiving the populace through their own media and propaganda.[17][18]

Such important new initiates and power-possessing beings in fact do nothing to help eradicate such processes of reciprocal destruction, but instead help to finance them. As Beelzebub notes:

"These terrestrial power-possessing and important beings, particularly the contemporary ones, at times do not frustrate such

---

[17] Beelzebub's reference to the *fire-water-copper-pipes* is curious. The Rothschild family adopted the sacred symbol of the *Star of David* or the *Seal of Solomon* as their family emblem and the name Rothschild refers to this 'red shield' in German. The Star of David is composed of two triangles depicting the elements of fire and water. This Seal of Solomon ended up also on the flag of the state of Israel, which some also refer to as Rothschild Land.

[18] In modern times, largely as a consequence of the truth movement over the internet, many more people have woken up to the powerful role played by secret societies within world affairs. These include such groups as the Illuminati, centred in the City of London, the Committee of 300, the Bilderbergers, the Council on Foreign Relations, Masonic and Luciferian orders, the Skull and Bones society, the Bohemian Grove crew, the Jesuits and the Black Pope, Zionist, Talmudic and Kabbalist orders. These are all such secret societies of 'initiates of new formation' and Hasnamusses, 'criminal gangs' which scheme the affairs and fortunes of humankind.

national affairs from which they might expect considerable gain personally for themselves or for the beings of their own caste. (pp. 1064-5)

My goodness, how things change and yet remain the same.

The Hasnamussian Sciences & the 'Intelligentsia'

When discussing the League of Nations, Beelzebub expressed his opinion that nothing will likely become of such a 'common-planetary society' mainly because "impartial Reason, proper to the presence of all three-brained beings who have already attained responsible age, is absent in them *(its members)*...." Beelzebub explains that their 'maleficent' education is particularly adapted to those young beings who will latter as a rule become 'power-possessing.' The capacities for 'sincere thinking,' the 'sensing of reality' and 'logical reflection' indeed "become a very rare luxury on this planet ...." Instead, their so-called 'education' mainly teaches them how best to "give oneself up to what is called 'self-calming' ..." and encourages such ignoble traits as "'egoism,' 'partiality,' 'vanity,' 'self-love,' and so on." (p. 1059)

Beelzebub explains to Hassein that the inherency towards the processes of reciprocal destruction has now become "fixed in their psyche during hundreds of centuries" and that it "can never be decrystallized in the course of a few decades." He suggests that such 'important' beings as might sincerely aim to eliminate warfare would best direct their energies towards "the eradication of the conviction ... of the virtue of two notions they have." The first of these concerns:

> "... the practice of exalting certain of the participants in these processes to what are called 'heroes' and rewarding them with honors and what are called 'orders'...." (pp. 1071-2)

Beelzebub explains that such hero worship becomes an 'automatic factor' within the psyche of the next generation which makes them especially vulnerable to "fall into that state into which it has already become without fail habitual for them to fall during these processes ...." Such misguided youths can be whipped into a frenzy or patriotic fervour most simply.

The second concrete step that might be taken towards the eradication of warfare would be:

> "... the abolition even of one of their illustrious 'sciences' from among their many *Hasnamussian sciences*,' invented by certain pimpled beings among them, in which it is nonchalantly proved that the periodic reciprocal destruction on the Earth is very, very necessary, and that if it did not exist an intolerable overpopulation would result on the Earth, and such economic horrors would ensure that men-beings would begin to eat one another. (p. 1072) [19]

---

[19] The reference to such 'pimpled beings' is elaborated upon in another of Beelzebub's comments on the socialization and education of an 'analytic-chemist,' an intelligentsia of the ruling classes:

> "For instance, some mama's darling, a young man, inevitably with a pimpled face — and he is pimpled because his mama considered herself a high-brow and thought it was "indecent" to speak of and point out certain things to her son, whereupon this son of hers, not yet having formed his own consciousness, did that which was "done" in him, and the results of these "doings" of his, as with all such young people, appeared on his face as pimples, which are very well known even to contemporary medicine. (p. 547)

[20] The Rockefeller family has been one of the prime promoters of the Malthusian philosophy, 'eugenics' and 'population control' in modern times. Adolph Hitler had received funding for his race theories and eugenics programs from the Rockefellers and allied financial and aristocratic interests. Bertrand Russell, one of the prime British intellectuals serving the plutocrats, theocrats and aristocrats with their desire for a 'new world order,' wrote:

> "At present the population of the world is increasing... If a Black Death could be spread throughout the world once in every generation, survivors could procreate freely without making the world too full... the state of affairs might be somewhat unpleasant, but what of it? Really high-minded people are indifferent to suffering, especially that of others.... Gradually, by selective breeding, the congenital differences between rulers and ruled will increase until they become almost different species. A revolt of the plebs would become as unthinkable as an organized insurrection of sheep against the practice of eating mutton." (*The Impact of Science on Society.*)

Bertrand Russell is a prime example of the pimpled intellectual depicted by Beelzebub, likely controlled by the same three principle motives ascribed by Beelzebub to the 'aristocrats' and the 'zevocrates:' *"The first concerns the question of food; the second consists of the recollections*

293

Of course, Beelzebub's description of the Hasnamussian sciences seems most bizarre and ridiculous, and yet this is only a parody of what actually occurs within the life of humanity. [20]

---

associated with the former functionings of the sexual organs; and the third relates to the memories of their first nurse. "(p. 1088)

Another author explains some of the current Hasnamussian objectives and plans being advanced under the euphemism of 'global government' or the 'new world order:'

> **"The Rockefeller** Foundation has the SAME agenda as the Illuminati and the Gates Foundation. David Rockefeller, a member of the Illuminati, is a founder and member of several organizations such as the Trilateral Commission, the Bilderbergers and the Club of Rome, whose purpose is to a) set up a One World Government, b) control ALL business throughout the world and, c) dramatically and rapidly reducing the population of the world from 6 billion to 500 million, by war, disease and famine." (Dr. L. Day, 2008)

The Hasnamussian science is thriving in modern times. Even the United Nations proposes in Agenda 21 that the ideal population for a sustainable earth would be 500 million. This is the figure carved in stone onto the Georgia Guide Stones erected in the state of Georgia, USA, by some Hasnamuss member of some 'special' and secret society. A message consisting of a set of ten guidelines or principles is engraved on the Georgia Guidestones in eight different languages with the statement: *Let these be guidestones to an age of reason.*" The first of these reads:

Maintain humanity under 500,000,000 in perpetual balance with nature.

This is the Hasnamussian science alive and well in modern times, supported by a plethora of other invented sciences. Humankind, in modern times, has never known life apart from the hidden influences of these terrestrial nullities, as Beelzebub describes.

A recent news item (October, 2010) entitled: *The Green Agenda Is About Getting Rid Of As Many Humans As Possible*, reads:

> The truth is that there are a growing number of environmental activists (including some very, very famous people) who are publicly advocating the end of our freedoms, the establishment of a Big Brother style world government and the systematic eradication of at least 90% of humanity all for the good of the environment. Unfortunately, this is not a joke and it is not an exaggeration. ... To these eco-fascists, climate change is the number one threat to the earth, and in order to eliminate that threat "democracy must be put on hold", an authoritarian world government must be established and we need to start getting rid of as many humans as possible. In a video, Gates describes how the number of people might be reduced.... *"The world today has 6.8 billion people... that's headed up to about 9 billion. Now if we do a really great job on new vaccines, health care, reproductive health services, we could lower that by perhaps 10 or 15 percent."*

Beelzebub explains that the eradication of such a Malthusian Hasnamussian notion would be a major step towards the prevention of such processes of reciprocal destruction. However, there would further need to be an eradication of other fanciful ideas:

> "... they would help towards this, that there might not reach to the beings of future times at least one of those idiotic ideas from the number of already without this sufficiently numerous similar ideas constantly arising there, which are transmitted from generation to generation as 'something' lawful and indubitable and which all together are partly the cause of the formation in their presences of those properties not one of which is becoming to three-centered beings of which there belongs also that property inherent in them alone which engenders in them even 'doubt in the existence of Divinity'; and owing chiefly to this doubt there has almost entirely disappeared from their common presences the possibility of the precipitation of those data which should without fail be precipitated in the presences of all three-brained beings, the totality of which data engenders in them the impulse, called the 'instinctive sensing,' of those certain cosmic truths, which are always felt even by all one-centered and two-centered beings, wherever they might breed in the whole of the Universe.

> "But the misfortune for all the other ordinary favorites of yours is that these power-possessing and important beings assembled from the whole of the planet do not begin to occupy themselves with these questions, considering them to be beneath their dignity.

> "What next! Such 'important' members of such 'important' societies suddenly occupying themselves with such trivial matters! (pp. 1072-3)

Of course, the important and power-possessing beings would not consider the life of the soul as something of interest or concern, as instead they promulgated those "idiotic ideas ... constantly arising there," which are passed from generation to generation as something 'lawful' and

---

Certainly, this is the Hasnamussian science of the day, along with quack sciences espousing inoculations, global warming due to human carbon emissions, genetically modified foods, chemtrail poisons—all *"invented by certain pimpled beings"* to prove "nonchalantly" the need for diseases, poisons and wars to maintain population control and for the infamous 'stock jugglers.'

'indubitable.' The sum of such idiotic ideas engenders in those strange three-brained beings "even '*doubt in the existence of Divinity.*" The consequence of such strange invented Hasnamussian philosophies and science is that such beings no longer attain to the "'instinctual sensing' of those certain cosmic truths."[21]

Beelzebub then launches into a long exposition about the varied 'and the 'crats'—many of whom are candidates for Hasnamusses. Beelzebub explains to Hassein that the true meaning of the word 'intelligentsia' would imply "force-in-oneself" and the capacity for objective reason. However, among your favorites, those called by this name are actually those beings "who are the exact opposite of what this word denotes," Instead, they should be called the 'unintelligent' and the "mechanogentsia." Beelzebub explains that these mechanogentsia can "give absolutely no direction at all to their being-functions" and are animated only by "external shocks" acting upon corresponding automatic perceptions as imposed through their maleficent education. Most importantly, Beelzebub explains the lack within the so-called intelligentsia:

> "But never do their outer manifestations in general nor those inner-being-impulses of theirs, which ought to be under the directive of their being-'I,' proceed according to their own wish resulting from the whole of their entire presence. (p. 1082)

However, these intelligentsia are especially those with that "'psycho-organic-need' of theirs to 'teach others sense' and to put them on the right road," and who "always have at least one 'victim' for their teachings."

Beelzebub views the so-called 'intelligentsia' as particularly affected by their superficial education and socialization:

---

[21] The Hasnamusses of the contemporary era are very intent indeed to squash within the populace any last semblance of a belief or feeling of the Divinity in life. A rash of recent publications are geared towards this end: Richard Dawkins, *The God Delusion*, 2006; Sam Harris, *The End Of Faith: Religion, Terror, And The Future Of Reason*, 2004; Carl Sagan, *The Varieties Of Scientific Experience: A Personal view Of the Search For God*, 2006; Daniel Dennett, *Breaking The Spell: Religion As A Natural Phenomenon*, 2006; Christopher Hitchens, *God Is Not Great: How Religion Poisons Everything*, 2007; Victor Stegner, *God: The Failed Hypothesis--How Science Shows That God Does Not Exist*, 2007. Such works are full of evidences of such bob-tailed reason as Beelzebub depicts.

"These freaks lose, so to say, that outer mask which thanks to the
same maleficent means existing there, called 'education,' most
of them little by little learned to wear from their childhood and
thanks to which they can very well conceal their genuine inner and
outer trifling significance from others, and in consequence they
automatically become slaves of others to the degree of humiliation;
or, as they themselves say there, they fall as regards all their inner
experience, under somebody's 'thumb'; for instance, under the
'thumb' of 'wife' or 'mistress,' or of such another who by some
means has ferreted out the inner insignificance of the given
terrestrial being, and thus the latter ceases to have for them this
artificial mask. (pp. 1077-8)

Beelzebub explains that it is just such 'freaks,' under someone's thumb,
who write various 'manuals' for the guidance and education of others. For
example, a contemporary being *whose heart as they say always 'sinks into
his boots' from fright when, for instance, a mouse runs past him,"* writes a book
on *"what must not be done on meeting a tiger;"* or another such a terrestrial
being *"under somebody's thumb"* writes a book on *"what must be done for the
good 'government' of others."* (p. 1078) Beelzebub portrays the intelligentsia
as striving always to conceal from others their inner insignificance or
'terrestrial nullity.'

Another Hasnamussian invention is that of 'policy.' Beelzebub explains that
such policies were created well before the contemporary era, back in the
period of Gemchania, but continue today:

"... beings of one community begin to pipe with full blast against
beings of another community that 'Hasnamussian music' they call
'policy,' that is, they begin to 'criticize' each other, to 'lower each
other's standing,' to 'down each other,' and so on, their aim being to
create what is called 'prestige' among the local beings in relation to
their own community.

"In the course of such a 'policy' one of the heads of a certain
European community in some way or other learned the 'secret'
how to influence the psyche of beings of other communities to
acknowledge the authority of and give supremacy to the beings of his
own community.

"Afterwards when the beings who had learned this secret—the principle of the action of which was called 'Ksvaznell' or 'inciting one against the other'—initiated the other heads of his community into it, and they all made it the basis of their 'policy'; then, indeed the beings of this community began everywhere and in everything to gain predominance.

"Although both the former heads of the beings of this community and also that being himself who had hit upon the secret Ksvaznell, already long ago perished, yet subsequent generations—continuing now of course automatically to employ this 'secret'—gradually not only took into their own hands almost the whole of this Gemchania, but also subordinated to their influence the very essence of all the beings breeding on that part of the planet Earth.

"In spite of the fact that two centuries have passed, yet at that period to which my further tale refers … it all continued in the same way.

"Having become proud of their success, the recent heads of that mentioned European community who had the luck, thanks to this same secret Ksvaznell alone, gradually to subordinate all to their influence and to grasp everything into their hands, wished to lay their 'paws' even on that which had until then been considered unattainable. (pp. 719-720)

The secret learnt within this community concerns how to 'incite one against the other,' so as to divide and conquer from within. And so these Hasnamusses of European origin began to spread the propaganda and lies through the communities to instigate such effects, to subordinate to themselves the control of the beings breeding on that ill-fated planet Earth. What a sad but 'cunning' Tale!

The 'Crats'

"And that is just as it is everywhere on Earth: donkeys are alike, they are only differently called."
Mullah Nassr Eddin (quoted by Beelzebub, p. 1090)

Beelzebub then explains to Hassein that many of the intelligentsia also go by other names, particularly by those Greek names ending in the term 'crat:' These include the Bureaucrats, the Plutocrats, the Theocrats, Democrats, Zevrocrats and the Aristocrats. The suffix crat is derived from the Greek and means 'to keep' or 'to hold,' according to Beelzebub, who then characterizes each of these types.

The Bureaucrats are the intelligentsia who look after the chancellery and who are completely controlled by their "automatic associations" to shocks coming from without. The bureaucrats manifest in a completely mechanical way without the participation of "any separate spiritualized being-part whatsoever of their common presence."

The 'plutocrats' are the intelligentsia and power-possessing beings described by Beelzebub as "scoundrels of the deepest dye" and "saturated by every kind of *Hasnamussness to the marrow of their bones.*" (p. 1084) These plutocrats are those who:

> "... were able very artistically to get all the honest, that is 'naïve,' fellow countrymen of theirs they came across, into their toils, thanks to which they became the owners of a great quantity of what is called there 'money' and 'slaves.'

"Here, bear in mind that it is just from these terrestrial types that most Hasnamuss-individuals arise. (p. 1083)

Beelzebub explains that when it was necessary to find some "very 'forceful' word" to denote them, the suffix 'plut' was borrowed from Russian, which means 'rogue.' These "terrestrial parasites" were quite content with such a title, not knowing its hidden significance, and "out of swagger, they go about in top hats, even on weekdays" and at other times, they "strut like turkey cocks." Beelzebub notes the influences of these "terrestrial monsters:'

"… these terrestrial types, thanks to what is called 'ill-gotten' gains, had already then acquired 'force and power' far greater perhaps than that of their kings. (p. 1084)

The Theocrats are next described as those 'intelligentsia' in who we find almost "the same 'perturbation' as in those who become plutocrats." However, whereas the plutocrats "act upon their surroundings for the satisfaction of their Hasnamussian needs through that function which is called among them 'trust,'" the Theocrats pursue the satisfaction of their Hasnamussian needs based on "faith." And thus, humankind has come to 'trust' the bankers and the power elites, and to have 'faith' in their crooked Hasnamussian priests and perverted religious figures. Appropriately, Mullah Nassr Eddin is quoted as having remarked: "Isn't it all one to the poor flies how they are killed? *By a kick of the hooves of horned devils, or by a stroke of the beautiful wings of divine angels?*" (p. 1086)

The Democrats do not tend to come from the 'hereditary *intelligentsics*' but were simple, ordinary terrestrial beings who became intelligentsia and only afterwards did the sacred function of 'Conscience' degenerate in them. However, when such Democrats become 'power-possessing beings,' "they have in themselves no inherited aptitudes at all for instinctually being able to direct others and in consequence are quite unable to direct the existence of beings *who happen to be in their power.*" (p. 1086)

The last two types, the Zevrocrats and the Aristocrats are distinguished by the names given to them, such as 'emir,' 'count,' 'khan,' 'prince' and so on, which titles always elicit 'vanity' in such beings, "up to their very death." These two types are very similar but one comes from a 'republican state organization,' while the other is from a 'monarchic state organization.'

Beelzebub describes both of these types as 'jokes of nature' and 'misconceptions' and he depicts their basic motivational patterns:

> "All the experiencings, however, of these aristocrats and zevrocrats there, according to my observation, can be reduced to only three series.
>
> *"The first concerns the question of food; the second consists of the recollections associated with the former* functionings of the sexual organs; and the third relates to the memories of their first nurse."
> (p. 1088)

Beelzebub was quite astonished and puzzled by how such beings, such 'jokes of nature,' with only these three areas of experiencing, could have as lengthy an existence as the other beings there. Beelzebub describes 'your favorites,' the strange three-brained beings on plant Earth, as delighting in having their zevrocrats and aristocrats take part in staging their 'puppet shows,' despite their being "quite vacuous and consequently feeble."

These are some of the various Hasnamusses, Intelligentsia and 'crats,' that dominate the world stage, as the power-possessing and 'important' beings on that ill-fated planet. Beelzebub often refers to that *'certain something'* in the Hasnamuss-individual, which is not simply put into words but is detected more in its blending with the spectrum of the abnormal being-impulses they manifest. Beelzebub explains that this 'certain something' will eventually cause *"what are called 'serious-retributing-suffering-consequences' for these individuals themselves"* in afterlife, but meanwhile, they have a greater effect on those around them and lead others to imitate and manifest the same undesirable qualities and impulses.

The Hasnamuss individuals, like the aristocratic, corporate, financial and religious elites, do not experience the impulses of *"being-self-shame"* or of Objective Conscience. The current crisis in the life of humankind attests to the horrors, suffering and desolation caused by these *"terrestrial nullities."* The pseudo-illuminate are such Hasnamusses, willing to spray you and your children with chemtrails, while poisoning your food, water and air, sickening you through genetically modified poisons and additives, infesting you with inoculations and pharmaceuticals, confusing your hearts and minds through all the lies and deceits of the corporate media in service of their Hasnamussian sciences.

Hasnamusses, Intelligentsia & Crats

The Hasnamuss are controlled by the three lower possibilities of money, sex and power, and do not attain to the awakening of the heart or to the possibilities inherent to the higher life of the soul. They are the product of lunacy and delusion. They feel self-satisfaction from leading you astray, engaging in every kind of depravity and they indeed have such *"irresistible inclinations to destroy the existence of other breathing creatures."* Such types came to rule the human race, all part of the *new world psychiatric disorder*. This is the scum that rose to the top of the waters of life and their crimes are the blood streaks through human history.

These are the types who form the United Nations, the secret and special societies, the plutocrats, theocrats, aristocrats and democrats who perpetuate the cycles of war, human violence and suffering:

> "As a rule, in consequence of the fact that these power-possessing or important beings there do not use the time foreseen by Great Nature for preparing themselves to become worthy responsible beings—owing chiefly to which during their responsible existence, even in their waking state, all kinds of associations in their common presences almost always flow automatically—therefore they themselves without any individual intentions and at times even half-intentionally try to do everything in such a way that the next process of reciprocal destruction should occur sooner, and they even hope that this next process should proceed on as large a scale as possible.

> "Such a monstrous need arises in their abnormal psyche because they expect certain egoistic profits from these processes, either personally for themselves or for their nearest, and with their degenerate mentation they even hope that the greater the scale of the next process, the greater the extent of the profits to be obtained, either personally for themselves or for their nearest. (p. 1062)

The pseudo-illuminate Hasnamusses are not so illumined and their false dual consciousness system and inner nullity has prevented the human race, your favorites, from maintaining normal conditions of being-existence or attaining to higher consciousness and the soul. Further, they have distorted and obscured the messages and teachings of all of the Sacred Messengers to such an extent, that the strange three-brained beings doubt even that they are a part of Divinity. Meanwhile, the archcriminal wars of the Hasnamusses stain the fabric of human history crimson red and new Hasnamussian inventions provide additional contrivances for their Hasnamussian impulses to destroy life on Earth.

And so, humankind came to be ruled by Hasnamusses, 'crats' and 'intelligentsia' of varied types. The situation is exactly as depicted by Mullah Nassr Eddin: "And that is just as it is everywhere on Earth: donkeys are alike, they are only differently called." (p. 1090)

The Future of Humanity

Beelzebub is not hopeful for humankind to eradicate these terrible processes from their planet due to the ongoing degradation of their strange psyche and the poor quality of your favorites' vibrations. Further, the artificial educational system and culture propagate the same falsities, lies, titillation, spin and rubbish. At the end of the chapter, on *Beelzebub's Opinion of War*, Beelzebub concludes with some of the deliberations of the Very Saintly Ashiata Shiemash, from "The Terror of the Situation":

> "'If it is still possible to save the beings of the Earth, then Time alone can do it.'
>
> "We can now only repeat the same in regard to this terrible property of theirs, of which we have just been speaking, namely, their periodic processes of the destruction of each other's existence.
>
> "We can only say now, that if this property of terrestrial beings is to disappear from that unfortunate planet, then it will be with Time alone, thanks either to the guidance of a certain Being with very high Reason or to certain exceptional cosmic events.
>
> Having said this, Beelzebub again began to look at Hassein with that same strange look. (p. 1118)

Of course, Beelzebub himself has been providing such guidance as a being of "very high Reason." However, aside from the guidance of a Being of high Reason or exceptional cosmic events, the situation of humankind does not look hopeful. Especially this is so given that the *Hasnamusses* and the Crats, the power-possessing beings and their 'special societies' insure the perpetuation of such horrors with ever new inventions of Hasnamussian science to make mass murder the 'merest trifle.'

On visiting America, during his final descent to the Earth, Beelzebub still held out some hopes for the beings of that country, noting:

"Concerning specially what is called the 'degree of degeneration' of the common presences of those who compose this contemporary large group on the continent America, in respect of the loss of possibilities for the acquisition of Being nearer to the normal Being of three-brained beings in general, I can tell you something somewhat consoling for them, namely, that in my opinion there remains among them the largest percentage of beings in whose presences the said possibility is not entirely lost. ...

"It seems to me that this has happened because there have migrated there, and still now migrate from the continent of Europe, beings chiefly from among what are called the 'simple beings' who are not, so to say, the 'hereditary offspring' of the European beings belonging to the 'ruling caste' in whom, thanks to transmission by inheritance from generation to generation during long centuries of predisposition to Hasnamussian properties, there is at the present time so much of what is called 'inner swagger' that it would never permit them to blend with the general mass in order to strive together with common efforts to become such three-brained beings as they should be. (pp. 1041-2)

Beelzebub regarded America as having some chance as "there were only very few of the 'offspring of the ruling caste'" and it was "still possible for 'our brother' to exist ...."   Unfortunately, America too has since fallen under the influences of such secrets and policies as the 'crats' have devised. In reference to the future of Jerusalem and Judaism, as recounted earlier, Beelzebub comments:

"The religion founded on the teaching of Saint Moses, although it existed for a long time and is still maintained after a fashion by its followers, yet, owing to the organic hatred formed in the beings of other communities towards the beings who follow this religion, due only to that 'maleficent' idea existing there called 'policy,' infallibly sooner or later they will doubtlessly 'croak it' as well and also 'with a crash.' (p. 733)

The teachings of 'normality-loving' Saint Moses certainly yielded to the spices of Zionism and the worship of the golden calf by Hasnamusses and power-possessing beings, with their secret Ksvaznell policies of dividing and conquering, and setting one against the other. Beelzebub, having witnessed the demise of many empires through his observations of Earth, foresaw Judaism as inevitably ending in also in such a 'crash,' perhaps not long after Christ birthplace is made into one of their favorite 'parking lots,' or humankind wake up to the multiple crimes being committed against them by such Hasnamusses and Crats.

ZERO
POINT
PROPOSAL
FOR THE
CRIMINAL
PROSE-
CUTION OF
THE

WORLD ELITES, SO-CALLED, FOR THEIR CRIMES AGAINST HUMANITY

The Restoration of Human Justice, the Rule of Law & the Enforcement of Canadian and International Anti-Terrorism Legislation against the True Terrorists of our Age

O dear, Canada as a democracy and sovereign nation has been lost; as have the U.S. and other western and European so-called democracies. Atrocious lies and deceptions have been intentionally perpetrated by our governments, the corporate media and the corporate/financial elite against the citizenry of our countries. These include lies about the 9-11 terrorist events, the lies of U. S., Canadian (and NATO) involvement in Afghanistan, Iraq and Libya, the selling off of national resources and the transfer of wealth to the international banksters, the poisoning and sickening of the Canadian and American population and environment through chemtrail poisoning, inoculations, GM foods, additives, and so much more. In total, these criminal activities of our government and the criminal cabals which control them violate all kinds of Canadian law—from the support and financing of terrorism, to accessories after the fact to mass murder, the obstruction of justice, criminal racketeering, the administration of toxic substances, theft and bank fraud, conspiracy to commit mass murder and much more—in addition to violating all standards of morality, decency and even common sense. As noted by J. E. Hoover, former head of the FBI: *"The individual is handicapped by coming face to face with a conspiracy so monstrous he cannot believe it exists."* The psychopathic elite, the plutocrats and such who came to deceive the human race, are both psychopathic and severely mentally disordered. As it happens, they are also then to be exposed for their "inner nullity" and insignificance. Perverts, pedophiles, psychopaths and parasites came to gain control of our nations, so-called *proud and free*—what a joke.

Unfortunately, the conspiracy theories were never simply just theories but these theories are supported by a vast wealth of criminal evidence of all kinds and are the only way of making intelligible the tragedy of what has been perpetrated within Canada as indeed around the world—all hidden from *the sheep people of the world* by the corporate media of lies. The corporate media of lies actually helped to stage the 9-11 events so as to traumatize and condition the American and world public to accept American war crimes to be perpetrated around the world, but particularly within the Middle East.

There is no doubt that the 9-11 attacks on the New York Trade Towers and such were a terrorist event. However, the American and Canadian governments, instead of prosecuting the true perpetrators of these crimes, have instead colluded with these criminal cabals in order to maintain the deception of the population and they have allowed a hate filled media to blame Muslims for these crimes. This has made the Canadian government co-conspirators and supporters themselves of this terrorist agenda. The Prime Minister and cabinet no longer serve the Canadian public but have joined forces with the terrorists with their plans for global dominance, a police state society and the pseudosciences of eugenics. This certainly maintains a supply of funds and media influence for the mainstream political parties. Our elected politicians have sold their souls and betrayed the Canadian people, as indeed governments around the world have betrayed their populaces. The Conservative party of Canada is now a terrorist organization, obstructing international justice, as are the Liberal, NDP and Greens parties. All have become complicit in supporting the terrorist activities and schemes of the so-called elites, failing to investigate 9-11 and allowing varied criminal corporate activities in service of their *new world psychiatric disordered* global government by criminal psychopaths and Satanists.

The Canadian people have been betrayed not only by our government but also by the criminal racketeering and treasonous activities of the RCMP, the provincial police services, the intelligence and military communities, and by the judiciary. Senior people within these services have failed to uphold the laws of Canada, their oaths of office or any semblance of morality. They have betrayed the trust of Canadians and without the restoration of justice within Canada, our future is only one of sickening, wars and violence, death camps, inoculations and implants, and all the deviant eugenics plans of the pseudo-elites and their so-called 'new world order,' which is really an *'old world psychiatric disorder.'* At this time in human history, the world has fallen into chaos, with world wide wars, disease and death.

Canada only has a future if we can reverse these trends and re-establish the rule of laws—the actual enforcement of the anti-terrorism legislation and the restoration of human justice within Canadian society. Fortunately, a world wide truth movement has gathered momentum, as people wake up to the crimes of their governments and the shadow elites who control them, and the intentional public deceptions of the corporate media. A huge volume of evidence has coalesced to reveal the truly cruel and despicable acts which have been perpetrated against the Canadian people and against peoples around the world.

Although the terrorist attacks of 9-11 were indeed tragic and the souls of the victims cry out for justice, at least the evidences surrounding this event can precipitate the exposure of who the true terrorists of our age really are. They are not Osama Bin Laden and his reindeer—but they are within our society and unfortunately they also control the Canadian government and police—as a shadow government, as they control the governments of the United States, Britain, and indeed almost all the countries of the world. These international terrorist organizations are indeed Zionists and Masons, banksters and corporate elites, and even royalties and whoring priests— quite a sad lot, should all be in Cuba where it is quite hot.

The enormity of their crimes and their betrayal of the Canadian people now make it impossible to any longer ignore the elephant in the room—the spider with all of its webs of deceit and lies and entanglements. Awakening to these facts is a shocking experience and must lead to a reconsideration of everything one thought one knew—about our country as a democracy, about the justice and police services within our society, and about the corporate media which has enabled such devious and unscrupulous schemes to be perpetrated against us as citizens.

If Canadians cannot address these crimes, Canada has no future other than your impoverishment, enslavement, sickness and death. This also will be the future for your children and grandchildren, if you have any. We are facing our last chance to save this beautiful nation of Canada, to save our own lives and rise up to protect future generations, and re-establish the rule of law and impartial justice within Canadian society and attempt to have a broader influence within the world community. Are there no nations left whose leaders still believe in truth or justice, or anyone who has still some nobility or uprightness of heart? Indeed, the situation of humanity is most tragic and so-much unnecessary suffering and despair has been our lot.

The zero point proposal is for the application of the anti-terrorist legislation around the world to the true terrorists of our age, as of the past ages. The criminal prosecution of these elites and the seizure of their assets would indeed *reduce all national debts world wide to zero.* All national debts to international bankster cartels would be reduced to zero and all sovereign assets returned to the peoples of respective nations. Furthermore, the government figures around the world who have participated in these crimes would be brought before truth hearings and be appropriately charged for their criminal involvement.

We have only to use logic and evidence and apply the principles of Canadian law against the true terrorists. IF this were done and the police actually functioned as the upholders of the law again, then instead of being controlled by these same cabals, then Canada would indeed be transformed as would all the nations of the Earth. Peoples around the world could enter a new era or age of wealth, health and longevity, and awakening unlike any in Canadian or world history. The actual application of the anti-terrorist

legislation around the world would bring about a world wide social and spiritual renewal, enabling new stages of the awakening of consciousness and human evolution--your evolution. There would indeed be innovations throughout all levels and sectors of our society.

According to Canadian legislation:

OFFENCES AGAINST PUBLIC ORDER

"terrorist activity" means:

(*a*) an act or omission that is committed in or outside Canada and that, if committed in Canada, is one of the following offences:

(*b*) an act or omission, in or outside Canada,

> (i) that is committed (A) in whole or in part for a political, religious or ideological purpose, objective or cause, and
> (B) in whole or in part with the intention of intimidating the public, or a segment of the public, with regard to its security, including its economic security ... and

> (ii) that intentionally

> (A) causes death or serious bodily harm to a person by the use of violence,
> (B) endangers a person's life,
> (C) causes a serious risk to the health or safety of the public or any segment of the public,
> (D) causes substantial property damage, whether to public or private property, if causing such damage is likely to result in the conduct or harm referred to in any of clauses (A) to (C), or
> (E) causes serious interference with or serious disruption of an essential service, facility or system ...

> and includes a conspiracy, attempt or threat to commit any such act or omission, or being an accessory after the fact or counselling in relation to any such act or omission ...

"terrorist group" means

> (*a*) an entity that has as one of its purposes or activities facilitating or carrying out any terrorist activity, or (*b*) a listed entity, and includes an association of such entities.

FINANCING OF TERRORISM

Providing or collecting property for certain activities

83.02 Every one who, directly or indirectly, wilfully and without lawful justification or excuse, provides or collects property intending that it be used or knowing that it will be used, in whole or in part, in order to carry out

> (a) an act or omission that constitutes an offence referred to in subparagraphs (a)(i) to (ix) of the definition of "terrorist activity" in subsection 83.01(1), or
>
> (b) any other act or omission intended to cause death or serious bodily harm to a civilian or to any other person not taking an active part in the hostilities in a situation of armed conflict, if the purpose of that act or omission, by its nature or context, is to intimidate the public, or to compel a government or an international organization to do or refrain from doing any act,

is guilty of an indictable offence and is liable to imprisonment for a term of not more than 10 years. 2001, c. 41, s. 4.

Providing, making available, etc., property or services for terrorist purposes

83.03 Every one who, directly or indirectly, collects property, provides or invites a person to provide, or makes available property or financial or other related services

> *(a) intending that they be used, or knowing that they will be used, in whole or in part, for the purpose of facilitating or carrying out any terrorist activity, or for the purpose of benefiting any person who is facilitating or carrying out such an activity, or*
>
> *(b) knowing that, in whole or part, they will be used by or will benefit a terrorist group, is guilty of an indictable offence and is liable to imprisonment for a term of not more than 10 years.*

2001, c. 41, s. 4.

FINANCING OF TERRORISM	
Freezing of property	83.08 (1) No person in Canada and no Canadian outside Canada shall knowingly
	(a) deal directly or indirectly in any property that is owned or controlled by or on behalf of a terrorist group;
	(b) enter into or facilitate, directly or indirectly, any transaction in respect of property referred to in paragraph (a); or
	(c) provide any financial or other related services in respect of property referred to in paragraph (a) to, for the benefit of or at the direction of a terrorist group.

Terrorist activity is defined so as to include activities which are *"in whole or in part for a political, religious or ideological purpose, objective or cause."* Certainly, the activities of the financial and corporate elites are for such "ideological purposes"—to bring about their so-called "new world order" and to support the population reduction programs propagated by such as Henry Kissinger, the Club of Rome, agencies within the United Nations (especially the World Health Organization), the varied Rockefeller and Tavistock think-tanks, and the pharmaceutical mafia. The criminal elites, so-called, also have criminal ideological purposes—to establish British/American/Israeli, and UN military dominance around the world and to institute a world wide fascist terrorist state, while reducing world population through war and varied forms of poisoning.

The political and ideological objectives of these groups, who actually staged the 9-11 terrorist attacks to advance their agenda, clearly are intended to *"cause death or serious bodily harm to a person by the use of violence, endangers a person's life, causes a serious risk to the health or safety of the public or any segment of the public, causes substantial property damage, and causes serious interference with or serious disruption of an essential service, facility or system...."* The psychopathic agendas of the pseudo-elites, the crème of the gangsters and banksters who have high jacked our nations, clearly violate all of these principles.

In order to reclaim Canada as a nation, these anti-terrorism laws have to be applied. The names of the individuals, banks and corporations involved in perpetrating the 9-11 attacks and serving to perpetuate the fraud, and trying to bring about the new world psychiatric disorder system are generally known and indeed largely matters of public record. The attendance sheets for the Bilderbergs, the names of those on the CFR and in the Rockefeller think-tanks, the identities of the corporations engaged in criminal practices, are all available within the public domain. Indeed, the fortunes of these terrorists should be frozen and seized within the domain of Canada, as indeed they should be around the world by the peoples of the respective countries involved, all under our respective anti-terrorist legislation.

Of course, not everyone in any of these groups is guilty by association and each individual needs to tried or heard separately so as to reveal their true involvement and the extent of their complicity. Such trials need to be held publicly and broadcast through the media to expose these individuals and to enable the awakening and education of Canadian and world citizenry.

Most likely, the seizure of the assets of this *international criminal cartel* would in fact pay off the Canadian national debt, as it would pay off the national debts around the world, as accrued to these terrorist organizations. The IMF and World Bank clearly show a history of involvement in terrorist and criminal activities around the world. The re-establishment of truth and justice within our societies, would indeed allow for seizure of the assets of the elites around the world. Clearly, such a transition within our society could enable a truly new age of wealth and abundance within nations around the world.

Of course, almost everyone considers that this could never be done and indeed it is not clear that it can, but this is the only hope for Canadians and for peoples around the world to climb out of the massive public debt and death traps set for them for these international criminal cabals, and to bring the real mass murderers and war profiteers to justice for their crimes against humanity.

Canadians must demand immediate public and criminal investigation of the lies of the 9/11 attacks on the US and for criminal investigations of the RCMP, CSIS and Military Intelligence in Canada, as well as into such other psychopathic policing services around the world: particularly, MI6, the Mossad, the CIA and NSA. In addition, we need investigations of the dominant political parties who have colluded in obstructing justice for the 9-11 events, for sacrificing Canadian soldiers in a war based on deception, for helping to perpetrate American war crimes and for colluding in advancing the new world order agenda. The psychopathic agenda of our shadow government is further enabling the impoverishment and sickening of citizens. A wide range of individuals within multinational banks and corporations, and the corporate media require to be charged for a wide range of criminal and treasonous activities. The wealth and assets of these banks, the multinational corporations and the corporate media found to be guilty of participating in these schemes, will all be seized by the national governments and held in trust for the peoples of the respective nations.

The general objective of these seizures will not be for the Canadian government to retain these assets but rather to evaluate their worth and then to enable the people who work for these corporations or businesses to assume ownership of the said companies and assets. Thus, for example, the media outlets will all continue to report the news and provide programming and most employees will retain their jobs, but the people who work for the media will come to own their own business over time while required to repay the Canadian government for the value of the assets (while paying 0% interest on their loans for a period of seven years). Corporations and business will come to be owned by the people who operate and maintain them, instead of the corporate criminals and mobsters, and will serve the true needs of Canadians. Anyone within the media who intentionally deceives the public in their reporting will be immediately fired and subject to criminal prosecution. The media will no longer be allowed to devise war propaganda, public deceptions, lies and disinformation, but will be dedicated to revealing to the public all the lies they have been told over the last decades of their existence.

The former government and corporate elite, senior officers and military personnel will face 9-11 truth hearings and be criminally sentenced for diverse crimes against humanity and the Canadian people, treason, war crimes and criminal racketeering. We need to use none of the criminal and torturous methods used by these people themselves. Their trials have to be made public and be reported impartially throughout the media. They will be retired from public and corporate life, and depending upon the severity of their crimes, released over time as they come forth to speak the truth and contribute to a renewed Canada.

I would recommend in all seriousness, that the primary group of these elites in Canada be held at the Montebello resort facility in Quebec, not far from Ottawa where these peoples will face public trials and hearings. The resort, which once hosted the three banditos—Calderone, Bush and Harper, conspiring to bring in the SPP can be renamed as the *Montebello Hospital for the Criminally Insane*—and reserved for those who have participated in attempting to create their new world psychiatric disordered society. The elites can all be elites together for intercourse among themselves. We will protect the Canadian people with a pack of guard dogs, as the police seem incapable of maintaining or upholding Canadian, international or humanitarian law.

Montebello Hostpital for the Criminally Insane will provide a nice facility for them, where they can enjoy each others fine company and celebrate their victories together. No staff will be required to work within the facility, but only to surround it so as to protect the people of the surrounding country. Food and supplies will be provided and the residents can cook and clean for themselves, and have all the internal politics and relationships as they may choose. We will provide them with GM and irradiated foods, Coca Cola and Pepsi with aspartame, fluoridated water, and a series of inoculations for flues, cervical cancer and viruses, and their own chip implants—to assured public safety and as a means of keeping records of their canteen funds. The residents will have access to TV's and radio where they can listen to all the past corporate media coverage of their own lies and deceits; although internet access will be restricted so that they can no longer infect the larger population with their *memes*.

As the truth of 9-11 is explored and those involved come forward to speak the truth, a whole web of criminality will be unravelled, which will eventually result in the complete paying off of Canada's national debt, as it would for all countries around the world, and for the return of a vast wealth to the peoples of Canada and all sovereign nations. Governments around the world would acquire a wide range of wealthy corporations and businesses, all of which can be revamped and used, and most employees will retain their jobs. The primary changes will be in ownership at executive levels. These corporate and business assets will be assigned financial values and continue to be worked by the people employed there. Over time, the government will be paid for the assets through the profits of the businesses. These funds will be loaned at zero percent interest. The value of legitimate stocks and investment in these companies by those not involved in the new world psychiatric disorder system will be honoured, such that innocent people will not lose their savings, pension funds and wealth through this period of transition. In fact, efforts need to be made to return monies to pension plans and individuals who wealth has been depleted over the past years through the criminal activities of these elites, enabled by the corruption of the mainstream political parties.

Charges will be brought against such corporate entities as the major pharmaceutical companies, Monsantos, the major oil companies and numerous other multinational companies who have assumed roles in the sickening of the national populations, for violating the human rights of planetary citizens, for corrupting the medical system, for intentionally undermining the manufacturing sector of our society and for the commission of bank fraud and criminal racketeering. The senior management within these companies will also be charged for crimes their companies have committed in foreign countries.

All of the major political parties need to be investigated for criminal racketeering, treason, and for allowing for the intentional poisonings of the Canadian peoples—through chemtrails, food additives, genetically modified foods, the fluoridation of the water, inoculation programs, and the use of invisible electronic and psychotropic weapons against the population. They need to be charged also with the theft of public funds and bank fraud, as accessories to mass murder and as co-conspirator in terrorist and treasonous activities. All of those involved in the criminal activities of the criminal elites of the New World Order fanatics will have all of their assets and wealth seized within Canada and held in trust for the Canadian peoples—to pay off the national debt and bring about a new century of investment in Canada for the peoples of Canada.

There will need also to be a series of criminal investigations into those professional bodies and groups which have maintained a conspiracy of silence about the programs perpetrated within our society and/or who participated actively in them. This includes investigations of the Medical and Psychiatric societies, Health Canada, the Psychological Associations, the association of University professors and academic circles. Doctors, psychiatrists and psychologists, who have a history of violating the Hippocratic oath will lose their licences; Pilots who have sprayed the citizenry of Canada with poisons will lose their licenses and face prison terms; Media personnel who have betrayed the public for so many years will be retired from public life and face prison terms for their roles as conspirators.

The media personnel can also receive David Rockefeller *mass murderer buttons* for their service to the psychopathic world elite, all the while intentionally deceiving their fellow citizens. Military and police personnel who have violated Canadian laws will be retired from their positions. Those academics who provided the rational and strategies for the new world psychiatric disordered system will be retired from academic life and charged for their conspiracies to commit mass murder through their eugenics plans. The finances of all of those involved in these areas will be reviewed and their ill-gotten gains from the past years and decades will be seized. Further, they will all be required to testify before public bodies and inquiries, or else to be imprisoned indefinitely until which time they choose to come forth to speak the truth.

Canada will issue arrest warrants for those individuals from foreign countries who have also been involved in the new world psychiatric disordered system; individuals such as David Rockefeller and mass murderers such as George Bush and Dick Cheney, Henry Kissinger, and eugenicist Bill Gates, and so on. Such terrorists will no longer to be protected by a corrupted police force if they attempt to visit Canada but would instead be arrested by police services. We will seek extraditions from foreign countries and seize the assets of foreign criminals present within Canada.

The restoration of justice within Canada is the only way to a new age within our country and indeed around the world. The crimes of the scumbag elites run as bloodstains through human history and we, the people of Canada and America, and world citizens, Will by the Grace of God, take back our countries and expose the criminality of the corrupted gangsters who have destroyed all the ideals upon which our nations are founded. Otherwise, we have no future except as sickened and enslaved citizens, with the mark of the Beast upon our right hand or forehead.

The elites are a serious group of psychopathic and perverted men and woman who rose to the top as torturers and demons within our modern society. Until this scourge is deal with, we will live in an increasingly nightmarish Orwellian world run by Zionist gangsters and war criminals, banksters and corporate criminals, perverted police, military and religious leadership. Humankind could be secure again to live natural lives when these new world order folk all have the mark of the Beast upon them and are safely tucked away for intercourse among themselves.

What sad and pathetic nations we have become and we have now to have the courage or 'uprightness of heart' to take back our countries and re-establish the rule of law — applying the anti-terrorism legislation to imprison these psychopaths before they destroy our country, your children and the larger world. This is our only hope, for ourselves, our children and grandchildren, for seven generations. By December 21, 2012, the aim is to achieve a world wide awareness of such a course of action, to bring about the reduction of all national debts of the world to zero, the imprisonment of these psychopaths around the world, and the liberation of humankind for a new age of abundance, health and spiritual awakening.

International Relations, National Security & The Role of the Military

"If the Nuremberg laws were applied, then every post-war American president would have been hanged." Norm Chomsky

If Canadians could wrestle control of our government from the so-called elites—the corporate and banking gangsters, we would face a major problem in re-evaluating our relationships with other countries which are similarly controlled by these same devious psychopathic groups. The United States has committed major war crimes against the peoples of Afghanistan and Iraq, and through the CIA and other agencies, have spread violence and chaos around the world over the last decades, all the while intentionally deceiving the American public. The activities of the CIA and these cabals are estimated to have been implicated in the mass murder of tens of millions of people around the world since the conclusion of the Second World War.

The criminal American, or should we say British-US-Israeli shadow government has perpetrated war crimes under the pretext of hunting down Osama Bin Laden and Muslim terrorists and invaded sovereign countries for purposes of imperialist world-domination—and for their gods of gold, oil and drugs, sex slaves, and military dominance. Almost two million people have died from the most recent near east excursions and many millions more left homeless, impoverished, sickened, traumatized and injured through these war crimes. In fact, the history of modern America is a history of mass murdering peoples around the world—Korea, Vietnam, Cambodia, Iran, Central and South America—to further American military dominance and in service of the international financers, aristocrats and corporations. The American government has been high jacked by criminal elements and Zionist controllers, and allowed the American public to be intentionally deceived about the causes of war and American criminal activity throughout the world. On the international level, the United States of America is one of the key terrorist organizations of modern times.

Israel is similarly guilty of terrorist activities and war crimes — ranging from Israeli involvement in the 9-11 attacks, the wars against Lebanon, Palestine, the ongoing genocide against the peoples of Gaza, and other terrorist attacks around the world — the 7/7 London subway bombings, the assassination of John Kennedy, the Mumbai attacks and so many more. The Zionist fanatics who control Israel also control the United States government as well as the Canadian government, along with other prominent gangsters.

We as Canadians have to realize that the United States, Israel and Great Britain are an axis of evil posing a far more serious threat to us than that of Muslim extremists, Iran, Korea, Russia and China, all put together. Of course, these countries are also run by other criminal gangs and pose threats as well which cannot be denied. However, the CIA, the Mossad, and MI 6 are terrorist organizations which have spread terror around the world through their black operations — hit teams, bombing, arming and financing terrorist groups, overthrowing popular governments and assassinating political and social leaders.

The United States has over seven hundred military bases in over 130 countries around the world and always serves the deviant and criminal ends of the corporate and banking elites, and not the true needs of the American people or those of other native peoples. Hollywood spews out movies making Americans out as if they are some big heroes while the lies of the wars are always concealed from the public. The military budget of the US, on so-called 'defence spending,' is equal to the military budgets of all other countries on earth combined. This has been part of the elite's plans to use the US military to gain world domination and to impoverish the American people through this means — along with their banking fraud and Wall Street racketeering. Weapons of warfare and for mass murder are the primary export of the US and the elites are happy to sponsor both sides of conflicts and arms build up.

Canada has participated in the war crimes of the American people against the peoples of Afghanistan and Libya and sacrificed our servicemen — not in the name of peace keeping nor protecting ourselves from foreign terrorist threats, but rather for the military-industrial and financial elites to further their fanatical plans for a new world psychiatric disordered state — a one world government with a group of psychopaths at its helm. The American dream turned into the American nightmare. Of course, the majority of the

American public are like the Canadian public—simply deceived like sheep through the corporate media and the brainwashing fashioned through the so-called educational system. The criminal invasion of the middle-east has constituted crimes against humanity and embodies the same type of new world psychiatric disorder agenda as conceived by Adolph Hitler and other Zionist and Communist fanatics through human history.

The Canadian government and superior officers within in the Canadian military, the RCMP and CSIS have intentionally deceived military personnel as to the real causes of the war in Afghanistan and allowed the citizens of Canada to be so deceived! They have become accessories after the fact to mass murder, war crimes and international terrorism. Canada now violates its own laws allowing uranium to be mined and exported for military purposes, while imprisoning native elders who protest the destruction and theft of their lands. In 2008, Prime Minister Harper has pledged $800 million towards vehicles for Canadian forces to be used in Canada and to be manufactured in the US. Apparently, these are likely trucks and prison vans to transport people to prison camps and jails, and to enable the increasing militarization of our society. This so-called *war on terrorism* has been a complete fraud—blamed on Muslims but concocted by the elites for your nightmare in a fascist state. The only terrorists that the police and intelligence community can find in ten years of the 'war or terror,' are those individuals set up and entrapped by the police services themselves! The RCMP make no effort, along with the Canadian government, CSIS, and the military to *capture the true terrorists of our age*. It has all been a fraud!

Why does the Canadian military allow Canadians to be sprayed from the skies with chemical poisoning, while we sacrifice our service men in a war based on deceptions and war crimes? Instead, the media and our governments divert attention elsewhere and intentionally deceive the Canadian public. The masters of war do indeed make millions and billions for the elites who scheme the whole thing and deceive the public through their Hollywood tales and corporate media, used as propaganda and all the deceits propagated through the educational system.

A responsible Canadian government could play a role within the international scene demanding that the world community face the ugly truths of 9-11 and the criminal activities of the elites. We demand that these people be exposed and prosecuted for their innumerable crimes against the people of Canada and against humanity. All NATO countries have deceived their own peoples about the underlying causes of the wars in Afghanistan and Iraq and have made no efforts to arrest the real terrorists! Similarly, the United Nations has betrayed the trust of the world's citizenry and has been complicit in concealing the criminal activities of the world elites. From its inception, the United Nations was built on land donated by the Rockefeller clan, while giving refuge to the worst of the Nazis through operation Paperclip, and it has always long served the agendas of the elitists and eugenicists, torturers and perverts.

Canada will take these concerns to the United Nations and demand 9-11 truth hearings be held before the international audience with exposure of the criminal activities of the United Nations in their contributions to the eugenics programs of the elites. Canada will similarly demand that the truth be brought out at the NATO meetings and that trials are held for the true world terrorists, mass murderers and their minions throughout the military and police communities who have enabled these crimes.

Canada respects the sovereignty of other countries and asks nations of the world to respect our sovereignty. Whether or not Canada would maintain its membership in the UN and NATO would depend upon the criminal activities of these groups being exposed to public scrutiny.

The truth shall set humankind free of these insidious influences and the corruption within our government, the corporate/financial communities and international bodies—such as NATO and the United Nations. At the same time, there is a need for international organizations and treaties if these can are not controlled by the international cartels of banksters and elitists.

The Canadian government would seek out opportunities upon the world stage to fashion treaties with countries supportive of the demand for truth and justice in the world—through the exposure and imprisonment of the criminal elites. We would seek to form alliances with countries or groups who similarly demand international justice and who will respect Canadian sovereignty. Canada desires to maintain 'fair trade' will any other country of the world, including our major partner of the US, but we will to live in truth and freedom instead of being imprisoned as slaves by a psychiatrically disorder group of Zionists, banksters, corporate criminals and professional deceivers. Canada will form alliances with similarly minded political, social and cultural groups around the world, all to expose the new world psychiatrically disorder scheme and to bring these people to justice worldwide.

Canadians must demand the immediate removal of all American, British and Israeli military personal, police and secret services from Canada, and all NATO or UN forces. Canada will renegotiate or overturn treaties allowing US, UN or any foreign military or police services onto Canadian soil. We demand that the HAARP facility in Alaska be shut down immediately until there is a full public exposure of HAARP uses and practices, and that all practices of chemtrail spraying and weather modification be stopped immediately, to be followed by public hearings and criminal prosecutions of those involved in these terrorist activities.

Canadian troops should be returned immediately from Afghanistan and all other corrupted UN and NATO involvements. Soldiers would be used on Canadian soil to defend our country from foreign forces and to secure the transition of Canada back to its democratic principles and charter. The military will be needed to provide security at facilities to be seized by the government, to take part in the imprisonment of corrupted gangsters who have committed such crimes against the people of Canada, and to disarm the quasi-military security forces which have been formed within our nation. The Military will further be required to hold public military hearings to charge the superior levels of military control and intelligence for their treasonous activities and their involvement of Canadian military in the illegal war crimes of the United States against the people of Afghanistan and Libya. These hearing will be public and covered extensively throughout the media.

It is incumbent upon the military to defend Canada from enemies both domestic and foreign, and at this time, Canada needs its Canadian forces to re-establish civil liberties, the rule of law and the principles of democracy within Canada. The Canadian peoples are being poisoned now from the skies through chemtrail spraying by actual terrorists. The real terrorist threat to Canadians is not to be found in the desecrated lands of

Afghanistan, but within Canada and the criminal elite who have highjacked the government of our nation. We demand that the Canadian military defend the Canadian people from the domestic terrorism and poisoning. Canadians need to support our military and provide more funding for our servicemen and women. There will be also be criminal investigations of medical and psychiatric experimentation conducted on Canadian public and servicemen/women. We do not want a government carrying on black operations against its own citizens and those who have done so, deserve to be exposed and prosecuted for their involvement.

Further, the Canadian people are currently at risk within our own country from whatever *false flag terrorist events* which the elites will stage in order to further advance their agenda or to prevent exposure and imprisonment. We need Canadian soldiers to help deal with this situation as the elites have an arsenal of weapons that can be used and are being used domestically. They have biological, nuclear and energetic weapons which they can use to stage false flag terrorist events within Canada, to tell you new lies and create new imaginary enemies while bringing about martial law and their fascist police state. The Canadian military needs to assume a role in helping to deal with the emergency situation as now exists within Canada, and as will be schemed by these fanatics.

The future contribution of Canadian soldiers to international efforts will be considered over time and according to circumstance. There are certainly aspects of a world government which could have served humankind if it has not been so infected with the poisons of the elites and their eugenics philosophies, their sexual perversions and greed. It is unfortunate that the United Nations was so corrupted from its inception, as indeed the Earth does require some form of international body to expose the criminal activities of the elites through modern history, and to revaluate all existing treaties, and such, which will require to be modified in light of the truths revealed.

The call is one for international law and order, and the application and enforcement of the terrorist legislation against those who have been perpetrating the nightmare scenario of these international criminal cabals. The wealth of these elites, of those who have and are participating in this old world psychiatrically disordered system, needs to be seized around the world, reducing all national debts world wide to zero, while bringing to justice, those corrupted politicians who have colluded within these global crime syndicates.

A New Age
Utopian Society
or an Old Age Nightmare?

When Karen and I woke up to the deception of 9-11, we realized shortly afterwards, that 9-11 was only a symptom of a much more pervasive sickness and evil which has overtaken the so-called democratic and civilized countries of the western world. Our country, our politicians, our media, our educators and doctors, our police and military have all been infiltrated from within through the past generations. Our society has become completely corrupted in a way that has effected almost every aspect of our lives and yet the masses of citizens are completely asleep to it all. The mass hypnosis of western society has been very effectively carried out while the sheep people are led to slaughter.

The sheep people have been intentionally 'socially engineered' and deceived about all major national and international events throughout the course of their lives. The elites have rewritten history, fabricated innumerable lies and falsities, and kept real knowledge and scientific inventions from the public. This massive public deception based on propaganda and lies has been perpetrated through the corporate media and Hollywood. While the citizens were lulled into sleep, the countries of America and Canada have been highjacked, as have the countries of Europe and around the world. Most people have a completely imaginary idea of what is really being done now within our society, and what our true history has been. Citizens imagine that their politicians serve them; that the media informs them; that their teachers educate them; and their doctors maintain their health. They imagine that the police actually capture the real criminals and terrorists, and that there is justice within our court and legal system. The TV, newspapers and magazines all maintain such deceptions, while a psychopathic elite laugh at the *goyem* being led to sickness, impoverishment and slaughter.

You are being sprayed with chemical poisons from your sky, whether or not you are intelligent and brave enough to look and see, and grasp the horror of this. The same people who are spraying you with chemtrails, or poisoning you with food additives and inoculations, are also, the same ones who brought you the 9-11 terrorist attacks, bombings, mass shootings, assassinations and terrorism around the world. As the motto of the Mossad suggests: *"By means of deception, we wage war"* – and they have, endlessly. Tens of millions of people have been murdered by these psychopathic elite and at this time they are bringing us ever closer to a World War III or IV, as Israel threatens new war crimes against the people of Iran, which could well escalate into broader world conflict. America, in service of the global elite, is positioning more and more weaponry around the world, so that the psychopaths can play their chess board games, sacrificing pawns and the masses of humankind. Global conflict is increasingly likely, as Russia and China are well aware of the psychopathic agendas of NATO and world Zionism.

This is really all so insane, so unnecessary and tragic. Humankind has never known life apart from the insidious activities of these elites through modern times. And now, for your nightmare, they are fashioning a police-surveillance state, spreading illness and poisons, while violating all the noble principles and ideals of our nations.

Humankind is at a turning point where either we descend further into the hell worlds that these psychopathic elite concoct for the human race, or else, we make the effort to take back our societies and demand the enforcement of our own and international anti-terrorism laws to bring *the real terrorist* to justice around the world. This needs to include the psychopathic elites and those government officials who have colluded in all of these schemes. Imagine that, that your members of Parliament think that it is quite fine that you citizens be sprayed from the sky with aluminium, barium, strontium and other poisons, or that Canadian soldiers die in criminal wars based on lies. They belie the truth with every word they utter and are a disgrace to us as a nation. The Houses of PARLIAMENT have become the Houses of CRIMINALS and your informative corporate media all deserve *thank you buttons* from David Rockefeller for helping to enable such multiple mass murders so effectively through the years.

Humanity's future lay in the balance and the only way of attaining a new age or utopian society is through the actual enforcement of the anti-terrorist legislation against the true terrorists of our age. Otherwise, there will be genocides on a scale that dwarf the atrocities of the past decades, while the Earth is increasingly desecrated and poisoned. Without the restoration of impartial justice, humankind will sink into a new dark age and it is only a matter of time, before you and your children and grandchildren are the victims of these psychopaths.

The re-establishment of law and righteousness within the world would truly bring about a new age—of prosperity, planetary healing and spiritual awakening. Humankind would discover all kinds of things they never knew—about history, their lives and most importantly, themselves. A RAPTURE could indeed sweep the world as the Stars shine, the truth is revealed and liberation music fills the hearts and minds of humankind once again. The elites can be tucked away in their camps for intercourse among themselves, with the mark of the Beast upon them, within the hells of their own design, and humankind can attain liberation from these forces of Satanism, Luciferianism and Zionism.

Imagine such a world, which would indeed be filled with wonder, love and discovery.

Secret of the Seventh Point
& the Significance of 11:37

Synchronicities are the jokers in nature's pack of card, for they refuse to play by the rules and offer a hint that, in our quest for certainty about the universe, we may have ignored some vital clues. (Peat, 1987, p. 7)

I am going to attempt to explain the background and significance of this cover illustration and of the 11:37 numerology in the title of this book. These things have multiple levels of meaning in light of the current crises in the life of humanity, especially as it ties into the significance of the Star of David on the Houses of Parliament, and what conspiracy theory suggests about the Rothschild, Zionist and Masonic agendas and hidden control of Canada, as of the US and European countries. Why is the *Star of David* or *Seal of Solomon* on the Peace Tower clock facing south towards the Masonic Lodge across the street? For that matter, why are those working under the 'peace tower' supportive of criminal wars based on lies and public deception? And further, why do they allow the chemtrail poisoning of their own citizens?

Personally, I feel that the Star of David on the Peace Tower clock is a very beautiful and inspiring sight, although unfortunately, most people have no idea of what it all means or of how your politicians belie its true meaning and significance. To me, it is significance that this Star of David has a central point, the life or moving principle at the center of the clock which moves the hands; so it is not empty inside like Solomon's Seal on Israel's flag and the Rothschild's shield. To me, the Star of David means that the Houses of Parliament really belong to those of us citizens 'upright of heart' and it is our task to reclaim our country from the insidious and criminal cabals who have highjacked the nation. We have to live up to the higher ideals embodied in the ancient symbol of the six pointed star with a seventh central point, instead of sinking into the soulless life of the new world order elites with their puppet politicians and media deceptions.

I took this picture of the clock on the Peace Tower of the Ottawa Houses of Parliament on September 17th of 2011. I spent that day on Ottawa's Parliament Hill from approximately ten in the morning till after six in the evening. I had gone out to support an Ottawa 9-11 truth group who were playing a new video from the *Architects and Engineers for 9-11 Truth* group, explaining the scientific evidence that Building 7 and the Two Towers were brought down by obvious controlled demolitions. From 4 pm to 6 that day, I conducted my bimonthly radio show through *www.bbsradio.com* from the Hill using my cell phone and interviewing members of the 9-11 group at the end of their day. The day was clear and sunny apart from the massive chemtrail spraying being conducted all over the Ottawa skyline throughout the day. While I was on the Hill, at different times through the day, I took short videos of the skyline documenting the chemtrail spraying with some dramatic shots of chemtrails highlighted behind the peace tower.

In the weeks after taking the videos, I began to learn how to use a media program to create a short documentary film, entitled: *A Day in the Life of the Chemtrail Poisoning of the Citizens of Ottawa by a Psychopathic Elite.* When composing this video, I used a tool which rotates the scenes to make the transitions between the video clips more interesting. In the photo above, the shot of the peace tower is being rotated in this way against a black background.

One day, a friend's son was helping me learn more of studio composition and we happened to stop the video at the frame of this photo as it was turning. The image immediately drew my attention and I asked my friend if there was any way that I could capture that image. I learnt then how to use the print screen button to seize a screen image and then to transfer it over into the Paint program, where I could save it.

So I happened to capture this transitional moment in my shot of the Peace Tower. It was only subsequently that I realized that the time on the clock was 11:37. This was a total coincidence as far as I was concerned, as I had no idea of what the time on the clock was when I happened to take the videos of it. I had not been aware of what the time was until the picture was extracted from the video.

For most people, this would not be much of any kind of coincidence, but for me, it had and has profound significance, as the number sequence of 1-3-7, and the alpha constant of science 1/137 are prominent in my writings and work on ancient metaphysics and modern science. Furthermore, these numbers have often come up for me in coincidental ways over the past years and I have considered them my magical numbers. Furthermore, the significance of these numbers ties into the meaning and significance of the Star of David or the Seal of Solomon.

A remarkable series of coincidences led to the capturing of this image with the clock set to this particular time of 11:37. I just happened to video the tower at that time although I had taken under ten minutes of video through the day with only about 10 seconds of a close up of the clock. Then it was coincidental that I happened to capture this photo in transition as I did, even still without realizing its significance. It was only subsequently, that I incorporated the number sequence of 11:37 into this book title and decided to explain some of its significance.

In *Synchronicity: The Bridge between matter and mind* (1987), physicist David Peat investigated synchronicity drawing from studies of Jung and Pauli, and with a background in Bohm's *Wholeness and the Implicate Orders* (1980). For Peat, *synchronicity* demonstrates the existence of 'a bridge' between mind and matter. Whereas science has tended to separate the study of mind and matter into separate sciences of psychology and physics, synchronous events demonstrate instances where mind and material processes arise together or influence each other in mysterious ways inexplicable in terms of the "causality principle." In effect, meaningful coincidences and patterns of events demonstrate that there is a level of causality, which is 'non-local' as such events cannot simply be explained in terms of 'local effects.'

Synchronicities are the jokers in Nature deck — events that demonstrate hidden orders of meaning and inter-relationships existing beyond the purely physical world of matter. Peat explains:

Synchronicities give us a glimpse beyond our conventional notions of time and causality into the immense patterns of nature, the underlying dance which connects all things and the mirror which is suspended between inner and outer universes. With synchronicity as our starting point, it becomes possible to begin the construction of a bridge that spans the worlds of mind and matter, physics and psyche. ... Synchronicity ... arises out of the underlying patterns of the universe rather than through a causality of pushes and pulls that we normally associate with events in nature. (pp. 2 &16)

Consider one example of a synchronous event used by Peat to demonstrate the enigmas poised by such fortuitous events or meaningful coincidences:

> One of the "classic" examples of synchronicity, told by Carl Jung himself, concerns a crisis that occurred during therapy. Jung's patient was a woman whose highly rational approach to life made any form of treatment particularly difficult. On one occasion the woman related a dream in which a golden scarab appeared. Jung knew that such a beetle was of great significance to the ancient Egyptians for it was taken as a symbol of rebirth. As the woman was talking, the psychiatrist in his darkened office heard a tapping at the window behind him. He drew the curtain, opened the window, and in flew a golden scarab ... Jung showed the woman "her" scarab and from that moment the patient's excessive rationality was pierced and their sessions together became more profitable. (Pp. 6-7)

To skeptics, it is easy to simply declare that this is just a 'chance' or random happening that a scarab arrived at that moment as the woman was exploring her dream, and that such a chance event really requires no explanation. Alternatively, the skeptic could question the integrity of the report or reporters, or somehow or other dismiss the possibility of such events as being meaningfully interrelated. To consider seriously such 'jokers' in life experience points to profoundly complex interrelationships of events, people and psychological dynamics, and beetles, all in some deep patterns of 'meaning'Dor information and intelligence all non-locally present. The skeptic will find no causal explanations in local four-dimensional reality and will dismiss the possibilities of non-local interrelationships to account for such happenings—such enigmatic bridges between mind and matter.

Peat, like Pauli and Jung, regards synchronous events as demonstrating how the physical world has to be linked in profound ways to the psychological world, in ways beyond local effects in our familiar four-dimensional space-time:

> Such curious events may ... indicate that a mutual process is unfolding out of the same ground and that this ground must

therefore lie beyond the individual consciousness that is located in space and time. ... evidence of some deeper, universal principle of hidden order. (p. 32)

Peat uses varied phrases to depict this deeper reality of hidden orders. He suggests *"everything causes everything else,"* and that *"the various phenomena of the universe arise out of the flux of the whole, and are best described as a 'law of the whole.'"* (p. 52) Further, *"within each element of matter and space-time is enfolded the entire universe."* (p. 67) And again, *"the operation of mind (has) resonances to the transformations of matter, and indeed, the two will be found to emerge from a deeper ground."* (p. 73)

Of course, for me, my photo happened to capture the clock at 11:37, which numbers have a profound meaning in my own mystical and occult studies and writings. I will elaborate upon some of this significance and meaning.

The six pointed star has an ancient history and is not only the *Star of David* or *Seal of Solomon* for Jews or Christians, but also the double triangle is a sign for Vishnu, the *Sri-Antara* of the Brahmins and the yogic symbol for the heart chakra. In magic, an upward turned triangle represents the element of fire and the downward turned triangle represents the element water. The six pointed star thus represents the interaction of these two primordial elements.

The first verses of the *Book of Genesis* in fact can be used to derive the six pointed star and a variation of this—a six pointed star with a seventh central point.

> Genesis 1: 1. In the beginning, God created the heaven and the earth.
> Genesis 1:2 And the earth was without form, and void; and darkness was upon the face of the deep. And the Spirit of God moved upon the face of the waters.
> Genesis 1:3 And God said, Let there be light: and there was light.

The Star of David is inherent to these verses. A six pointed star represents the heaven and the earth as created by God, above and below, as well as representing the spiritual and material nature of a human being. Verse 2 describes the universe before creation as absorbed into nothingness and without form, which is totally consistent with modern scientific views of "vacuum genesis" or creation out of the apparent nothingness and plenum of the quantum vacuum. This is *creation ex nihilo*. In verse two, the Spirit of God then moves across the face of the waters and this also can be depicted by the Star of David, with the elements of fire and water. In verse 3, God says let there be light—and we might take this light as emerging as a first point of supernal lux established within the centre of the Star of David. So both the more widely known version of the six sided Star of David and the variant with a seventh central point are both suggested as a symbol by the first verses of Genesis. The ancient symbol is not inherently evil and the high jacking of the symbol by demon possessed families should not deter serious study of its significance—especially of its variant, with a central point.

The symbol of the double triangle with a central point is especially emphasized within *The Secret Doctrine* of occult scholar H. P. Blavatsky. The symbol depicts the sacred geometry inherent to the Kosmos and the nature of the Dhyan Chohans (Divine Intelligences) who sculpt the void through the processes of creation.

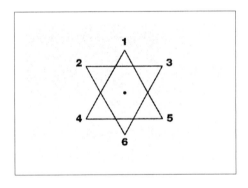

… the "Six-pointed Star" … is the symbol, in almost every religion, of the *Logos* as the first emanation. … The six-pointed Star refers to the six Forces or Powers of Nature, the six planes, principles, etc., etc., all synthesized by the seventh, or the central point in the Star. … In its Unity, primordial light is the seventh, or highest principle … the light of the unmanifest Logos. … The former is symbolized by the Central Point in the double-Triangle; the latter by the hexagon itself, or the "six limbs" of the Microprosopus …. (H. P. Blavatsky, *Secret Doctrine*, 1888, pp. 215-6)

This archaic symbol replicated here is from *The Secret Doctrine*. The figure has three aspects—a central point, an upward turn triangle representing fire and spirit, and a downward turned triangle representing the element water (or material creation). The central point represents the laya centre or the first point, the living entity and the Logos, while the triangles represent the inherent spiritual and material nature and forces manifested within the matrices of existence. Understanding this symbol is of profound significance, especially with the central point which is often excluded—as in the Rothschild red shield or on the flag of Israel, which are empty inside. The primary symbol of Theosophy is the Seal of Solomon with the Egyptian *ankh* in the centre to represent the 'living entity.'

God is first One, then Three and then Seven. This is a basic principle of intelligent design elaborated within *The Secret Doctrine* and throughout the mystical literature, including Kabbalah, Christianity and Hinduism. These profound principles are embodied within this symbol which has a unitary, triune and sevenfold nature. Just as white light can be divided by a three sided prism to yield a spectrum of colors, so also the nature of Deity is described as triune and sevenfold.

In a chapter *"The Hexagon with the Central Point, or the Seventh Key,"* Blavatsky wrote:

Pythagoras viewed the hexagon formed of two crossed triangles as the symbol of creation, and the Egyptians, as that of the union of fire and water (or of generation), the Essenes saw in it the Seal of Solomon, the Jews the Shield of David, the Hindus the Sign of Vishnu (to this day); and if even in Russia and Poland the double triangle is regarded as a powerful talisman — then so wide-spread a use argues that there is something in it. It stands to reason, indeed, that such an ancient and universally revered symbol should not be merely laid aside to be laughed at by those who know nothing of its virtues or real Occult significance. (S. D. III, p. 105)

Blavatsky quotes an occultist, from *Things Concealed*, depicting the Seal of Solomon with a central point: *"The seventh key is the hieroglyph of the sacred septenary, of royalty, of the priesthood (the Initiate), of triumph and true result by struggle. It is magic power in all its force, the true "Holy Kingdom." In the Hermetic Philosophy it is the quintessence resulting from the union of the two forces of the great Magic…."* Blavatsky then concludes: *"The force of this key is absolute in Magic. All religions have consecrated this sign in their rites."*

The Star of David with a central point is also the symbol for the Heart Chakra, the central chakra within a human being and the origin of the I experience, and of consciousness and life within the material body. There are three chakras above and three below the heart chakra. Most people, humankind asleep, are ruled by the three lower chakras—associated with the motivations of money, sex and power, These motives are lower material desires yet they come to dominate the ego and mind of the masses, especially those of the psychopathic elite. In spiritual evolution, the first level of awakening or self realization involves the awakening of the fourth chakra. The light of the Self inherent to the Heart can then illuminate the higher chakras, the throat, brow (or third eye) and crown chakra, yielding different types of mystical experiences, powers and states of samadhi. Unfortunately, most people are ruled by their three lower chakras and do not realize the latent faculties and powers within themselves.

Blavatsky stresses the importance of the 'heart doctrine:'

> "Learn above all to separate Head-learning from Soul-Wisdom, the "Eye" from the "Heart" doctrine. But even ignorance is better than Head-learning with no Soul-wisdom to illuminate and guide it. ... The "Doctrine of the Eye" is for the crowd, the "Doctrine of the Heart," for the elect. ... "Great Sifter" is the name of the "Heart Doctrine...." Blavatsky, *The Voice of the* Silence, 1889

The famous Illuminati symbol is of the 'eye' in the triangle. However, Blavatsky suggests that the 'heart doctrine' is a deeper teaching than that of the 'eye doctrine.'

The Star of David embodies these sacred principles of design and can be represented by the number 1/137. The 1 in the numerator of this fraction indicates the Deity or the Absolute, or the fundamental Unity; while the 1 below indicates the emergent point or logos, which then is divided by three and yields seven. This number 1/137, more than any other number, embodies the Secret Doctrine's arcane wisdom teaching concerning creation physics and metaphysics.

Modern science is basically founded upon a dualistic perspective in which it always contrasts opposing principles—such as matter and energy, waves and particles, observers and the observed, the mind and the body, conscious and

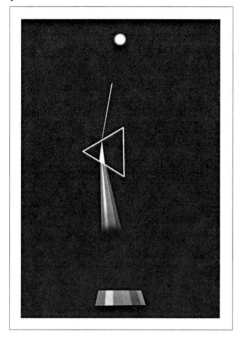

unconscious, science and religion. In contrast, mystical and spiritual science suggests that the Divine Principles of a Triune and Sevenfold nature are embodied within all phenomena of nature. Thus, the One is divided by three and yields seven—just as white light divided by a prism creates a spectrum of colours. Time, space, matter and energy—all of the four elements of modern science—can be regarded separately in such a 1-3-7 analysis, akin to the mathematical nature of light!

Whereas modern science has considered mainly matter and energy, within time and space, an occult perspective suggests a trinity of intelligence, energy and matter, or spirit, soul and body; upon seven planes or dimensions of being existence. An occult perspective offers a far more multidimensional model of human and cosmic existence, than does modern science. Scientists still think that there is only 'the material world' and deny the existence of the 'immaterial world,' in their typical dualistic philosophy of life.

These principles of the Law of Three and the Law of Seven are found within Christianity, Judaism and Kabbalah, Islam and Sufism, Tibetan Buddhism and Hinduism, in the Fourth Way teachings of G. I. Gurdjieff, and elsewhere. Blavatsky provides this succinct summary of these esoteric principles in Kabbalah.

> The entire system of the Kabalistic numerals is based on the divine septenary hanging from the Triad (thus forming the *Decade*)… which, finally, all merge into the ONE itself: an endless and boundless Circle. (*S.D. I*, p. 239)

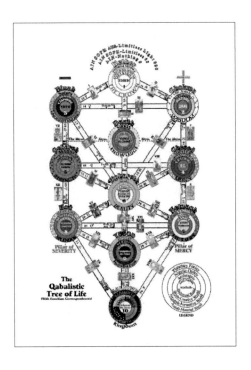

The *Tree of Life* is said to exist within the Garden of Eden, an indicator of its secret knowledge! The other Tree inside the Gates of Eden is the *Tree of Knowledge of Good and Evil*, suggesting a dualistic paradigm. Even the serpent, symbolizing the line of thinking that leads one astray, is double-tongued, saying one thing and doing another, like the madmen who deceived the masses of humanity. In Kabbalah, the *Tree of Life* is said to be hidden within the *Tree of Knowledge of Good and Evil* — and similarly, the study of dualistic science might eventually lead to an understanding of the higher laws and Divine Principles.

The number 11 also has particular meaning in Kabbalah as a magical number representing an individual who has mastered the 10 Sephirot of the *Tree of Life* and is established in the 11th I AM principle. 11 is considered the number of practical magic. In a sense, the combination 11:37 thus represents my response to that combination of 9/11.

The numbers 11:37 have long had deep meanings for me in terms of such occult studies. These same numbers also have profound meaning in modern science and are related to the 'alpha constant.' Peat mentions another remarkable coincidence concerning these numbers and the life and death of physicist W. Pauli:

> One of the most curious of these stories about Pauli concerns the number 137. One of the great unsolved mysteries of modern physics is the value of the fine structure constant, for while the other fundamental constants of nature are all immensely small or enormously large, this fine structure constant 1/137 turns out to be a human-sized number. This number 137 and its place in the scale of the universe particularly puzzled Pauli and continues to challenge physicists today. It was a mystery that Pauli was to take to his death, for on being admitted into the hospital, the physicist was told that he was being put into room 137. According to one version of this story,

on learning of his room number, Pauli said, "I will never get out of here." The physicist died shortly after." (p. 22)

Surely this is an unusual number — 1/137. It is the first of the constants of nature, the 'fine structure constant' and it is represented by the first letter of the Greek alphabet — 'alpha.' It is the only "human sized number" of the constants of Nature and it is also a prime number. We will consider the meaning and interpretation of alpha and review some of the comments offered by modern physicists as to its enigmatic nature.

At a website dedicated to this number, *www.137.com*, C. Mann (2001) provides some basic definitions:

> Now, alpha is nothing more, nothing less than the square of the charge of the electron divided by the speed of light times Planck's constant. Thus this one number contains in itself the guts of electromagnetism (the electron charge), relativity (the speed of light), *and* quantum mechanics (Planck's constant). All in one number! Not only that, this number isn't like the gravitational constant or the universal gas constant, full of meters and kilograms and degrees Celsius. Alpha is a pure dimensionless number—little wonder that people have been fascinated.

It is not easy to understand the meaning and interpretations of alpha, as it pops up in different contexts and different authors explain it differently. Mac Gregor (2007) in *The Power of Alpha*, notes in this regard:

> The mystery about — is actually a double mystery. The first mystery—the origin of its numerical value —»1/137 has been recognized and discussed for decades. The second mystery—the range of its domain—is generally unrecognized. (p. 69)

Different sources define the fine structure constant in different terms. It is described as the 'coupling constant' or a "measure of the strength *of the electromagnetic force governs how electrically charged elementary particles (e.g., electron, muon) and light (photons) interact.*" In physics, the number 1/137 is the strength of the electromagnetic force relative to that of the strong force. The strong force binds particles within the nucleus of the atoms, and the three quarks in each of the protons and neutrons. This law applies on a micro-level with a range of .00000000000001 or 10^{-13} centimeters, in a different order of scale from that in which we live our lives (seemingly). In contrast, the electromagnetic force determines all the phenomena of our everyday world — our perceptions, thoughts, and the heartbeat, the structures of the body and of the world around us. The number 1/137 thus represents in a way this bridge between worlds, on different orders of scale as we pass from a higher to a lower dimension.

Another author describes alpha as "the probability that an electron will emit or absorb a photon." L. Susskind (2006) explains:

> Roughly speaking the probability that any particular electron will radiate a quantum of light is given by the fine structure constant —. In other words, only one lucky electron out of 137 emits a photon. That is the meaning of —: it is the probability that an electron, as it moves along its trajectory, will capriciously emit a photon. (p. 49)

M. Born and A. Miller (2009), in *Deciphering the Cosmic Number: The Strange Friendship of Wolfgang Pauli and Carl Jung*, provide another perspective, noting:

> If alpha were bigger than it really is, we should not be able to distinguish matter form ether (the vacuum, nothingness), and our task to disentangle the natural laws would be hopeless difficult. The fact however that alpha has just its value 1/137 is certainly no chance but itself a law of nature. It is clear that the explanation of this number must be the central problem of natural philosophy. (p. 253)

Alpha shows up within different contexts and has long puzzled scientists. Mann notes: "The great physicist Heisenberg told his friends that the problems of quantum theory would disappear only when 137 was explained, and spent years trying to explain it." Similarly, one of the greatest physicists of the last century, R. Feynman is reported to have said that "physicists ought to put a special sign in their offices to remind themselves of how much they don't know. The message on the sign would be very simple. It would consist entirely of one word, or, rather, number 137." (www.137.com) Feynman himself penned these prophetic notes on the mysterious alpha constant.

> There is a most profound and beautiful question associated with the observed coupling constant, — the amplitude for a real electron to

emit or absorb a real photon. … Immediately you would like to know where this number for a coupling comes from … Nobody knows. It's one of the greatest damn mysteries of physics: a magic number that comes to us with no understanding by man. You might say the "hand of God" wrote that number, and "we don't know how He pushed his pencil." …. we don't know what kind of dance to do on the computer to make this number come out, without putting it in secretly! (p. 129)

From a mystical perspective, this expression 1/137 can be used to depict the basic metaphysical teaching of *The Secret Doctrine* and it is intrinsic to the Kabbalah. From an occult perspective, 1/137 is clearly a magical number, secretly encoded into the Kosmos. It is then doubly peculiar that this enigmatic number is found by scientists at the heart of being. Just as white light is divided by a three sided prism to yield a spectrum of seven colors, so also we can conceive of the Light of Brahman, the supernal lux of the Kabbalah and the Divine Light of Blavatsky, as entailing similar patterns of intelligent design — as above, so below.

Mann relates another paradoxical story:

> The best explanation of the mystery ever given to Victor Weisskopf, another leading theorist from that time, was provided by Gershom Scholem, one of the most eminent scholars of Jewish mysticism. When Scholem met Weisskopf, he asked about the prominent unsolved problems in physics. Weisskopf said, "Well, there's this number, 137 …." And Scholem's eyes lit up! He said, "Did you know that one hundred thirty-seven is the number associated with Cabala?"

1/137 is a very mysterious number indeed, basic to *The Secret Doctrine*, Kabbalah and modern physics. Perhaps, the mysteries of alpha were written in from the beginning, "put in secretly" as a principle of intelligent design and a key to understanding the dynamics of light and creation.

Of course, to the materialist science philosopher, these enigmas of 1/137, the alpha constant, and the principles of mystical creation, are only additional fortuitous coincidences in a universe devoid of spirit and soul, or cosmic design. As Blavatsky explains, the unholy trinity of modern science is that *inert matter*, *senseless force* and *blind chance*! And so the physicists can post the number 1/137 on their doors to remind themselves of how little they know, while failing to understand the truth under their noses all the while. If synchronicities show a link between mind and matter, then perhaps the formula of 1/137 is a clue to the nature of divine mind and the principles of mystical creation. My goodness, what an unusual synchronicity that the paradoxical alpha constant of science, which enables us "to distinguish matter from ether (the vacuum, nothingness)," takes on the numeric values of *The Secret Doctrine* and Kabbalah, and the principles of intelligent design and then it then finds its way onto the Peace Tower at just the right time on that fateful day.

I must be an electron that absorbed and emitted too many photons! Anyway, this background portrays something of what these magical numbers 11:37 mean to me, and why it had such significance and thus ended up on the cover of this book. The Star of David on the Peace Tower similarly does not imply that all is hopeless as the Zionists and Masons have been in control all along. Instead, we must take this sacred symbol as a sign to those of us *upright of heart*, that it is incumbent upon us to rise to the occasion and to take back our country while reestablishing the rule of law and impartial justice.

Aren't you tired of being ruled by war mongers, international criminal cabals and banksters, perverts, pedophiles and parasites? Imagine what the restoration of justice and international law would really mean within Canada as around the world. The human race became a rat race, controlled and deceived by a pseudo-master race. What a horrifying and tragic, yet spectacular Tale!

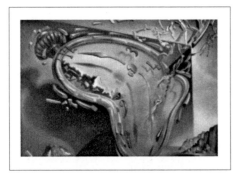

A final coincidence occurred just the other day, when I was explaining to a friend something of the significance of the title. My friend noticed an art piece by Salvador Dali which I have on my wall, representing the distortions of time and reality. I had never realized that it also suggests such a magical time of 11:37.

The hour is late, 23 minutes to noon.

Dragonfly Tales & the Magic of Nature

A Tribute to Karen T. Hale
November 19, 1955 - May 6, 2011

On May 6, 2011, Karen died quite unexpectedly and suddenly at home of the age of 55. Karen's body was cremated and her funeral service held on an unlucky Friday, May 13, 2011. Karen will be missed by her family and friends. Karen has been my love and friend over the past twelve years and had become a dedicated truth researcher since our 'rude awakening' in August of 2006.

Karen is and was a remarkable woman, quite unlike any I have ever known. Karen and I shared varied quite epic adventures through that period. Many unusual things happened to us which to this day I do not understand. To me, through the last year of my time with Karen, she was my *sweetheart* and no other word captures one of Karen's essential qualities, her inherent goodness and kindness.

Karen had asked on several occasions through our years together that one day I would write about her and the things I had witnessed, or which we had experienced together, or as she had witnessed of me. I always laughed at the thought, never thinking that I could lose her so suddenly, when so many things were left undone and incomplete between us, and while we faced such a battle before us. And then, suddenly one day, the love of my life died in my arms at home, a true spiritual warrior who was determined to carry forward our struggle for truth and righteousness.

Karen and I both knew that we were on an adventure together, awake in a madcap time in a world of sleepwalkers, with horrendous events unfolding on the world stage.

At this time, I am struggling with the grief of my loss and remorse over things that had happened between Karen and I through those years and I am not ready to write of such things as we experienced, or which Tales as Karen recounted to me. If I manage to *live to tell*, I hope to write an autobiography as part four of the *Within-Without from Zero Point* series and to recount, as I can recall, what happened to us. It is a wild tale, the significance of which I do not understand even now. As a fool who knows nothing, I hope eventually to share something of these tales and capture something of the enchantment of this woman. To me, Karen is 'missing in action,' lost to an enemy so insidious that most people, ordinary people, cannot believe it exists. And yet it does.

Karen and I met when she came out to attend lectures which I was giving at the Zero Point Centre in Kemptville, Ontario in 1999. Karen came for teaching as she was ever seeking and open to different ideas and influences. She did not mean to so engage the heart of the teacher, but she was such a charmed and gifted women, that she did. At the same time, Karen was at times quite strange and troubled, and unable even to deal with the regularities or irregularities of everyday life. Our times together were certainly a madcap and epic Tale, ending on a tragic yet triumphant note twelve years later.

Karen had issues and struggles in her life even before we met and before we stumbled upon 9-11 Truth, which set off periods of mania and madness in us both, as well as experiences of rapture and bliss, illumination and fearfulness. In ways, the insanity of what is being done in our society, ranging from the wars based on lies, to the spreading of sickness through inoculations, chemtrails and foods, all the weapons of the hidden world of the elites, drove us in our researches, studies and efforts. At times, this drove a wedge between us, although we eventually abided through it all over the years. Karen and I learned together and her love always supported me through my efforts on internet radio, my website and in my writings.

Through the last months of her life, Karen and I both felt that we were elders and that we had some responsibility to attempt to do something to combat the madness of this all. How could our world have become so controlled and fashioned by such deviant and perverted groups as has happened? These people are seriously psychiatrically and spiritually disturbed!

Karen spent too many hours at the computer, ever searching out new information and understanding, and she smoked too much, both of which must have put a strain on her heart, as she died of a massive heart attack; although at the moments of her death, Karen thought that she was under attack by their psychotronic weapons, which do exist.[22] I have to suspend judgement on this as I have had to do with respect to other things which happened to us, individually or together.

Karen was an individual, who like myself, takes on the suffering of others, helping to bear *the sorrow of our Endlessness*, as is taught in the Gurdjieff teaching. When we awoke up to the criminality of our own government and media, the lies of 9-11 and the perversions of the old world psychiatric disorder, we began to realize the horror of it all and to take such suffering upon ourselves while struggling to do something. We had not known that we lived in such a world gone mad.

These elites are really so pathetic and have none of the nobility of heart of Special K., a nickname I had for Karen, like that of Missy. Karen died with a nobility of heart that most people cannot imagine as they are so distracted by Lady Gaga and such ridiculous things as the elites fashion for their little minds.

It is unfortunate that Karen so seldom wrote in her life, as when she did, she always saw things so differently than others. When she added her own webpage to my site, she penned this verse, which was so insightful and prophetic of things to come:

---

[22] Karen had reported loud ringing in her ears, dizziness and heart palpitations before her death from a heart attack. She thought that she was under attack, which I had tended to dismiss as a possibility at that time. Only subsequently did I learn that her symptoms exactly correspond to those attributed to the 'murder meters.' Karen was definitely sensitive to electromagnetic sources and would no longer even be in the same room as a television. She died while within 20 feet of our meter. Are we to selectively become the victims of such insidious foul play?

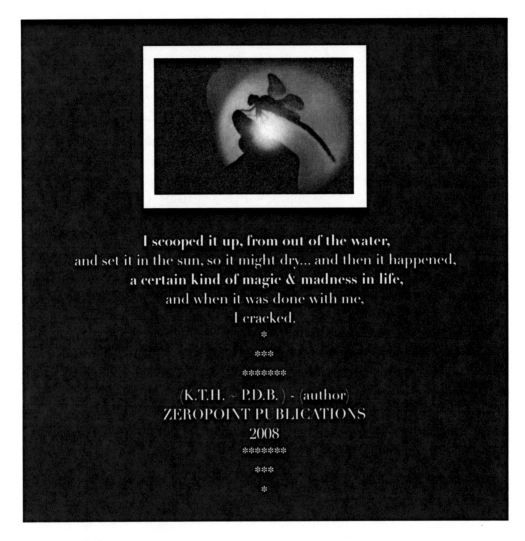

I scooped it up, from out of the water,
and set it in the sun, so it might dry... and then it happened,
a certain kind of magic & madness in life,
and when it was done with me,
I cracked.
*
***
******
(K.T.H. ~ P.D.B.) - (author)
ZEROPOINT PUBLICATIONS
2008
******
***
*

On September 11, 2006, Karen and I had been the only two truth activists on Canada's Parliament Hill, with posters to the effect that 9-11 was an inside job and distributing written materials which explained aspects of the fraud and public deception actually being perpetrated by our governments. I could never have imagined as a person asleep, the extent of the crimes of our governments against us. Since awakening, Karen and I lived in the fire exposing ourselves to risks, as I still do, trying to awaken an almost brain dead public who share no uprightness of heart and moral outrage at what has been done to us as Canadian and world citizens.

After the Dawson College shooting in Montreal, Karen and I travelled to Montreal to distribute a research paper i had written, based on our observations of the fraudulent media coverage, trying to expose this incident as another *false flag* black operation. The Canadian shadow government wanted new laws to prohibit semi-automatic weapons and this was another of their concocted shooting sprees as they have committed around the world whenever they want to further disarm the citizens. Aren't they cunning and illuminated?

Karen has supported me throughout in my work and was the most able and apt truth researcher, always moving on to new discoveries and insights. A remarkable, sensitive and talented woman, Karen felt morally outraged by what is being done by the psychopathic elites and Masonic goofballs, and strove tirelessly to contribute to my work and together to the larger world wide truth movement.

Five minutes before her death, Karen had insisted that I photo her with a T-shirt on which she had made up, featuring a remarkable image by Truther and inspired artist David Dees, depicting the royal wedding against the backdrop of human carnage and suffering created by such self-styled little 'elites.' What a pathetic joke. Karen was so caring for others, especially for the disadvantaged and had a hard time bearing the sadness and horror of it all.

Coincidentally, Karen was standing in front of a Mexican picture of mother Mary and so the halo of the Divine Mother appears surrounding her. Of course, this was just another coincidence in this peculiar universe of wonder.

Lastly, the following is a poem which Karen wrote, wanting it to be illustrated as a children's book, explaining certain principles of higher magic. The basic principle of magic is that every man and every woman is a Star, having a divine source element or God-spark within. The references in the poem to a 'jar,' relate to a line by the poet Kabir, who in describing mystical life and creation, states: "Inside this jar are seven oceans and innumerable stars."

Of course, we are not talking of the little Hollywood glitter stars, but to the real Stars of the Holy World. This is the seventh principle to which we might attain through understanding of the mysteries of our own Selves and Hearts.

You are a Star

You are a star birthed from within without the night
you are a star reflecting some light
you are a star, that's what you are
you are a star

You are a star that cries out *I am* before flight
you are a star that's been pushed out into the light
you are a star that's what you are
you are a star.

You are a star filled with luminous light
you are a star blissful and bright
you are a star that's what you are
you are a star.

You are a star a pearl of great price
you are a star stuck in a jar
you are a star
that's what you are
you are a star.

You are a star turned topsy-turvy from the flight
you are a star filled with limit-less light
you are a star that's what you are
you are a star.

You are a star playing hide & seek in God's place
you are a star within a heart space
you are a star that's what you are
you are a star.

You are a star that heals with a smile
you are a star
that's who you are
you are a star.

You are a star reflecting sunlight
you are a star
no matter where you are,
you are a star
stuck in a jar.

You are a star in a jar!

K. T. H.

Thank you Karen for your love and support,
your courage and service to humankind
against the insurmountable odds we faced together.
You are a Star, an inspiration to me and loved ones
to carry forward a cause of righteousness and truth
in a world gone mad.

Karen sweetheart, you earned your Star
Through our Epic Adventures, Life and Love
May I look into your beautiful face once again
And be inspired by your example of living in Love and Truth
Despite the horror and sadness of it All.

KAREN — YOU ARE A STAR.

About the Author

Christopher P. Holmes was born in Sussex, England at 7-7:30 am, October 7, 1949. His father, William, was a Canadian military officer, a graduate of RMC, stationed in England during the war where he met Diane, who became his bride and mother to three sons. Christopher has lived his life in Canada since his early years, throughout the province of Ontario. He received a B.A. from Carleton University in Ottawa and M.A. and Ph.D. degrees in psychology from the University of Waterloo. He worked as a professor at York University in Downsview Ontario from 1977 to 1990 and then within the Ontario Ministry of Corrections from 1990 to 2002. Over the past ten years, Christopher has worked independently as a writer and researcher under the Zero Point logos.

Christopher's primary interests have long been investigations of human consciousness and psychology as a *science of the soul*. He has experienced varied states of enlightenment and realization through his life which has fuelled his desire to understand the mysteries of consciousness and creation. His work explores the interface between mysticism and science, especially as pertains to consciousness and to studies of creation physics and metaphysics.

Christopher considers himself a mystic, a psychologist and scientist, and most recently, a truth activist and spiritual warrior in a world gone mad.

Zero Point Publications
Box 700, Kemptville, Ontario, Canada K0G-1J0

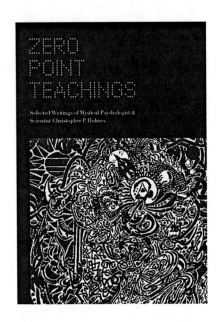

ZERO POINT TEACHINGS
Selected Writings of Mystical Psychologist & Scientist

Christopher P. Holmes

The zero point teachings are a portal of some sort and I invite you to consider an alternative view of the nature and structure of reality--to view the world in a magical and mystical way. The basic concept is that all living beings, including you, have a zero point centre within connected to the higher dimensional physics of the heart. This is the means by which "the Gods and other invisible powers clothe themselves in bodies"—as explained by mystic scholar Madame Blavatsky in The Secret Doctrine (1888). Just as the scientists now conceive that our huge universe grew from an infinitesimal singularity out of the quantum vacuum, so also, I am suggesting that you also have such a hidden zero point or singularity source condition--a singular I within the Heart. Further, we ourselves emerge "out of nothingness" in some mysterious way unknown to modern science and contemporary understanding, but consistent with modern views of the physics of the quantum vacuum, as void and plenum, filled with light and zero point fields.

> Mystic Aivanhov (1976) elaborates upon the significance of the zero point concept: "I ... engraved the symbol of the knowledge of the Initiates: a circle with a point in the center. ... Understand me once and for all: I am speaking from experience, for me it is not mere theory, all my life has been based on this symbol of the circle with its central point. This center which is in us, we must find ." (Love and Sexuality, I, pp. 25-6)

ISBN 978-0-9689435-7-1

www.zeropoint.ca

$24.95 Cdn

PSYCHOLOGICAL ILLUSIONS
Explorations of the Gurdjieff Fourth Way Teaching

Christopher P. Holmes

Psychological Illusions

Explorations of the G.I. Gurdjieff
Fourth Way Teaching

Christopher P. Holmes

The central illusion of humankind is that we *"know self."* The components of this illusion concern the different powers or capabilities which men and women think that they possess but which in reality they do not. Four primary illusions or misunderstandings concern the faculties of consciousness, the unity of I, the possession of will (or the capacity to do) and the existence of the soul. The fourth way psychology begins with a study of humans as they are under the conditions of mechanical life and then describes the psychology of man's *possible evolution*. Humans can awaken and experience new states of consciousness, achieve a unity of "I" and real will, and thus attain the soul. Unfortunately, wrong ideas and convictions about the nature of consciousness, unity and will, are major obstacles to self knowledge. If we can begin to understand these illusions, then there is a chance of escape, of awakening and evolution.

According to Beelzebub, the central character in Gurdjieff's *Tales*, the three-brained beings on planet Earth are microcosmoses or *"similitudes of the Whole."* As such, they have the possibility of not only serving local cosmic purposes, feeding the earth and moon as part of organic life on earth, but also of experiencing sacred being-impulses, attaining varied levels of objective reason and individuality and even of *"blending again with the infinite."* (1950) As a microcosm of the macrocosm, a human being can potentially coat higher being-bodies for the life of the soul, instinctually sense cosmic truths and phenomena, and maintain existence within the subtle realms of being after death—achieving different levels of immortality. Unfortunately, humankind came to exist only in waking sleep states of automated consciousness, perceiving reality topsy-turvy, conditioned by pleasure and self love, and wasteful of their sacred sexual substances. Human beings no longer realize their deeper cosmic purposes and possibilities, or attain real "I."

Psychological Illusions explores the psychology, metaphysics and cosmology of the fourth way teaching. This includes material on the *Ray of Creation*, the fundamental cosmic laws, the alchemical crystallization of *higher being-bodies* for the life of the soul, and the miraculous possibilities existing for the evolution of the individual human being. The Gurdjieff fourth way teaching is a profound and coherent system of esoteric teaching about the horror of the situation for humanity asleep, living under their psychological illusions.

ISBN 978-0-9689435-2-6

www.zeropoint.ca

$24.95 Cdn

"THE SLUG"
On G. I. Gurdjieff's Beelzebub's Tales to his Grandson

Christopher P. Holmes

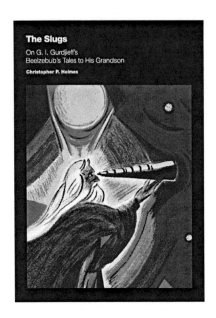

The Slugs provides an overview, explanation and interpretation of G. I. Gurdjieff's masterpiece Beelzebub's Tales to His Grandson, undoubtedly one of the most profound and mysterious books of the sacred literature in the modern world. The framework of ideas, claims and objective science offers a fundamentally alternative view of the nature of life, the origins and history of the Solar System and humankind, the nature of the human psyche and psychopathology, and a science of the soul. In the light of The Tales, most of modern thought and philosophy is so much 'pouring-from-the-empty-into-the-void.' The 'sorry scientists' of 'new format' have no conception of the great inscrutable mysteries of Nature and the subtle inner dimensions and alchemy of human beings. Beelzebub's Tales is a work not only of myth, allegory, history and fantasy, but about the secrets of 'objective science' and the psychology of the soul.

Gurdjieff's masterful Tales also provides a shocking portrait of the "strangeness of the human psyche" and explains how humans' essential consciousness and the divine impulses of faith, hope and love, passed into the 'subconsciousness,' while a 'false consciousness system' replaced it, crystallized around their egoism and associated unbecoming being-impulses. Beelzebub as a cosmic figure of higher reason observes the horrific "processes of reciprocal destruction," or war as periodically occurs on Earth, and asks how such phenomenal depravities come about and why humans cannot eradicate such an arch-criminal particularity in their psyche. The strange three-brained beings perceive reality "topsy-turvy," are mechanized to "see nothing real" and squander their sacred sexual substances solely for pleasure and their multiform vices. Beelzebub's portrayal of the "Hasnamusses," individuals who lack the Divine being-impulse of 'conscience,' the 'intelligentsia' and the 'crats,' provides vivid images of the psychopathology of the world's so-called 'elites' with their special societies or "criminal gangs," their "international five o'clocks" and "Hasnamussian sciences." The future of humanity is bleak indeed without the guidance of a being of such a higher intelligence as Beelzebub himself. The Slugs, like Gurdjieff's Tales, provides searing and illuminating insights into human psychopathology, the cause of war and the horror of it all.

The Author: Christopher P. Holmes is a mystic scientist and consciousness researcher, a clinical and forensic psychologist, and truth activist. He has studied the Gurdjieff work for over thirty five years and pursued broad investigations of human consciousness, the physics and metaphysics of creation, the mysteries of love and esoteric mystical teachings.

ISBN 978-0-9689435-4-0

www.zeropoint.ca

$21.95 Cdn 2nd Edition

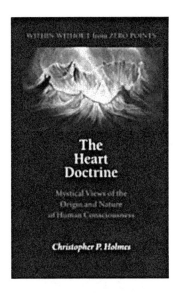

WITHIN-WITHOUT from
ZERO POINTS I

THE HEART DOCTRINE
Mystical Views of the Origin and
Nature of Human Consciousness

Christopher P. Holmes

" ... "material points without extension" are Leibnitz's monads,
and at the same time the materials out of which the 'Gods' and
other invisible powers clothe themselves in bodies.... the entire
universe concentrating itself, as it were, in a single point."

H. P. Blavatsky, The Secret Doctrine, I. Cosmogenesis, 1888

Modern psychology and science have been dominated by "the head doctrine"–the assumption that the material brain produces consciousness. In contrast, mystics claim that the origins of consciousness and Self are related to the mystical dimensions of the Heart. We are individual "eyes" or "I"s of "THAT," the divine unity within which we live, move and have our being. Mystical experiences involve penetrating various veils of nature which allow for the awakening of consciousness and the Heart, the realization of higher Space dimensions, and experiences of the unity of things within the inner life. Most importantly, human beings have a zero point centre and this is the means by which higher dimensional influences bring life and consciousness into the living being. These are the deep mysteries explored by the fool at the zero point.

Within-Without from Zero Points is an extremely unusual and provocative series which juxtaposes the most advanced concepts in modern science with mystical and spiritual teachings. It provides a sweeping scope of inquiry into the ultimate mysteries of consciousness, life, creation and God.

"My mission is to help uncover the forgotten, deep heart teachings of Jesus. ... The information you have gathered on the zero point has been a powerful validation of my own inner meditation practice and intuitions. Hence it has greatly enhanced my faith and the effectiveness of my meditation. Thank you so very much for your labors." **John Francis, *The Mystic Way of Radiant Love: Alchemy for a New Creation.***

"... if Christopher Holmes' articulation of 'the heart doctrine' had been restricted to citing and commenting upon those awe-inspiring teachings, he would have accomplished a great deal by establishing the foundation of an alternative paradigm to that which dominates contemporary approaches to the study of consciousness. However, when he introduces the mysterious concept of "the zero point," his arguments take on a level of significance which is, in my opinion, unparalleled in modern consciousness research. ..."
James A. Moffatt

ISBN 978-0-9689435-0-2
www.zeropoint.ca

$24.95 Cdn

UPCOMING

WITHIN-WITHOUT FROM ZERO POINTS II

MICROCOSM-MACROCOSM
Scientific and Mystical Views on the Origin of the Universe, the Nature of Matter & Human Consciousness

Christopher P. Holmes

" ... "material points without extension" are Leibnitz's monads, and at the same time the materials out of which the 'Gods' and other invisible powers clothe themselves in bodies.... the entire universe concentrating itself, as it were, in a single point." H. P. Blavatsky, The Secret Doctrine, I. Cosmogenesis, 1888

"... all the so-called Forces of Nature, Electricity, Magnetism, light, heat, etc., are in esse, i.e., in their ultimate constitution, the differentiated aspects of that Universal Motion. ... for formative or creative purposes, the Great Law modifies its perpetual motion on seven invisible points within the area of the manifest Universe." Madame H. P. Blavatsky, The Secret Doctrine, 1888

"It is necessary to notice that in the Great Universe all phenomena in general, without exception wherever they arise and manifest, are simply successively law-conformable 'Fractions' of some whole phenomenon which has its prime arising on the Most Holy Sun Absolute." G. I. Gurdjieff, 1950

Mystical accounts of states of Union, or unity with the world or universe on varied levels, attest to the fact that there is some kind of inner magic and alchemy going on within the inner cosmos of human consciousness—a metaphysics and physics to consciousness and the human heart.

Microcosm-Macrocosm explores the newest theories in physics and creation science–including materials on superstrings, higher dimensions, singularities, the quantum vacuum and the holographic principle. It also draws from ancient metaphysics–particularly The Secret Doctrine of H. P. Blavatsky (1888), esoteric Judaism and Kabbalah, and the cosmology and metaphysics of G. I. Gurdjieff. This is a challenging and provocative work with deep insights into the Divine Mystery teachings and a unique critique of modern science philosophy. It provides a shocking alternative view of the zero point origins of human consciousness and cosmos.

UPCOMING

WITHIN-WITHOUT from ZERO POINTS III

TRIUNE MONADS IN SEVEN DIMENSIONAL HYPERSPACE
Scientific and Mystical Studies of the Multi-Dimensional Nature of Human Existence

Christopher P. Holmes

Monads draws from the teachings of Madame Blavatsky, Kabbalah and Judaism, Gurdjieff, and a wide range of mystical doctrine about the multidimensional nature of human existence. Esoteric teachings identify the abode of the 'I' as within the human heart, where a triune Monad element is established within a Seven Dimensional Eternal Parent Space which underlies and sustains our normal physical four-dimensional space-time complex. Such ideas from mystical sources bear profound relationships to theories in advanced physics as to the nature of Space itself, quantum interconnectedness and higher dimensional superstring elements at zero point levels. A triune and sevenfold Monadic Essence spins a Web of Spirit, Soul and Matter within a Seven Dimensional Virual Reality out of the Aethers of the void and plenum, the quantum vacuum. In order to illustrate the necessity for such an alternative understanding of reality, this work examines evidences for out-of-body experiences, Sheldrake's fields of extended mind, enigmas posed by heart transplant patients and twin studies, and an interpretation of other paranormal investigations.

UPCOMING

WITHIN-WITHOUT FROM ZERO POINTS IV

A FOOL AT THE ZERO POINT
An Autobiographic Tale about the Strange Case of Professor Z, the Mysteries of Love and Ecstasies of the Heart & the Horror of It All

Christopher P. Holmes

Christopher, by the grace of God, will provide an autobiographical account of his life experiences, his psychical and mystical experiences, his life struggles and relationships, and an account of awakening to the horror of it all. This work includes materials on Christopher's struggles for academic freedom at York University, his twelve years of work in correctional centres as a forensic psychologist, his life and loves, and his awakening to psychopathology of the world elites with their plans for committing genocide against the human race.